Presidential Spending Power

LOUIS FISHER

Presidential Spending Power

PRINCETON UNIVERSITY PRESS, PRINCETON, NEW JERSEY

Copyright © 1975 by Princeton University Press
Published by Princeton University Press
Princeton and London
ALL RIGHTS RESERVED
Library of Congress Cataloging in Publication Data
will be found on the last printed page of this book
PRINTED IN THE UNITED STATES OF AMERICA
by Princeton University Press, Princeton, New Jersey
Second printing, with corrections, 1976

Contents

Acknowledgments

IN these frenetic times I was pleased to find a number of friends and colleagues willing to read the manuscript. Those who managed to review the entire draft include Samuel M. Cohn, formerly with the Office of Management and Budget, now with Nathan Associates; Professor Fred I. Greenstein, Princeton University; James P. Pfiffner, University of Wisconsin; David F. Reynolds, U.S. Department of the Interior; Allen Schick, Congressional Research Service; and James L. Sundquist, The Brookings Institution. Portions were read by Lester A. Fettig, Senate Government Operations Committee; Professor John H. E. Fried, Lehman College; Gerald L. Kamens, Agency for International Development; Walter J. Oleszek, Congressional Research Service; Professor Morris S. Ogul, University of Pittsburgh; Professor Harry Howe Ransom, Vanderbilt University; Morton J. Schussheim, Congressional Research Service; George H. Strauss and others, from the Office of Management and Budget; Rexford G. Tugwell, Center for the Study of Democratic Institutions. My wife, Alice, carried the greatest burden by reading the first draft.

A number of other agency officials read certain chapters, asking that their names be withheld here. I am indebted to all for improving the quality of the book. For shortcomings that remain I take credit.

Dozens of other executive officials, while not readers of the manuscript, have sharpened my insights and understanding of the budget process. For that beleaguered and much abused assemblage of professionals, I want to express my appreciation. Let me single out, from the Office of Management and Budget, the names of Candice Bryant, Phillip Dame, Michael Griffin, Jeanne King, Sidney Orkin, and Joyce Walker. Their skills and talents serve the Nation well.

I owe a heavy intellectual debt to Lucius Wilmerding, Jr., author of that classic work on budget execution, *The Spending Power: A History of the Efforts of Congress to Control Expenditures*. Published three decades ago, in 1943, it retains freshness and relevance for our problems today.

During the development of my project over the past decade, I have had occasion to present various bits and pieces to professional meetings, journals, and magazines. A paper on "Presidential Spending Discretion and Congressional Controls" was presented at the 1971 Annual Meeting of the American Political Science Association, held in Chicago. That paper, greatly augmented, was published under the same title in the Winter 1972 issue of *Law and Contemporary Problems*. Also in 1972 I published *President and Congress: Power and Policy* (New York: The Free Press: A Division of The Macmillan Company). Chapter 4, entitled "Spending Powers," contained my earlier effort to sketch out the development of the executive budget and the types of discretionary powers. I am grateful to The Free Press for permitting me to reprint some of that material here.

Much of the material on impoundment first appeared in "Funds Impounded by the President: The Constitutional Issue," *George Washington Law Review*, October 1969; "The Politics of Impounded Funds," *Administrative Science Quarterly*, September 1970; and "Impoundment of Funds: Uses and Abuses," *Buffalo Law Review*, Fall 1973. In the area of covert financing, I delivered a paper called "Dark Corners of the Federal Budget: Confidential and Secret Funds," to the Center for the Study of Democratic Institutions, Santa Barbara, Calif., November 5, 1973. Other articles on the subject include "Executive Shell Game: Hiding Billions from Congress," *The Nation*, November 15, 1971, and "Secret Spending: Dark Corners in the Budget," *The Nation*, January 19, 1974.

On June 15, 1973, I presented a paper, "Congressional Control of Budget Execution," to the Select Committee on Committees of the U.S. House of Representatives. An article, "Reprogramming of Funds by the Defense Department," was published in the February 1974 issue of *The Journal of Politics*. Another article, "Congress, the Executive and the Budget," appeared in the January 1974 issue of *The Annals*, published by the American Academy of Political and Social Science. I was able to refine and test my ideas when invited to speak to executive officials, particularly at the Federal Executive Institute at Charlottesville, Virginia, and the Executive Seminar Centers at Berkeley, California, and Oak Ridge, Tennessee.

Sanford Thatcher, of the Princeton University Press, gave early encouragement to the project and was a steady source of good judgment. Polly Hanford of the Press set records from week to week in expediting production.

This book marks a continuing effort to pull together material from politics, law, and economics, keeping all of those forces in historical perspective. With disconcerting frequency I find myself spread thin by the effort. Robert L. Heilbroner, a former professor of mine at the New School for Social Research, is capable of spanning the disciplines with remarkable equanimity. I am happy to dedicate this book to him.

L. F.

April 1975
Rockville, Md.

Presidential Spending Power

Introduction

In an essay remembered for its grace and insights, Woodrow Wilson described administration as "the most obvious part of government; it is government in action; it is the executive, the operative, the most visible side of government. . . ."[1] But when it comes to administration of the budget, we find nothing that is obvious, very little that is visible.

Our priorities here are peculiar. We fix upon the appropriations process, watching with great fascination as Congress goes about its business of making funds available to agencies. What happens later—the actual spending of money—rarely commands our attention. Billions of dollars are impounded, transferred, reprogrammed, or shifted one way or another by the President and his assistants. Billions more are used in confidential and covert ways, without the knowledge of Congress and the public. In many cases the decisive commitment to spend funds is made not by Congress but by executive officials. In this entire area of budget execution our knowledge is sketchy and primitive.

Why this lack of interest in the spending phase of the budget cycle? It is as though we visited the race track, watched the horses parade back and forth in front of the stands, saw them line up in the starting gate, and then went

3

home just as the bell sounded. The outcome of the race does not interest us. We do not see the budget cycle to its completion.

Please understand my purpose. I am not "poaching" here on the territory of Aaron Wildavsky and Richard Fenno, who have described so well the ins and outs of agency budgeteering and the response by Congress to agency budget requests. I focus on what agencies do once they get the money. Whenever necessary I enter the areas of budget preparation and the appropriations phase, but my primary direction is budget execution.

The first two chapters describe the evolution of Presidential spending power, with the year 1921 dividing the two chapters. Here I try to identify and explain the various forces that have led to large delegations of spending power to the President. In those chapters, and others, it is of course a convenience and a simplification to speak of "Presidential" power. Many of the discretionary spending actions are taken at the departmental or agency level, often with little participation or knowledge by the President and his immediate advisers.

Subsequent chapters focus on specific types of discretionary actions. Chapter Three discusses the general issue of broad grants of spending authority versus line-item control. It logically leads to the next chapter, on reprogramming, which involves the shifting of funds within appropriation accounts. Chapter Five covers transfers: the shifting of funds from one appropriation account to another. Most of that chapter concerns the financing of the Cambodian war from 1970 to 1973. The remaining five chapters are devoted to the timing of obligations, impoundment, covert financing, and executive commitments.

To the uninitiated, and even to the seasoned budget analyst, this book may appear at times to be exhaustive in its details. That is not so. I have broken new ground, a lot of it, but there is much more to discover, much more to understand. As a result of conversations over the years with agency budget officials and committee staff, who have patiently educated me on inside practices, I am aware of transactions so convoluted and intricate that I wonder if it is ever possible to reach bottom. I do not discuss here all the subtleties, stratagems, and jugglings that are at work. Accept my book as an introduction, a developed one perhaps, but an introduction nonetheless. Most of it is comprehensible to the layman. Frequently you must tackle technicalities and details; otherwise you cannot play the game.

As for generalizations and prescriptions, I do what I can. Others will do more in the future. I hope my book will be a catalyst. In the next few years I anticipate a number of congressional hearings on budget execution and administrative discretion. New legislation is likely. Budget execution will probably command greater attention in the professional journals, and citizens and public interest groups will adopt a more alert posture. To attempt at this point a definitive work would be pointless and futile. A lot of hard climbing is ahead before we attain the necessary perspective. In the meantime we should be a little suspicious of bold generalizations and spectacular reform proposals.

I am uncomfortably aware of the maxim: "Where you stand depends on where you sit." For the past five years I have been a staff member of Congress. The writing of this book has depended heavily on congressional documents: committee reports, committee hearings, debates in the *Congressional Record*, studies by the General Accounting Office, my own work with legislation, and other sources of a distinctly legislative nature. And yet it would give me no pleasure at all to present this material with a congressional bias. To compensate for my daily routines I have made a point of reaching out to executive officials, meeting with them often, understanding their point of view, appreciating events in as broad a perspective as possible. I hope I have presented the basic facts and events in such a way that the reader is free to draw conclusions different from mine.

To gain an adequate appreciation of the budget one ends up going through Nietzsche's three metamorphoses: the load-bearing camel, capable of strength and endurance; the freedom of the lion, able to break with givens and conventions; and finally the child, representing innocence and a new beginning, an act of creation and the promise of new values. There is something new to be found if we are open to the discovery.

Several years ago I was greatly impressed by a remark made by George Mahon, chairman of the House Appropriations Committee. He was asked by another member of the House: "Do you understand the budget?" His response: "Not too well."[2] I was delighted by that. It was refreshing to have a man of Mahon's experience and learning make such an admission. Later that day a House staffer stopped by my office and I repeated the story to him. He looked at me with disbelief: "I don't understand. I have several friends who are budget analysts and they're right on top of things."

Those of us involved in Federal budget matters should find such a statement amusing. No one is "right on top of things." No one ever will be. Especially is that the case with the discretionary actions of executive officials in the spending of Federal dollars. If Congress wants to retain the power of the purse, if it intends to exercise greater control over budget priorities, it must improve its understanding and oversight of the spending process. Otherwise we stand the risk of having the important work of representative government discharged increasingly by nonelected administrative officials and political appointees.

A word of explanation. This book was not written in response to the legislative ferment that gave rise to the Congressional Budget and Impoundment Control Act of 1974. The book had its origin, I am somewhat pained to admit, more than a decade ago. For several years I compiled information and played with various forms of organization. I tested some ideas in professional papers, journals and magazines, public forums, and in my work with the Congressional Research Service. The appearance of this book one year after the budget reform act may be timely, but it was not the stimulus for my efforts or my interest. I mention the act for yet another reason. It was passed with the assumption that Congress can rely on the appropriations process to control budget totals and budget priorities. That is a very shaky premise. What is done by legislators at the appropriation stage can be undone by administrators during budget execution. Congress acknowledged that in part by adding an impoundment control title to the act. I am confident that Congress will discover, as it tries to implement the act, that impoundment is not the only means by which the executive branch can rearrange priorities and dictate spending levels. Only a systematic exploration of the entire area of budget execution, followed by the necessary statutory and nonstatutory controls, will assure Congress a decisive voice in shaping the budget and determining how public funds shall be spent.

1

Presidential Budgeting
(1789-1921)

In budgetary circles the year 1921 is used as a point of origin for Presidential spending power. In that year the Budget and Accounting Act directed the President to formulate a national budget; a Bureau of the Budget was created at the same time to provide him with technical assistance. On the basis of that statutory responsibility and staff capability, Presidents have since extended their influence and control over financial matters.

It is convenient to identify pivotal statutes, but all too often they become the secular counterpart of the Creation. We assume that nothing existed before, that all was void and darkness. This perception dominates the literature on the Federal budget. We are led to understand that, prior to 1921, Presidents had little to do in framing the financial program of the Federal Government. Individual spending agencies transmitted their budget requests to Congress in what was called a "Book of Estimates." The Secretary of the Treasury could have played a coordinating role, but studies conclude that his handling of budget estimates was routine and perfunctory.

According to this point of view, Presidents and their Secretaries of the Treasury were passive bystanders during those years, mechanically forwarding budget estimates to Congress without revision or comment.[1] The year 1921 thus appears to be an abrupt turning point, a dramatic cleavage between past and present procedures for the budget. But rarely does history divide into such neat periods. Watersheds are difficult to find. A closer look at the 19th century shows that it was not so barren of budget leadership by the Administration. Such Presidents as John Quincy Adams, Van Buren, Tyler, Polk, Buchanan, Grant, and Cleveland did take a hand in revising budget estimates before they were sent to Congress. A number of Secretaries of the Treasury assisted them in that task.

Unless we appreciate the developments of the 1789-1921 period, and comprehend the political and economic forces that were part of the momentum building up to the Budget and Accounting Act, we may wrongly conclude that Presidential spending power began with a statute and can be ended with a statute. Yet that is not so. The power is an accumulation of numerous statutes, financial panics, wars, a splintering of congressional controls, and demands from the private sector for economy and efficiency.

ESTABLISHMENT OF TREASURY DEPARTMENT

One of the first responsibilities awaiting Congress in 1789 was the creation of executive departments. The Departments of Foreign Affairs and War were recognized as executive in nature and assigned directly to the President. Those departmental heads were under no obligation to come before Congress and present reports. Both departments had retained their identity as administrative agencies during the transition from the Articles of Confederation to the Constitution. Robert Livingston and John Jay held the post of Secretary for Foreign Affairs from 1781 to 1790, while Henry Knox served as Secretary of War from 1785 to 1794.[2]

The administration of financial matters was more difficult to resolve. Robert Morris had been Superintendent of Finance from 1781 to 1784, at which point the management of finances fell back to the Board of Treasury. The experiment with a single executive in the finance area was marked by controversy and uneasiness. In 1789, when the First Congress had to decide the administrative structure for finances, there was considerable discussion as to whether control should be vested in a single executive or under a Board of Commissioners. Elbridge Gerry warned that such power in the hands of one man would create innumerable opportunities for embezzlement, peculation, and for "defrauding the revenue, without check or control, and it is next to impossible he should remain unsullied in his reputation, or innoxious with respect to misapplying his trust." He argued that a board would permit the selection of commissioners from each section of the country: Eastern, Middle, and Southern. But Jeremiah Wadsworth of Connecticut, drawing on his own experience during the Confederation, called a Board of Treasury "the worst of all institutions." Even with good men there was a lack of system, fixed principles, and responsibility. That sentiment prevailed.[3]

The remaining issue narrowed down to the scope of power to be delegated to the Secretary of the Treasury. It was proposed on June 25, 1789, that the Secretary not only digest plans for the improvement and management of the revenue but also *report* them. John Page of Virginia objected to that as a "dangerous innovation" and a threat to the privilege of the House of Representatives to originate all bills for raising revenue. He feared it would establish a precedent "which might be extended, until we admitted all the ministers of the Government on the floor, to explain and support the plans they have digested and reported: thus laying a foundation for an aristocracy or a detestable monarchy."[4] Benjamin Goodhue chided his colleagues for exhibiting suspicion and jealousy toward the fledgling Department of the Treasury:

> We certainly carry our dignity to the extreme, when we refuse to receive information from any but ourselves. It must be admitted, that the Secretary of the Treasury

11

will, from the nature of his office, be better acquainted with the subject of improving the revenue or curtailing expense, than any other person; if he is thus capable of affording useful information, shall we reckon it hazardous to receive it?[5]

Thomas Fitzsimons of Pennsylvania suggested that the bill be amended by striking out the word "report" and inserting *prepare* in its place. The bill enacted into law reflected that change: ". . . it shall be the duty of the Secretary of the Treasury to digest and prepare plans for the improvement and management of the revenue, and for the support of public credit; to prepare and report estimates of the public revenue, and the public expenditures. . . ." He was also required to "make report, and give information to either branch of the legislature, in person or in writing (as he may be required), respecting all matters referred to him by the Senate or House of Representatives, or which shall appertain to his office."[6]

Prior to the creation of the Treasury Department, Congress had appointed a committee of three on April 29 to prepare and report an estimate on supplies and revenues. On July 24 a 10-man Committee on Ways and Means was appointed, but it was disbanded several weeks after the establishment of the Treasury Department.[7] Its duties were absorbed by the new Secretary of the Treasury, Alexander Hamilton, who found himself in an office he had anticipated earlier in Federalist 36: "Nations in general, even under governments of the more popular kind, usually commit the administration of their finances to single men or to boards composed of a few individuals, who digest and prepare, in the first instance, the plans of taxation, which are afterwards passed into law by the authority of the sovereign or legislature."

Congress originally anticipated a close working relationship with the Secretary of the Treasury. Before long, however, some Members found the contact too close for comfort. When Hamilton asked to come before Congress in 1792 to answer questions concerning the public debt, legislators protested the practice of mixing the two branches. They objected to having the heads of departments originate legislation or even voice an opinion that might influence Congress.[8]

Congress stepped up its attack on Hamilton. A House resolution in 1793 claimed that he had violated appropriation laws, ignored Presidential instructions, failed to discharge essential duties, and had committed an indecorum against the House. On every single count he was exonerated, but criticism continued. A new charge in 1794, regarding a pension claim, was later dismissed by Congress as "wholly illiberal and groundless." Legislative investigations persisted until Hamilton, in December 1794, satisfied the critics by announcing his intention to resign. During his tenure as Secretary his activities had spanned the entire breadth of the Cabinet, bringing influence to bear not only on Treasury but also on the Secretaries of State and War and on the Attorney General.[9]

REFORMS BY JEFFERSONIAN REPUBLICANS

In March 1794, during Hamilton's last year as Secretary of the Treasury, the House revived its Ways and Means Committee. It operated as a select committee for one session but was not reappointed. Steps were taken in December 1795 to reestablish the committee, this time to function on a permanent basis. Although it was not until 1802 that Ways and Means was formally included in the House Rules as a standing committee, it had existed and functioned in that capacity ever since December 1795. The Senate continued to refer general appropriation bills to select committees until 1816, at which point it established the Committee on Finance as a standing committee. Within a few years the committee firmly established its control over tariff and appropriation bills in the Senate.[10]

During the early 1800s, Congress handled the nation's finances with little difficulty. An abundance of customs revenue easily covered the modest expenses of the national government. By possessing responsibilities over both revenue and appropriation, the House Ways and Means Committee, together with Senate Finance, had an opportunity to maintain a coherent picture of national financial needs. Supervision of *expenditures*, however, was a weak point. Among its other duties, the House Ways and Means Committee had been directed in 1802 "to examine into the state of the several departments, and particularly into the laws making appropriations of moneys, and to report whether the moneys have been disbursed conformably with such laws." A separate House Committee for Public Expenditures was established in 1814 to relieve Ways and Means of that responsibility, and in 1816 the House further divided the labor by setting up six separate committees to oversee the expenditures of the Departments of State, Treasury, War, Navy, and Post Office, as well as expenditures for public buildings. The work of the expenditure committees never received high marks.[11]

Annual estimates of expenditures originated in the various bureaus and agencies of the executive branch. An act in 1800 made it the duty of the Secretary of the Treasury "to digest, prepare and lay before Congress at the commencement of every session, a report on the subject of finance, containing estimates of the public revenue and public expenditures. . . ." The financial policy of Jefferson's Secretary of the Treasury, Albert Gallatin, depended on a systematic budget and close scrutiny of bureau estimates. His principal goals included reduction of the national debt and elimination of excise taxes. To reach those goals he first had to estimate the revenue from customs, postage, and public lands, and then subtract the annual payment on the debt. That left him with the amount of $2,650,000 to run the Government, requiring stringent economies in the naval and military establishments.[12]

Gallatin's interest in the War and Navy Departments was of a continuing nature. He objected to Navy estimates in 1803 on two grounds: the merits of the requests and the competence of Robert Smith, Secretary of the Navy. He told Jefferson that the estimates were much beyond what was necessary. It was later suggested that Gallatin serve as Secretary of State in Madison's Administration, on the understanding that Smith would take over as Secretary of the Treasury. As Henry Adams observed, Gallatin "dryly remarked that he could not undertake to carry on both Departments at once, and requested Mr. Madison to leave him where he was."[13]

Financial recommendations by Gallatin, who had previously served on the House Ways and Means Committee, were routinely accepted by the Cabinet and by Congress. John Randolph, chairman of the committee, was a close personal friend. During committee meetings it was "doubtless . . . under Gallatin's directing eye that Randolph exacted promises from Secretaries Dearborn and Smith to pare the expenditures of the War and Navy departments a further $600,000."[14] Gallatin's financial reports in future years, particularly during 1807-08 and 1811, demonstrate a continuing effort to relate estimated expenditures to anticipated revenue, and to present financial options for the foreign policy issues facing the Administration.[15]

EXECUTIVE CONTROL, 1817-1865

President Monroe complained on several occasions that Treasury reports were being sent to Congress without first being communicated to him. It has been reported that matters between Monroe and his Secretary of the Treasury, William Crawford, became so strained that personal communications between them ceased altogether. According to an account by John Quincy Adams, a visit by Crawford concerning the nomination of certain customs officers resulted in a confrontation in which Crawford raised his cane, as in the attitude to strike, and exclaimed: "You damned infernal old scoundrel!" Monroe seized the tongs at the fireplace in self-defense, applied a retaliatory epithet, and ordered Crawford to leave. Adams said that the two men never met afterwards.[16]

During his own Presidency, John Quincy Adams was kept much better informed about budget estimates. At one point, when his Secretary of the Treasury pressed for reduction of departmental estimates to the lowest possible level, Adams cautioned that it was advisable to include a little padding. Congressional committees felt an obligation to "retrench something from the estimates presented to them; and if some superfluity be not given them to lop off, they will cut into the very flesh of the public necessities."[17]

The struggle between Andrew Jackson and the Second United States Bank opened a new chapter in the contest over the spending power. Congress frequently treated the Secretary of the Treasury as *its* agent, delegating to him— rather than the President—the responsibility for placing Government money either in the national bank or in State banks. Jackson wanted the funds deposited in State banks but had to remove two Secretaries of the Treasury before finding someone willing to execute his plan. A Senate resolution censured Jackson for acting in derogation of the Constitution and the laws. In defense, Jackson contended that the Secretary of the Treasury was "wholly an executive officer" and could be removed whenever the President was no longer willing to be responsible for the Secretary's actions. Jackson regarded the safekeeping of public funds as an executive, not a legislative, responsibility.[18]

Van Buren shared that attitude. The financial panic of 1837 required even greater Presidential leadership over the budget. Van Buren's First Annual Message stated that the condition of the country made it necessary to keep budget estimates as low as practicable. The Departments were therefore asked to "prepare their estimates accordingly, and I am happy to find that they have been able to graduate them on so economical a scale." His last annual message,

16

on December 5, 1840, also referred to the need to reduce expenditures because of the recession.[19]

The Whigs had gained control of the White House in 1840. Upon entering office, William Henry Harrison warned of the "unhallowed union of the Treasury with the executive department," declaring that the essential difference between monarchy and the American Presidency was the former's control over public finances. It was a great error, he said, for the founding fathers not to have made the Secretary of the Treasury entirely independent of the President.[20] John Tyler, who succeeded Harrison, reiterated that sentiment in his inaugural address:

> I deem it of the most essential importance that a complete separation should take place between the sword and the purse. No matter where or how the public moneys shall be deposited, so long as the President can exert the power of appointing and removing at his pleasure the agents selected for their custody the Commander in Chief of the Army and Navy is in fact the treasurer.[21]

Realities of office eventually taught Tyler that the separation between sword and purse could not be so complete. In his Second Annual Message, in 1842, when the country was still in the midst of a business slump, he said that departmental heads had paid "every proper attention" to the interest of the country, and that the "reduction in the annual expenditures of the Government already accomplished furnishes a sure evidence that economy in the application of the public moneys is regarded as a paramount duty." The following year he told Congress of his concern that the Treasury would be exhausted because revenue was not as high as estimated and expenditures were exceeding Treasury calculations. He later reported that every effort had been made "to retrench all superfluities and lop off all excrescences. . . ."[22]

Executive budget leadership increased in 1844 with the election of James K. Polk as President. Drawing upon his legislative experience as chairman of the Ways and Means Committee, he became an active participant in controlling departmental estimates and in determining the level of Federal expenditures. In his first year in office he directed his Cabinet to pay close attention to the estimates submitted by bureau chiefs, who were "favourable to large expenditures, and in some instances included objects which were unconstitutional, especially in regard to internal improvements."[23]

Polk's interest in budgetary matters was fully aroused two years later when he learned that his decision to call up volunteers for the Mexican crisis might have to be postponed. The reason: insufficient funds. After an investigation pointed in the direction of the Quartermaster Department, the President said he was "astounded" by its expenditures and equally appalled by the condition of the Department's books. The situation darkened when Quartermaster General Jesup returned to Washington to offer an explanation. He finally admitted to having requisitioned $2 million to be transferred to New Orleans, allowing two bankers to act as transfer agents. They deposited $400,000 with the quartermaster in New Orleans and kept the balance for stock speculation. Polk said the disclosure nearly made him sick.[24]

After that experience he intensified his scrutiny of departmental estimates. He reviewed them with Cabinet members and sometimes even with bureau chiefs in the War Department. He warned of padding in the estimates from military departments, which were in the habit of estimating for "very large and sometimes extravagant sums. They do this for two reasons, first, because they suppose their own consequence depends somewhat on the sums they may [have] to disburse in their respective branches of the service during the year; and secondly, because they say their estimates may be cut down by Congress." When cutbacks by Cabinet members seemed too timid, he intervened to reduce items or eliminate them altogether.[25]

18

The Presidents who immediately followed Polk extolled the virtues of frugality and economy in their annual messages, but considered the level of Federal spending a legislative prerogative. An exception to this pre-Civil War period was James Buchanan, generally regarded as one of our less assertive Presidents. The financial panic of 1857-58 may explain his interest in budgetary affairs. He told Congress that the heads of departments had been instructed to reduce their estimates "to the lowest standard consistent with the efficiency of the service. . . ." The budget estimates of the Treasury, War, Navy, and Interior Departments "have each been in some degree reduced. . . ."[26]

We can assume that Civil War financing required Lincoln to review departmental estimates, and yet solid evidence is lacking. We do know that Lincoln did not trust the loyalty of departmental officials. At the time of the firing on Fort Sumter he said that the "several Departments of the Government . . . contained so large a number of disloyal persons that it would have been impossible to provide safely through official agents only for the performance of the duties thus confided to citizens favorably known for their ability, loyalty, and patriotism." Every department was "paralyzed by treason," he said.[27] Under such conditions he would have done well to review departmental estimates before they were sent to Congress.

Congressional Organization

The ability of Congress to maintain a coherent picture of national finances was weakened by two developments during the 19th century: division of the general appropriation bill into separate pieces of legislation, and splintering of the money committees in both Houses.

The first development began in 1794 when Congress passed two general acts, one for the support of Government and one to support the military establishment. In 1799

Congress passed a separate appropriation bill for the Navy Department (created the previous year) and during the 1820s it enacted separate appropriation bills for fortifications (1823), pensions (1826), and rivers and harbors (1826). Separate appropriations were provided for the Military Academy in 1834, the Indian Department in 1837, the Post Office in 1844, and for the Legislative, Executive, and Judicial branches in 1856.[28]

The money committees lost large portions of their jurisdiction after the Civil War. The Senate Finance Committee's responsibility over appropriation measures was handed out to two new committees: an Appropriations Committ- was justified as a means of dividing the "onerous labors of the Finance Committee with another committee." The resolution was taken up by unanimous consent and agreed to.[29]

Under the strain of Civil War financing, the House Ways and Means Committee found it increasingly difficult to discharge its responsibilities. In 1865 its jurisdiction was reduced to revenue bills, its other responsibilities parceled out to two new committees: an Appropriations Committee and a Committee on Banking and Currency. Proponents of that division of labor credited Ways and Means with faithful and diligent service but said that "no set of men, however enduring their patience, studious their habits, or gigantic their mental grasp, when overburdened with the labor incident to the existing monetary condition of the country growing out of this unparalleled civil strife, can do this labor as well as the people have a right to expect of their Representatives." The newly created House Appropriations Committee was reminded that the "tendency of the time is to extravagance in private and in the public," and that their full labors would be required to restrain excessive and illegal appropriations.[30]

Presidents continued to play a part in controlling the budget. On December 6, 1869, President Grant told Congress that the estimate for the War Department was "as low as it is believed can be relied on. The estimates of bureau officers have been carefully scrutinized, and reduced wherever it has been deemed practicable." Four years later, in the midst of the depression of 1873, the House of Representatives appealed to the executive branch for assistance in balancing the budget. Henry Laurens Dawes of Massachusetts announced that the Secretary of the Treasury had recommended a tax increase of approximately $40 million. Dawes introduced a resolution to require departmental heads to reduce their estimates of expenditures "to the end that all possible effort at reduction be exhausted before new burdens be imposed upon the people." James Garfield, chairman of House Appropriations, offered a substitute resolution that placed directly upon President Grant the responsibility for having estimates revised. There was some opposition from those who considered Congress fully competent to make whatever reductions were required, but the resolution was adopted.[31]

FRAGMENTATION OF APPROPRIATIONS COMMITTEES

In the period after 1865, House Appropriations came under fire for exercising too much control over legislative committees. Resentment deepened after adoption of the "Holman Rule" in 1876. That provision gave House Appropriations authority to retrench expenditures by reducing the number and salary of Federal officials, the compensation of any person paid out of the Treasury, and the amounts of money covered in an appropriation bill. In an article published three years later, James Garfield said that the construction given the Holman Rule resulted in putting a "great mass of general legislation" in appropriation bills. And then, in a prophetic warning:

If this rule be continued in force, it will be likely to break down the Committee on Appropriations, and disperse the annual bills to several committees, so that the legislation on that subject will not be managed by any one committee, nor in accordance with any general and comprehensive plan.[32]

Step by step the powers of House Appropriations were reduced. Through suspension of the rules, the Committee on Commerce gained control over funding of the rivers and harbors bill in 1877. An effort in 1880 to restore that bill to the Appropriations Committee was defeated. The House gave the Committee on Commerce the "same privilege in reporting bills making appropriations for the improvement of rivers and harbors as is accorded to the Committee on Appropriations in reporting general appropriation bills." The Committee on Agriculture and Forestry also gained the right, in 1880, to receive estimates and report appropriations in its area.[33]

In 1885 the House Appropriations Committee was stripped of six additional areas: consular and diplomatic affairs, Army, Military Academy, Navy, Post Office, and Indian affairs. This fragmentation has been explained as an act of reprisal against the committee chairman Samuel J. Randall, who had opposed his party's low-tariff policy. Personal animosities flavored the dispute. During his service as Speaker in 1877, Randall had demoted William Morrison by transferring him from the chairmanship of Ways and Means to that of Public Lands. Morrison bided his time, waiting for his moment of revenge. The opportunity came in 1883, after the Democrats regained control of the House. Morrison led the opposition to Randall's reelection as Speaker. John G. Carlisle, the new Speaker, promptly put Morrison back as chairman of Ways and Means. Randall was made chairman of Appropriations. When Morrison reported out a tariff-reduction bill, Randall helped defeat it by siding with the Republicans. In retaliation, Morrison helped strip Randall's committee of six areas of jurisdiction.[34]

(Behind this weakening of House Appropriations was the conviction among many congressmen that economy had been carried too far) Charles Lore of Delaware regarded the breakup of House Appropriations as an opportunity to consider measures which younger members wanted for their districts. Suppose it did lead to greater spending, he asked; would a legislator "come here and wear his boy's roundabout which he has outgrown and when he had come to man's stature? Would he take his old coat split up the back like a locust?"[35] Speaker Thomas Reed also emphasized the new needs pressing upon the country:

> But Mr. Carlisle and Mr. Morrison would not have been able to strip the Committee on Appropriations of its bills merely because they wished to deprive Mr. Randall of power. Behind them and behind the movement were the growing needs of the country. When economy is carried to extreme and becomes parsimony, it is only a hindrance and a stumbling-block instead of a virtue. In 1885 economy had become parsimony, and the real needs of the country had been repeatedly sacrificed to a mere show of figures.[36]

The appropriations process also fragmented on the Senate side. In 1877 the rivers and harbors appropriation bill was assigned to the Senate Committee on Commerce. Not until 1895, however, did Senator Fred Dubois introduce a resolution to distribute the bulk of Senate Appropriations' jurisdiction to ten other committees. He maintained that it was physically impossible for the Appropriations Committee to give adequate consideration to all the budget requests. The glut of appropriation bills at the end of each session interfered with debate and limited the opportunity for amendments. Other Senators expressed a desire to put an end to the "monopolistic dominance" of the Appropriations and Finance Committees. The dismantling of Senate Appropriations finally occurred in 1899. In addition to the referral of

rivers and harbors bills to Commerce, six other appropriation bills were dispersed to legislative committees. The
agriculture bill went to Agriculture and Forestry; the Army
and Military Academy bill to Military Affairs; the Indian
bill to Indian Affairs; the naval bill to Naval Affairs; the
pension bill to Pensions; and the Post Office bill to Post-
Offices and Post-Roads.[37]

Party leaders shouldered some of the responsibility
formerly held by House Appropriations. The Speaker acted
as a partial restraint on spending by refusing to recognize
Members who put forth extravagant proposals. Thomas
Reed, Speaker in the 1880s and 1890s, used his recognition
power to resist demands for an omnibus public buildings
bill, despite the fact that 308 Members had signed a petition
urging its passage. An article by Rollo Ogden in 1897 recommended stronger party control as a means of controlling
national expenditures. That control was to be exercised
either through the party caucus or through the Speaker,
giving him the "power over legislation, including appropriations, which he now wields secretly, and to insist upon his
having an acknowledged public responsibility, as leader
of his party, as well as the private one which he now really
has."[38]

Joseph Cannon, during his years as Speaker, also used the
power of recognition to curb spending. More than two-thirds
of the Members had signed a petition asking to have a public buildings bill considered by unanimous consent or under
suspension of the rules. When Cannon learned that the bill
contained $20 million, he notified the chairman of the com-
mittee that he would not recognize him. Cannon is reported
to have said: "I will not recognize any one to move to
suspend the rules to pass that bill, but if two-thirds of this
House has the courage of its convictions, as indicated in
that petition, it can remove me as Speaker, and put in a
Speaker who will acquiesce in their wishes and pass the
bill."[39]

24

"Protector of the Purse"

In the years following the Civil War the President, not Congress, emerged as the more trusted guardian of the purse. This image was simplistic, of course, in the sense that special interests could (and did) exert influence on executive decisions. Yet implicit in the budget reform proposals of the early 20th century was the belief that economy could be better achieved by augmenting the power of the President.

Congress was especially vulnerable for its handling of rivers and harbors bills. President Arthur, in vetoing one in 1882, put his finger on the root cause behind such legislation. Citizens from one State, learning that public revenues were being used for projects elsewhere, insisted on projects for themselves. "Thus," Arthur noted, "as the bill becomes more objectionable it secures more support." Although Congress promptly passed the bill over his veto, Arthur received favorable publicity for his effort. A cartoon by Thomas Nast shows the President armed with a rifle, watching an oversized vulture, perched upon the Capitol, consume his veto message. At the bottom of the cartoon were these words of encouragement: "President Arthur, hit him again! Don't let the vulture become our national bird."[40]

Another heavy drain on the Treasury was the pension system, sanctified by an aura of patriotism and self-sacrifice. Frauds had followed the Revolutionary War and the War of 1812, but the full measure of chicanery by pension claimants and their agents was not felt until after the Civil War. Federal outlays for military pensions reached record heights from one decade to the next: $29 million in 1870, $57 million in 1880, $106 million in 1890, and $139 million at the turn of the century. The last veteran's benefit for the Revolutionary War was not paid out until 1906—123 years after that war had ended.[41]

Veterans met slight resistance from Congress, while Cleveland stands as the only determined counterforce among the

Presidents. In his first term he vetoed 304 bills—almost three times as many as all Presidential vetoes before him. A full 241 of the Cleveland vetoes were leveled at private and general pension bills.[42] Even those statistics do not capture the poor quality of pension legislation. Forty-two pension bills were killed by pocket vetoes. Other bills became law without Cleveland's signature because he lacked time to study them.

On a single day in 1886 he was handed nearly 240 private bills—granting new pensions, increasing their benefits, or restoring old names to the list. A check by the Pension Bureau revealed that most of the claims had been there before and had been rejected. Some disabilities existed before the claimant's enlistment; others were not incurred in the line of duty; still others had their origin after discharge. Denied relief by the Bureau, individuals turned to their Congressmen for assistance through private bills.[43]

Cleveland's vetoes of pension bills in 1886 earned a reputation for their sarcastic quality. One claimant, who enrolled in the Army on March 25, 1865, entered a post hospital a week later with the measles. He returned to duty on May 8 and was mustered out of the service three days later. Cleveland observed that 15 years after this "brilliant service and this terrific encounter with the measles," the claimant discovered that the measles had somehow affected his eyes and spinal column. Cleveland found no merit to the claim. He bristled at another pension request from a widow whose husband had joined the service and deserted several days later. "Those who prosecute claims for pension," said Cleveland, "have grown very bold when cases of this description are presented for consideration."[44]

Within the space of three days, during June 1886, Cleveland turned out 43 pension vetoes. A Thomas Nast cartoon captures the President in his new role as protector of the purse. Cleveland is shown manfully blocking the door to the U.S. Treasury while thwarted pension agents slink from his presence.[45]

26

Cleveland's steadfast position on pension abuses may well have cost him the 1888 election. The Grand Army of the Republic, acting in the role of self-appointed spokesman for veterans, campaigned vigorously against him. The crucial loss of Indiana and New York, which Cleveland had carried in 1884, appears to have been the price of his numerous pension vetoes. The newly elected Benjamin Harrison promptly repaid the G.A.R. by appointing James Tanner, a former member of their Pension Committee, to the post of Commissioner of Pensions. Cleveland was reelected in 1892, however, and continued to decry the "barefaced and extensive pension frauds," the pension agents who urged "reckless pension expenditure, while nursing selfish schemes," and the "increasing latitude clearly discernible in special pension legislation."[46]

STUDIES ON ECONOMY AND EFFICIENCY

Expenditures by the national government increased sharply at the end of the century. On top of pension bills and rivers and harbors projects, Federal outlays were further swelled by the Spanish-American War and construction of the Panama Canal. After 28 uninterrupted years of budget surpluses, from 1866 to 1903, the nation encountered deficits for the next six years.

Congress initiated a number of inquiries into work methods of the executive departments. The Cockrell Committee (1887-89) exposed some of the reasons for huge backlogs in administrative work: time-consuming and duplicative routines, hiring of proxies, unnecessary record-keeping, and reliance on copyists who transcribed by hand instead of utilizing typewriters, carbon paper, and duplicating machines. The Cockrell-Dockery Commission (1893-95) also investigated into executive operations, resulting in new accounting proposals for the Treasury Department.[47]

A decline in customs revenue in 1904, coupled with a sharp rise in expenditures reflecting a $50 million right-of-

27

way payment for the Panama Canal, produced a sizable deficit for the Roosevelt Administration. On his own initiative, President Roosevelt appointed the Keep Commission in 1905 to determine how the executive branch might conduct its business on the "most economical and effective basis in the light of the best modern business practices." He stressed the need to eliminate duplication of work, wasteful habits, superfluous letter-writing, and inordinate attention to paper work. He recalled one naval officer who prided himself on his ability to determine, from a big case of papers, the number of bottles of violet ink assigned to the captain of each battleship.[48]

Congress tried to tighten its control over budget deficiencies in 1905 by requiring appropriations to be apportioned by monthly or other allotments, "as to prevent undue expenditures in one portion of the year that may require deficiency or additional appropriations to complete the service of the fiscal year." Departmental heads were allowed to waive or modify the apportionment requirement—a freedom invoked with such frequency that Congress rewrote the legislation the following year. Waivers or modifications were prohibited "except upon the happening of some extraordinary emergency or unusual circumstance which could not be anticipated at the time of making such apportionment. . . ."[49]

As a result of larger receipts from customs and from internal revenue in 1906 and 1907, the budget moved back to a surplus position, but only temporarily. Revenues fell in 1908 and new legislation pushed pension costs from $139 million in 1907 to over $161 million in 1908. Heavy deficits reappeared in 1908 and 1909; another deficit of $73 million was forecast for fiscal 1910.[50]

Responding to this new rash of deficits, Congress directed the Secretary of the Treasury in 1909 to estimate revenue for the coming year. If a deficit appeared likely, he was to recommend reductions in appropriations. If he considered that impracticable, it was his responsibility to recommend

28

loans or new taxes to cover the deficiency. At the same time, President Taft directed his departmental heads to make their estimates "as low as possible consistent with imperative governmental necessity." The Secretary of the Treasury reported to Congress that there could "scarcely be more scrutiny" of budget estimates than was given by the President and his Cabinet.[51]

Taft estimated that he had reduced the fiscal 1911 budget by $42.8 million. He advised Congress that departmental estimates were "cut to the quick, so to speak, and any assumption on the part of Congress, so often made in times past, that the estimates have been prepared with the expectation that they may be reduced, will result in seriously hampering proper administration." He reinforced his control over departmental estimates by issuing Executive Order 1142, prohibiting bureau officers or division chiefs from applying to Congress for legislation or appropriations except with the consent and knowledge of the head of the department. Furthermore, no request from Congress for information was to be satisfied "except through or as authorized by the head of his department." To his chagrin, Congress cut deeply into his budget requests, forcing him to come back later for supplemental appropriations.[52]

COMMISSION ON ECONOMY AND EFFICIENCY

This experience convinced Taft that neither he nor Congress had adequate information with which to make intelligent decisions on the budget. At his request, in 1910, Congress appropriated $100,000 to finance an investigation into more efficient and economical ways of conducting the public business. Taft used the money to set up a five-member Commission on Economy and Efficiency. Over the next two years the Commission prepared comprehensive reports on the management of executive departments.[53]

In June 1912, Taft submitted to Congress the Commission's proposals for a national budget. The President would be made responsible for reviewing departmental estimates and organizing them into a coherent document. The latter would then serve as the basis for intelligent legislative action. The Commission said that the budget was the "only effective means whereby *the Executive* may be made responsible for getting before the country a definite, well-considered, comprehensive program with respect to which *the legislature* must also assume responsibility either for action or inaction."[54]

Those proposals were not adopted during Taft's Administration. His party did not control the House of Representatives in 1911-13, where support was essential, and the Presidential election year of 1912 was close at hand. There was little likelihood that Taft would remain in office. Moreover, the financial embarrassment of the Nation had eased considerably. Taft himself had cut expenditures by his review of departmental estimates, while receipts from the 1909 tariff bill exceeded any customs revenue in the history of the country. Passage of the 16th Amendment (proposed in 1909 and ratified in 1913) promised even larger revenues from an income tax. In this case, however, adoption of a direct income tax would become one of the conditions for budget reform. Prior revenues had come from a system of indirect taxation that the ordinary taxpayer did not see or feel (revenue from tariff duties, taxes on tobacco, or liquor, etc.). Direct taxes would heighten the public demand for economy and efficiency.[55]

On June 10, 1912, President Taft directed departmental heads to prepare two sets of estimates: one for the customary Book of Estimates and a second for the national budget recommended by his Commission. Since the budgetary situation had improved, and legislators feared that Taft might exercise budget powers to reduce programs in their districts, Congress moved to block his plans. An act of August 23 directed administrative personnel to prepare estimates and to submit them to Congress only in the form required by law.[56]

Once again the two branches had locked horns on the budget issue, each contending that its prerogatives were at stake. Congress considered the budget format to be part of its spending prerogative. Taft regarded the form in which he transmitted recommendations to Congress as purely an executive matter. He went ahead with his plan to submit two budgets, but the model budget for the fiscal year ending June 30, 1914, was almost completely ignored by Congress. After leaving office, Taft lamented that dust was accumulating on the reports of his Commission.[57] It took the financial shock of World War I to finally precipitate action on budget reform.

BUDGET AND ACCOUNTING ACT

Although Woodrow Wilson entered office in 1913 with a keen interest in budget reform, he appeared to seek co-ordination and accountability simply by centering control of all appropriations in a single committee. On the other hand, John Fitzgerald, chairman of the House Appropriations Committee, called for bolder action: Presidential formulation of estimates (to fix responsibility) and a system that would make it as difficult as possible for legislators to increase the amounts proposed by the President. For increases by Congress, Fitzgerald suggested a two-thirds majority.[58]

The war in Europe soon diverted the Government's attention from budget reform legislation, and yet executive budgets were adopted by a number of States and by municipal governments. Moreover, in 1916 the three major parties all agreed on the need for budget reform at the national level. Republicans, rebuking the Democratic Administration for failing to sponsor the proposals of the Taft Commission, pledged the GOP to the establishment of a "businesslike budget system." The Progressive Party also endorsed a national budget. Democrats limited their recom-

31

mendations to a return by the House to a single Appropriations Committee "as a practicable first step towards a budget system." The year 1916 also marked the creation of the Institute for Government Research, a private association set up to promote efficiency and economy in Government operations. Forerunner of the Brookings Institution, it published a series of influential studies on budget reform, concluding that the "essence" of a budget was that "it shall be formulated by the executive and by the executive alone."[59]

After 1916, World War I pushed Federal expenditures to record levels—from about $700 million before the war to upwards of $12.7 billion and $18.5 billion by 1918 and 1919. Deficits reached unprecedented magnitudes. The total national debt—slightly over $1 billion in 1916—soared beyond $25 billion by 1919. It was a foregone conclusion that debt management problems after the war would require modernization of the budget process and an increased financial responsibility for the executive branch.

In his annual message to Congress in December 1917, President Wilson repeated his party's platform on budget reform by urging the House to centralize appropriations in a single committee. The precise degree to which Wilson scrutinized the budget estimates is not known, but his record does not seem unlike Taft's. The estimates were generally taken up in the Cabinet meetings, where the Secretaries of the departments presented their estimates and plans. If individual estimates exceeded the total amount determined by the President and his Cabinet, the Secretaries would have to make whatever reductions were necessary.[60]

In March 1918, Congressman Medill McCormick introduced a number of bills and resolutions calling for unification of departmental estimates by the Secretary of the Treasury, creation of a House budget committee to replace the Committees on Ways and Means and Appropriations, establishment of an independent audit of departmental accounts, and reorganization of the Treasury Department. He proposed that a 40-man House budget committee be given jurisdiction over both revenue and appropriations, with power to reduce but not add, unless requested by the Secretary of the Treasury upon the authority of the President, or unless the committee could muster a two-thirds majority of its members. Members of the House would not be able to add to the budget on the floor, except to restore what the President had originally submitted.[61]

Critics of executive budget-making considered it a diminution of legislative power. "Uncle Joe" Cannon, Speaker of the House from 1903 to 1911, warned that an executive budget would signify the surrender of the most important element of representative government: "I think we had better stick pretty close to the Constitution with its division of powers well defined and the taxing power close to the people." Edward Fitzpatrick, author of a budget study in 1918, characterized the executive budget concept as a step toward autocracy and a Prussian-style military state.[62]

President Wilson continued to withhold his support for a national budget. From the Peace Conference in Paris, in February 1919, he cabled Swager Sherley, the new chairman of House Appropriations: "I hear you are again endeavoring to work out a budget system plan. I hope you will succeed." But it was Wilson's position that reliable studies on the budget could begin only after Senate action on the peace treaty, for that would decide the level of defense spending, disposal of military surplus property, and demobilization of the economy.[63]

In June 1919 the House passed a resolution to create a Select Committee on the Budget. The resulting committee report criticized the lack of internal executive checks on departmental estimates:

> The estimates are a patchwork and not a structure. As a result, a great deal of the time of the committees of Congress is taken up in exploding the visionary schemes of bureau chiefs for which no administration would be willing to stand responsible.[64]

Economy and efficiency, said the committee, could be secured only by making an officer responsible for receiving and scrutinizing requests for funds by bureau and departmental chiefs: "In the National Government there can be no question but that the officer upon whom should be placed this responsibility is the President of the United States."[65] A bureau of the budget, to be located in the office of the President, would assist him in that task. To protect the President's responsibility, the bill reserved to him alone the right to submit budget estimates to Congress, unless either House requested such information from other executive officials.

The bill that passed the House on October 21, 1919, did not provide for an "executive budget." It was executive only in the sense that the President was responsible for the estimates. It was legislative in the sense that Congress had full power to increase or reduce the estimates. Increases could be made in committee or on the floor by simple majority vote.[66]

Wilson finally announced, on December 2, 1919, his support for a national budget. The Senate, preoccupied with the peace treaty, did not act until the following spring. The bill reported by the Senate Special Committee on the National Budget differed from the House version in certain respects. It recommended that the budget bureau be placed not in the President's office but in the Treasury. The committee felt that it would be necessary for the director of the bureau to set his judgment against that of a Cabinet member. In the event the President sided with the director on any serious issue, it would result in the resignation of the Cabinet officer. Placing the budget bureau in the Treasury Department, the committee decided, would facilitate adjustment of such differences without constant appeal to the President. Moreover, placement in Treasury would permit coordination between expenditures and revenue.[67]

The bill that came out of conference reached an imaginative compromise by placing the budget bureau directly under the control of the President but making the Secretary of the Treasury the budget director. Wilson vetoed the bill because it provided for removal of the Comptroller General and the Assistant Comptroller General by concurrent resolution (which is not submitted to the President for his signature). Wilson regarded the removal power as an "essential incident" to the appointing power of the President. The House vote to override the President was 178-103, short of the necessary two-thirds margin. The House then modified the vetoed bill to meet Wilson's objection but no action was taken on the Senate side.[68]

Congress passed a new bill early in 1921, signed into law by Warren G. Harding. The Budget and Accounting Act created a Bureau of the Budget, to be located in the Treasury Department, and authorized the President to appoint his own budget director. The Budget Bureau was given authority to "assemble, correlate, revise, reduce, or increase the estimates of the several departments or establishments," except estimates for Congress and the Supreme Court, which are included in the budget without revision.[69]

Removal of the Comptroller General and the Assistant Comptroller General was to be by joint resolution, a form of legislation which must be submitted to the President for his signature. Wilson's objection had been satisfied, but only in part. The initiative for removal of the Comptroller General still lay with Congress.

2

Presidential Budgeting
(1921-1975)

THE Budget and Accounting Bill prompted both Houses of Congress to centralize their own controls over the budget. In 1920, immediately after passage of the bill on the House side, the House acted to consolidate jurisdiction over all appropriations in a single committee. It was anticipated that the Appropriations Committee would first parcel out its work to subcommittees and then bring the budget before Congress "in one measure."[1] That objective was made clear during floor debate in 1919:

> MR. JONES OF TEXAS. Is it planned to have the budget presented en masse to the House?
> MR. TAYLOR OF COLORADO. Oh, yes.
> MR. JONES OF TEXAS. Or will it be submitted separately?
> MR. TAYLOR OF COLORADO. It will be submitted en masse to the House and considered systematically and consecutively as the great national budget. . . . one great appropriation committee of 35 will bring the President's budget, with such changes as they agree upon, all at one time, so that it may be considered at once.[2]

In 1922 the Senate changed its rules to give appropriations jurisdiction to a single committee. In order to secure sufficient votes to pass the resolution, three members each from seven authorization committees were made ex officio members of the new Appropriations Committee. That feature remains in the Senate rules today. Three members of certain designated committees, to be selected by their respective committees, serve as ex officio members of the Appropriations Committee whenever the annual appropriation bill in their area is being considered.[3]

This appearance of centralization in 1920 and 1922 was soon offset by several factors. Instead of waiting for all subcommittee products to come before Congress "in one measure," Congress acted on them one at a time. Moreover, the subcommittees enjoyed a substantial degree of autonomy because of the intense specialization required. The full Appropriations Committee, honoring a norm of reciprocity, was expected to defer to subcommittee recommendations.[4]

PRECEDENTS DURING 1920s

Following the 1921 act, administrative regulations extended the Budget Bureau's control over spending levels. The first Budget Director, Charles G. Dawes, issued a circular setting forth procedures for establishing reserves and effecting savings. Appropriations from Congress were to be treated as a mere ceiling on expenditures rather than as a directive or invitation to spend the full amount. Dawes ordered the budget officer from each executive department or independent establishment to obtain from each bureau or branch an estimate of the portion of appropriations considered indispensable for carrying out activities. After review by the Budget Director and approval by the President, the estimated savings would be designated a "General Reserve." The amount approved by the President for expenditure under an appropriation title would represent the "*maximum* available for obligation during the fiscal year." Since further savings would be attempted during the course of the year, each bureau was to withhold additional sums from obligation in order to supplement the General Reserve.[5]

37

As a result of Dawes's circular the apportionment process now had two objectives: to prevent deficiencies (as required by statute) and to effect savings (as directed by administrative regulation). At the end of the year, in another circular, Dawes required agencies to make periodic reports of apportionments and any waiver or modification permitted by law. That his directives fell something short of being self-executing was underscored a few months later when Dawes issued another circular, this time protesting that funds previously reported by a department as a "saving" had been spent without consultation with the Budget Bureau.[6]

The philosophy of treating appropriations as a ceiling—as permissive in nature—was later reiterated by President Harding. In a meeting on June 18, 1923, with the Business Organization of the Government, he emphasized that while appropriations represented the maximum amount of business for that year, they were not a measure of the minimum amount that might be performed:

> Therefore, in planning your expenditure program for the coming fiscal year and apportioning your funds under such program, you should not only carefully guard against any of your activities being carried on at a rate which would require additional appropriations for the fiscal year, but should arrange to conduct your business with a minimum of expense consistent with efficient administration. I expect you all to effect some savings from your appropriations for the coming fiscal year. To accomplish this and also to enable you to have funds on hand with which to meet unanticipated requirements, you should not fail to set aside a reasonable reserve from your appropriations.[7]

Announcements from the Budget Bureau and the President would remain largely hortatory so long as individual agencies retained authority to apportion funds and to waive that process. Not until later, in 1933, did the Budget Bureau gain control over apportionments.

The Budget Bureau, under Dawes, acquired other responsibilities. New procedures were established to control the flow of legislation. While there was no specific statutory authority for that function, the Budget Bureau maintained it was implied in the Budget and Accounting Act. Section 206 prohibited agencies from submitting their financial proposals to Congress unless first requested by either House. Under a broad interpretation, it could be argued that Congress expected the Budget Bureau to review all departmental reports to Congress on proposed or pending legislation.[8]

A circular issued by Dawes in 1921 prescribed Budget Bureau clearance for all legislative proposals originating in the departments, or referred to them by Congress, insofar as the proposals might "create a charge upon the public Treasury or commit the Government to obligations which would later require appropriations to meet them. . . ." In his study on this development, Richard Neustadt has pointed out that the impulse behind this procedure came not from the Budget Bureau but from the House Appropriations Committee, which was concerned about the lack of control and discipline on agency requests.[9]

Now known as "central clearance," the process has three main facets: a review of agency proposals being sent to Congress (to determine if the proposals are "in accord with the program of the President"); coordination of departmental advice on legislation that originated in Congress; and recommendations to the President as to whether he should sign or veto enrolled bills presented to him by Congress. Studies in recent years have emphasized greater intervention by White House staff in the clearance process, relegating to the Budget Bureau routine actions that did not command Presidential attention. The Budget Bureau also established a procedure to clear proposed Executive Orders and proclamations, considered by the Bureau for much the same purpose as reports on legislation.[10]

39

REORGANIZATION UNDER ROOSEVELT

Economic collapse in 1929 led to broader Presidential authority over expenditures. After deficits appeared in 1931, for the first time in a decade, President Hoover asked for authority to effect savings by reorganizing the executive departments. In 1932 he received authority (subject to a one-House veto provision) to make partial layoffs, reduce compensation for public officials, and consolidate executive agencies in order to effect savings. When he issued orders to regroup and consolidate a total of 58 agencies, the House of Representatives disapproved the orders on January 19, 1933, preferring to leave reorganization changes to the incoming President. In his last two days in office Hoover signed two more economy measures, authorizing his successor to effect further reorganization and to reduce military spending in accordance with an economy survey ordered by the President.[11]

Once in office, Franklin Roosevelt requested authority to reduce veterans' benefits and the salaries of Federal employees. Despite opposition from some members of his own party, he obtained that authority in the Economy Act of 1933. On the basis of that authority he issued Executive Order 6166 to reorganize, transfer, and abolish certain executive agencies and functions. His order transferred the functions of "making, waiving, and modifying apportionments of appropriations" from departmental heads and bureau chiefs to the Budget Director.[12] Instead of allowing individual bureau chiefs to adjust apportionment schedules at their own convenience, he placed that decision in the Budget Bureau. The Bureau no longer had to rely merely on indirect pressures to influence agencies, such as its power to review and revise their budget estimates. Several decades would pass before there was full appreciation of the relationship between apportionment authority and Presidential impoundment.

40

Other Executive Orders were issued during this period to increase Presidential control over expenditures. A number of Government corporations and agencies had funds at their disposal which were not derived from annual appropriations. Three Orders in 1935 required them to submit budget estimates, together with proposed apportionment of their expenses, to the Budget Director for his approval.[13]

BROWNLOW COMMITTEE

In 1936 President Roosevelt appointed a Committee on Administrative Management, headed by Louis Brownlow, to study the executive structure of the Government. In its remarks on fiscal management, the committee included among the list of major defects two items of special interest: inadequate staffing of the Budget Bureau (at that time it had about 40 employees) and interference by the General Accounting Office with basic executive responsibilities. Control over expenditures was "essentially an executive function," the committee said, to be discharged through an *accounting* system installed in the Treasury. Expenditures would then be made subject to an independent *audit* by GAO to examine and verify that the Administration had faithfully discharged its responsibility.[14] The committee believed that the

> settlement of accounts and the supervision of administrative accounting systems are executive functions; under the Constitution they belong to the Executive Branch of the Government. The audit, by the same reasoning, should operate under legislative direction. The Comptroller General today straddles both positions.[15]

Accompanying the committee's report were two staff studies bearing directly on the budget issue: "Financial Control and Accountability" by A. E. Buck, and "The General Accounting Office" by Harvey C. Mansfield. Buck took the position that current direction of spending and current

41

budgetary control were "essentially executive functions." Congress should therefore vest the major responsibility for those functions squarely with the President, "without hampering restrictions of one kind or another." He recommended that the Budget Bureau be made an integral part of the Treasury Department and proposed that the following GAO functions be transferred to the Treasury Department: final settlement and adjustment of claims for or against the Government, the keeping of general accounts, and the prescribing of departmental accounting system.[16]

Mansfield also criticized the failure to distinguish between audit (to be exercised by the GAO) and control ("the power to pass on expenditures and prevent their being made," which was a feature of executive management). He maintained that GAO had interfered repeatedly with the proper discharge of administrative responsibilities: "Instances abound of practices required by decisions of the Comptroller General that are maddening to observe when better results could be obtained more quickly and less expensively by different practices."[17]

A separate study by the Brookings Institution, prepared for Senator Byrd's select committee, was not so harsh on the GAO. The study did conclude that the compromise of the Budget and Accounting Act of 1921—attaching the Budget Director to the President but placing the Budget Bureau in Treasury—should end. The Budget Bureau "should be removed from its anomalous position in the Treasury Department and be given independent status under the President." As to its investigative work, the Bureau had "suffered from the too rigorous application of the philosophy that it could not conscientiously recommend economy for other administrative units without practicing the strictest economy itself."[18] That attitude had resulted in inadequate staffing and investigation.

On the basis of recommendations by the Brownlow Committee, Roosevelt proposed in 1937 that Congress establish general principles by which the President could reorganize the executive branch on a continuing basis. He emphasized that although reorganization could improve efficiency and morale, it was not intended as an instrument for major spending reductions.[19] To do that would require elimination of programs and activities.

Nevertheless, the reorganization proposal gradually acquired a cost-saving reputation. In January 1938 the House considered a proposal by Clifton Woodrum, who recommended that the President be authorized to reduce any appropriation whenever he determined, by investigation, that such action would help balance the budget, reduce the public debt, and serve the public interest. Opponents charged that the President could use the authority to dominate Congress and intimidate opposition. Maury Maverick, Democrat of Texas, argued that legislators would hesitate to challenge the President since he "could single out any district or portion of America to have appropriations or not to have appropriations, as he pleased." John Ditter, Republican from Pennsylvania, warned that the reorganization bill put the public purse at the disposal of the President and made the civil service a "ready tool of the Executive for political appointments." Roosevelt's Court-packing proposal had already been described as a scheme to destroy the independence of the judiciary. The reorganization plan was now characterized as a companion move to deprive Congress of its vital spending prerogative.[20]

A different version of the reorganization bill finally passed in 1939, stating that continuing deficits made cutbacks desirable and directing the President to effect savings by consolidating or abolishing agencies for more efficient operation. Reorganization would take effect after 60 days unless voted down by both Houses. Of the five purposes identified in the act, spending reduction, like Abou Ben Adhem, led all the rest. Any appropriation unexpended as a result of the act would be impounded and returned to the Treasury.

Roosevelt strengthened his control over the budget by using the reorganization authority to transfer the Budget Bureau from the Treasury to the newly formed Executive Office of the President. In Executive Order 8248, signed September 8, 1939, he defined the functions and duties of the Budget Bureau.[21]

GROWTH OF BUDGET BUREAU POWERS

Budget Director Dawes was fond of describing his work in modest terms: "One must remember that the Bureau of the Budget is concerned only with the humbler and routine business of government. Unlike cabinet officers, it is concerned with no questions of policy, save that of economy and efficiency."[22] And yet assisting the President in the formulation of the budget was a policy involvement, for that decided which programs to include and at what funding level. Policy was also involved in creating the concept of "General Reserves," encouraging agencies to spend less than Congress had appropriated, and providing central clearance of legislative proposals.

Under the pressure of World War II, the Budget Bureau expanded from its prewar level of approximately 40 people to around 600. Executive Order 8512, issued in 1940, made the Bureau responsible for supervising methods of financial reporting by government agencies. The Federal Reports Act of 1942 required the Budget Director to coordinate Federal reporting and statistical services in order to eliminate duplication and waste. Other statutes and Executive Orders during the war created new tasks, including review of public works projects and budget review of wholly owned Government corporations.[23]

The idea of using the Federal budget as an instrument to promote economic stability gained adherents during the Hoover and Roosevelt Administrations. It evolved from a one-shot, "pump-priming" effort, which would be discontinued once the private economy recovered, to the permanent notion of compensatory fiscal policy. The former was a temporary expedient, the latter a guiding policy to be used from one Administration to the next. After the Budget Bureau was transferred to the Executive Office of the President, a Division of Fiscal Analysis was established to analyze the impact of budgetary operations, expenditure programs, tax programs, and debt management on the economy as a whole. During World War II the Fiscal Division prepared programs for economic stabilization.[24]

Compensatory fiscal policy was a major part of the conceptual development that led to the Employment Act of 1946, which established three broad objectives for the Federal Government: maximum employment, production, and purchasing power. The original version—the Full Employment Bill of 1945—had delegated spending powers to the President. In cases where the private sector failed to provide for full employment, the bill directed the President to prepare a program of Federal investment and expenditures that would close the gap. He was further directed to review Federal programs on a quarterly basis and to alter their rate as he considered necessary for ensuring full employment.[25]

Those provisions were deleted from the bill that became law. However, the Act was interpreted by postwar Presidents as containing an implicit objective of combating inflation. The objective of price stability could be drawn from the goal of maximum purchasing power. Thus, the potential was there for assertive Presidents to invoke the Act when using the budget for stabilization purposes, in some cases delaying expenditures, at other times accelerating them.

Subsequent statutes added to the power of the Budget Bureau. On the basis of the Intergovernmental Cooperation Act of 1968 and a Presidential memorandum of November 8, 1968, the Bureau issued rules and regulations with regard to improved administration of grants-in-aid to the States;

45

special or technical services to State and local units of government; and the formulation, evaluation, and review of Federal programs and projects having a significant impact on area community development.[26] At the direction of President Nixon, Federal Regional Councils were established in ten regions, consisting of the top regional officials of the major grant agencies.

The Budget Bureau also provides assistance to the Director and to the President in formulating executive branch personnel management goals and in coordinating management of personnel systems throughout the executive branch. The Director and the Chairman of the Civil Service Commission are the President's agents for comparability findings used to adjust the Federal pay system. Agency employment levels are controlled by personnel ceilings which the Budget Bureau establishes for each agency. Furthermore, the Bureau provides leadership and coordinates agency actions in evaluating the use, disposition, and acquisition of Federal real property, and it develops a central management mechanism for Government procurement policy.[27] Much of the responsibility over procurement moved to the General Services Administration in 1973.

Changes During Nixon Administration

The nearly five years of the Nixon Administration marked a turbulent period for the Budget Bureau. The Bureau was replaced by a new office, of uncertain charter and purpose, and became embroiled in repeated confrontations with Congress.

OFFICE OF MANAGEMENT AND BUDGET

On March 12, 1970, President Nixon sent to Congress a message and reorganization plan in which he proposed that the Budget Bureau be replaced by an Office of Management and Budget (OMB). Nixon explained that the dominant

46

concern of the new agency would no longer be preparation of the budget but rather "assessing the extent to which programs are actually achieving their intended results, and delivering the intended services to the intended recipients."[28] The plan was scheduled to take effect on July 1, 1970, unless disapproved by either House.

The main issue to Congress was not the change in names or the emphasis on program evaluation. Upgrading the management function of the Budget Bureau had been debated and studied for decades. In 1937 the Brownlow Committee criticized the Bureau for failing to achieve usefulness and effectiveness as an "instrument of administrative management." By emphasizing its task of preparing the budget, it had only partially developed its supervision over budget execution by spending agencies. The Budget and Accounting Procedures Act of 1950 directed the President, through the Budget Director, to evaluate and develop improved plans for the "organization, coordination, and management" of the executive branch. In 1955 the Hoover Commission reiterated the claim that the Budget Bureau's responsibility for preparing the budget had overshadowed its overall management and policy functions. In order to revitalize and emphasize the management functions of the Bureau, the Commission recommended that its name be changed to "The Office of Budget and Executive Management."[29]

President Nixon's plan for an OMB was challenged on other grounds, such as the very premise upon which the plan rested. Nixon said that the plan "recognizes that two closely connected but basically separate functions both center in the President's office: policy determination and executive management." He proposed that two separate agencies assist him: a Domestic Council for the first function, an OMB for the second. The Domestic Council "will be primarily concerned with *what* we do; the Office of Management and Budget will be primarily concerned with *how* we do it, and *how well* we do it." The plan assumed that "policy" (for the Domestic Council) could be separated from "administration" (for OMB), a bifurcation that has been rejected as impracticable for many decades.[30]

The split between the Domestic Council and OMB was actually more "political vs. technical" than "policy vs. administration." The Council would serve as staff support for John Ehrlichman, the first Director. Part of the Council's responsibility was to keep closer watch over the functioning of the bureaucracy, including OMB. And while the Council was touted as a planning and policy formulation organization, it could not monopolize those activities. OMB continued to function in the policy area. In some cases, because of their experience and expertise, OMB staff were drafted into Domestic Council operations.[31]

Part of the President's reorganization plan proposed to vest in OMB the responsibility for developing new programs to "recruit, train, motivate, deploy, and evaluate the men and women who make up the top ranks of the civil service, in the broadest sense of that term." Representatives of the American Federation of Government Employees, AFL-CIO, appeared before Congress to oppose the plan, claiming that it would undermine the Federal employee merit system:

> Let us be frank about it. The way one selects the top career levels of the civil service, "in its broadest terms," will decide the way one selects the intermediate and lower levels. If the top levels are selected in a manner essentially different [from] the lower levels, no one with any drive and initiative will want to come in at the intermediate or lower level. Political influence, special interests, manipulations, exceptional criteria will creep into the system, whether we like it or not, and no matter how upright the administrators are.[32]

The President of the National Federation of Federal Employees also opposed the plan.[33]

Also disturbing to Congress was the transfer to the President of functions that had been vested by law in the Budget Bureau or in its Director. At least 58 such statutory provisions were identified. Since Congress had created the Bureau, and had prescribed certain powers and duties for it, Congress could reasonably expect the Bureau to report and give an account of its performance. In contrast, the degree of legislative oversight over the new Office of Management and Budget would be less. The House Committee on Government Operations reported that Congress "cannot expect quite the same response when the self-same statutory functions are vested in the President, for the President represents the head of a separate branch of Government. . . ." Although President Nixon had stated his intention to delegate the statutory functions to the OMB Director, he would be free at a later date to transfer some of those functions elsewhere in the Government.[34]

On April 29 a subcommittee of the House Government Operations Committee voted 4-3 to reject the plan. On the following day John Blatnik, subcommittee chairman, and Chet Holifield, ranking majority member of the full committee, introduced alternative legislation. A principal purpose of their bill was the creation of an Office of Management and Budget without transferring statutory functions to the President. The bill also omitted reference to the development of career executive talent. Later that same day, on April 30, opposition to the President increased when he announced his decision to send U.S. forces into Cambodia to clear out Communist sanctuaries. Sentiment was strong against any proposal that would augment Presidential authority.[35]

On May 8 the full House Government Operations Committee reported a resolution to disapprove the reorganization plan. In addition to the objections already discussed, the committee said that the selection of the Executive Director of the Domestic Council violated a section of the

Reorganization Act which requires that officers authorized by a reorganization plan either be confirmed by the Senate or be in the competitive civil service. The President's plan would render the Executive Director and his large staff "not accountable to Congress and beyond the power of Congress to question. Large and important areas of domestic concern could be completely concealed from the Legislative Branch."[36] A separate statement by Clarence Brown, Republican from Ohio, objected to the design of the Domestic Council and the idea of separating policy from management:

> As one Member of Congress, I do not intend to sanctify the establishment of a permanent new layer of power in the White House which will be able to operate under the protection of executive privilege which will protect it from being called to account by Congress and which can stand between the Congress, the cabinet, the BOB, or the CEA, on the one hand, and the President on the other. I further do not believe it wise to attempt to separate policy from fiscal and managerial responsibility as is herein being attempted through creation of the Domestic Council and by downgrading the Bureau of the Budget. Since such a split is, in practical terms, impossible, the most logical result will be "all power to the Council."[37]

This type of opposition did not materialize in the Senate. When a subcommittee of the Senate Government Operations Committee held hearings on May 8, subcommittee chairman Abraham Ribicoff announced that he was "inclined to favor this plan." As a former member of the Kennedy Cabinet, Ribicoff expressed the view that "the most backward bureaucracy in the Federal Government is the Bureau of the Budget. Nothing moves when it gets there. They stalemate. They are people without imagination. And they frustrate the work of members of the Cabinet. . . ." From the Cambodian invasion, and the reaction to it which sent thousands of angry protestors to Capitol Hill, he drew a different lesson. The situation highlighted the need to make Government more responsive. Ribicoff said that every institution in the world was under attack: governments, corporations, universities, churches, and the courts. The great problem was how to change the institutions without violence. That was where "thoughtful people of good will have to exercise their intelligence to try to change institutions so institutions can work in modern society." While Ribicoff did not want the President interfering with Congress, neither did he want Congress interfering with the President: "I would like to give the President as much responsibility as he could possibly use to coordinate this great bureaucracy of ours."[38] The Senate's decision not to act on a resolution of disapproval represented implied support for the reorganization plan.

The House Government Operations Committee had already decided to disapprove the plan, triggering a furious lobbying effort by the White House. On May 11 six members of the President's Advisory Council on Executive Organization, using the stationery of the Council (in violaticn of law), mailed letters to Members of Congress urging them to support the President. Two days later the House upheld the President, voting 193-164 in favor of the plan. On July 1 President Nixon issued Executive Order 11541, prescribing the duties of OMB and the Domestic Council. All budget functions transferred to the President were delegated to the OMB Director, such functions to be carried out by the Director "under the direction of the President and pursuant to such further instructions as the President from time to time may issue."[39]

CONFIRMATION OF OMB DIRECTOR

A combination of factors converged in 1973 to trigger a new legislative effort to curb the President's budget power. The heavy-handed use of impoundment, on an unprecedented scale, was a major consideration. Added to that was a growing awareness on the part of Congress of the policy-making role played by the Budget Bureau, particularly after its transition to the Office of Management and Budget.

Another factor behind the opposition to OMB was President Nixon's choice of Roy Ash as Director. Ash was the former president of Litton Industries, which had more than a half-billion dollars in disputed contract claims pending against the Navy. Gordon Rule, a senior procurement official with the Navy, told the Joint Economic Committee that the selection of Ash was a mistake. He warned the committee that the military-industrial complex was being supplanted by a military-industrial-executive department complex.[40] Assisting Ash, as OMB Deputy Director, was Frederic V. Malek.

The Senate Government Operations Committee, without even holding hearings, reported out a bill to require Senate confirmation of the Director and Deputy Director of OMB. The present incumbents would be permitted to retain their positions for 30 days following enactment of the bill. The committee's action received unanimous support from its members, Republicans as well as Democrats. The committee concluded that OMB had developed into a "super department with enormous authority over all of the activities of the Federal Government. Its Director has become, in effect, a Deputy President who exercises vital Presidential powers."[41]

The Senate began debate on the bill three days later. Senator Robert Byrd of West Virginia offered an amendment to require reconfirmation of the OMB Director and Deputy Director with the beginning of a new presidential term. He later clarified his amendment to provide that nothing in the bill would impair the President's power to remove the occupants of the office prior to the new presidential term. The amendment was agreed to by voice vote. As amended, the bill passed the Senate by a vote of 63-17, well in excess of the margin needed to override a veto.[42]

While the bill was being debated, Ash was sworn in as OMB Director. That created a new problem: could Congress constitutionally remove him from office? To meet that issue, Senator Griffin suggested it might be more satisfactory to simply abolish the office of OMB Director and recreate it later, making it contingent on Senate confirmation.[43]

The issue of the removal power was explored on March 5 and 9, 1973, when the House Government Operations Committee held hearings. The two major bills before the committee were the bill adopted by the Senate and essentially the same bill as introduced by Jack Brooks of Texas. But by the time the House hearings began, Brooks had also decided to meet the removal issue by abolishing the two offices and establishing them later subject to Senate confirmation. Furthermore, he proposed to vest most of the functions of the OMB directly in the Director, in effect restoring the situation to what prevailed prior to Reorganization Plan No. 2 of 1970.[44]

Some of the arguments against the Brooks bill were made from the standpoint of preserving the prerogatives of the House. John Rhodes, member of the House Appropriations Committee, warned that Senate confirmation of the OMB Director would dilute the power of the House in appropriations and fiscal matters. The main thrust of the Administration's opposition was that the Senate confirmation role should not extend to the "inner circle" of Presidential advisers; the removal of Ash and Malek would trench upon the prohibition in the Constitution regarding bills of attainder; and the Constitution prohibited sophisticated attempts (i.e., the Brooks bill) as well as direct legislative attempts to interfere with the President's removal power.[45]

The House Government Operations Committee reported out the Brooks bill on April 6. The report advanced five arguments in favor of Senate confirmation: (1) it would help restore the balance between Congress and the President in the budgetary process; (2) it recognized the contemporary power of the OMB Director; (3) it corrected the anomaly of the OMB Director and Deputy Director being appointed without benefit of Senate advice and consent, while top officers in other parts of the Executive Office of the President were subject to confirmation (for example, the Director of the Central Intelligence Agency and the Chairman of the Council of Economic Advisers); (4) it vested certain functions directly in the OMB Director rather than in the President; and (5) it protected and reinforced the requirement of Senate confirmation by preventing the President from delegating OMB functions to other agencies and leaving OMB an "empty shell."[46] With the exception of Alan Steelman of Texas, every Republican on the committee filed dissenting views.

When the bill was taken up on the House floor, Steelman offered an amendment to have Senate confirmation apply not to the incumbents but to future nominees. In this way he hoped to defuse both the partisan problem (the charge that the bill was aimed at Ash) as well as the constitutional issue (regarding the removal power). His amendment failed by a vote of 130-263, after which the House passed the Brooks bill 229-171. The Senate concurred in the House version and the bill was sent to the President.[47]

President Nixon vetoed the bill on the ground that it would require the "forced removal by an unconstitutional procedure. . . ." While he did not dispute the authority of Congress to abolish an office, he said that such power "cannot be used as a back-door method of circumventing the President's power to remove." Although the Senate was able to override the veto, it was sustained by the House.[48]

Both Houses passed new legislation, this time applying the confirmation process only to future OMB Directors and Deputy Directors. In addition, the Senate Government Operations Committee provided that the functions transferred to the President by Reorganization Plan No. 2 of 1970 would be transferred back to the OMB Director. The House Government Operations Committee limited its bill to confirmation, making no effort to change the functional allocation resulting from the 1970 reorganization plan. This time the committee's action was unanimous, reported out by a vote of 39 to 0.[49]

The House version became law on March 2, 1974. It provides that the OMB Director and Deputy Director shall be appointed by the President, by and with the advice and consent of the Senate. The provision applies to each office after the individual holding it ceases to hold the office.[50]

The law requiring confirmation of OMB Directors and Deputy Directors is regularly included among the "reassertions" of the 93d Congress. Implementation of the law, however, has been less impressive. It was first applied to the OMB Director on January 29, 1975, when the Senate Government Operations Committee held a hearing to question the nominee, James Lynn.

The committee had only organized the previous day. The transcript of that meeting suggests that Lynn would be subjected to close interrogation, particularly by Senator Lee Metcalf and his staff assistant. Because of several factors—the President's budget being due within a week, the parlous condition of the economy, and the Senate's scheduled recess of February 7-17—committee chairman Ribicoff wanted to hold the hearing immediately. Metcalf, about to go abroad on a trip, agreed to an exploratory hearing on January 29 on the condition that he have an opportunity to question Lynn at a subsequent hearing.

Instead, the hearing was completed in one day. The lack of preparation by committee members and their staff was painfully obvious. From the desultory questioning it appeared that the committee was discharging an unwanted, embarrassing task. No one in the room would have known that the hearing constituted an act of congressional reassertion.

OMB'S RECORD

Although the Budget Bureau had received its share of criticism—for negativism, parsimony, and behaving like the

55

"abominable no-man"—it had also enjoyed a reputation for being nonpartisan and professional in outlook, staffed mainly by career administrators with impressive credentials and expertise. In contrast, OMB was considered highly politicized, its operations increasingly dominated by short-term political appointees who had little understanding, appreciation, or patience for Congress as a coequal branch.

A panel of the National Academy of Public Administration remarked in 1974 that the emergence of a "powerful White House staff which has progressively assumed the role of speaking for the President has seriously diminished the responsibilities of the career, professional staff of OMB and its capacity to provide the kind of objective and expert counsel to the President which characterized earlier operations. . . ." The Brownlow Committee in 1937 had recommended that the position of Assistant Budget Director be filled under civil service rules, preferably by promotion from the career service. It also recommended that division chiefs be appointed from the career service. But OMB developed a system of five associate directors heading up Management and Operations; National Security and International Affairs; Human and Community Affairs; Economics and Government; and Natural Resources, Energy, and Science. With but one exception they were recruited from outside the Government, generally business administration types with little understanding of Congress or the agencies.[51]

The system of associate directors created a problem of layering inside OMB. Careerists, who formerly had access to assistant directors in the Budget Bureau, now had to operate through a new layer. This resulted in delays, frustration, and poor communication. Knowledgeable staffers with "institutional memory" could not inform new policymakers that, for example, the "square wheel" they thought to be a remarkable innovation had been tried twice before and found wanting, and why it had failed. Further, they had less opportunity to thrash out the issues face-to-face with the policy-makers. Many would not put on paper what they would have said orally. Nor could they utilize tone, gesture, or varying forms of emphases and remonstrations to register their point. Staff turnover was high. Senior staff people, who had distinguished themselves during their service with the Budget Bureau, preferred to resign or retire in order to escape the deteriorating situation at OMB.

The conceptual assumptions underlying the 1970 reorganization plan proved faulty. Distinctions could not be maintained between policy and administration, political and technical, or even management and budget. The budget of the Domestic Council was eventually slashed and its range of operations curtailed, allowing OMB to retrieve some of the functions that had slipped away. As OMB Director Ash told the House Appropriations Committee in 1974: "So I think [OMB] is restoring a line more or less as it theretofore was, because there was a time, at least to my second-hand knowledge, many functions that were OMB's daily work tended to get caught up in the Domestic Council and are now changed."[52]

In the backwash of Watergate, confrontation politics, and Nixon's resignation, OMB groped for new moorings. Several weeks after the resignation a task force advised President Ford to curb OMB's policy role. It concluded that OMB had become too involved in departmental policy processes. The same theme was propounded on February 3, 1975, when Senator Abraham Ribicoff announced that the Senate Government Operations Committee had reported favorably on the nomination of James Lynn to be the next OMB Director. He quoted the following from Lynn's testimony during the confirmation hearing: "Each agency should have primary responsibility for providing the President with policy advice in that agency's area."[53]

The problem with OMB was not its deep involvement in "policy" or its interference with agencies. That is inevitable for any central budget staff. What OMB lacked was political judgment, the kind of judgment that becomes second nature to professionals who have worked with Congress and the agencies, who are capable of the give-and-take, compromise, and good-faith efforts that are required in the policy process. OMB became the captive (temporarily we hope) of abstract theories of organization, doctrinaire views of management, and impractical claims of constitutional power.

3

Lump-Sum Appropriations

THE choice between lump-sum and line-item appropriations has been debated in America for at least the last two centuries. James Madison, drawing on his experience with the Continental Congress, expressed surprise that some delegates still failed to distinguish between general classes of appropriations and expenditures in detail. Without that distinction the Secretary of Congress could not buy "quills or wafers without a vote of nine States entered on record. . . ." Unless one vote of appropriation extended to a "*class* of objects, there must be a physical impossibility of providing for them; & the extent & generality of such classes can only be determined by discretion & conveniency."[1]

ADVOCACY OF LINE-ITEMIZATION

This practical view of administration gave way during the early years of the national government to sharp partisan clashes. The literature speaks of two separate and rival camps: the Federalists as advocates of lump-sum appropriation and executive spending discretion, versus the Jeffersonian Republicans as spokesmen for line-itemization and legislative control. While it may excite the imagination and be conceptually appealing to construct such a neat scenario, the facts do not support it.

The first appropriation act of 1789 provided lump sums for four general classes of expenditures: $216,000 for the civil list, $137,000 for the War Department, $190,000 to discharge warrants issued by the previous Board of Treasury, and $96,000 for pensions to disabled veterans. The appropriation acts for 1790 and 1791 also provided lump sums, but the funds were to be spent in accordance with the detailed estimates given Congress by the Secretary of the Treasury.[2]

Beginning with the appropriation act of December 23, 1791, Congress narrowed executive discretion still further by using a "that is to say" clause. For example, a little over a half million was appropriated for the military establishment, that is to say, $102,686 for troop pay, $48,000 for clothing, $4,152 for forage, and similar earmarkings for nine other categories. By 1793, appropriations were descending to such minutiae as $450 for firewood, stationery, printing, and other contingencies for the Treasurer's office.[3] Thus, long before the Jeffersonians had gained control of the Presidency, the practice of granting lump sums had been abandoned.

Jefferson's Secretary of the Treasury, Albert Gallatin, advised him to seek "specific appropriations for each object of a distinct nature. . . ." Jefferson went beyond that, in his first message to Congress, by announcing that it would be prudent to appropriate "specific sums to every specific purpose susceptible of definition. . . ." Hamilton promptly denounced that goal as "preposterous." While he agreed that it was "just or proper" for Congress to appropriate specific sums for specific purposes, nothing could be "more wild or of more inconvenient tendency" than to implement Jefferson's proposal.[4]

The trenchant quality of Hamilton's response no doubt reflected his assumption that Jefferson had used his message to indirectly reproach the Federalists (i.e., Hamilton) for financial mismanagement. Jefferson exceeded the bounds of reasonableness. Gallatin himself knew that it was impossible for Congress to foresee in all its details, the necessary application of moneys, and a reasonable discretion should be allowed to the proper executive department. The most proper way would perhaps be not to enter into so many details, not to make specific appropriations for every distinct head of service, but to divide the general appropriations under a few general heads only. . . .[5]

In an 1802 report to Congress, Gallatin cautioned against excessive subdivision of the appropriations, especially in the case of the War and Navy Departments, "beyond what is substantially useful and necessary." Jefferson himself, as President, recognized that "too minute a specification has its evil as well as a too general one," and thought it better for Congress to appropriate in gross while trusting in executive discretion. It was preferable to make a temporary trust to the President, which could be "put an end to if abused."[6]

EMERGENCY PERIODS

Lump-sum appropriations are especially noticeable during periods of war and national depression, when the crisis is great, the requirements uncertain, and the conditions ripe for large delegations of legislative power. A Civil War act provided for $50 million to pay two- and three-year volunteers, $26 million for subsistence, $14 million for army transportation and supplies, and another $76 million for assorted items, to be divided among them "as the exigencies of the service may require. . . ."[7]

On the eve of the Spanish-American War, President McKinley asked Joseph Cannon, chairman of House Appropriations, to come to the White House. McKinley said he needed substantial sums of money to prepare for war. Cannon, who had reviewed the Treasury reports prior to visiting the White House, felt certain he could appropriate $50 million without a bond issue or imposing new taxation. When he suggested that the President send a message to

Congress the next day, recommending the appropriation, McKinley resisted. He was still negotiating with Spain, he explained, and a message would be interpreted by Europe as equivalent to a declaration of war.

Cannon agreed to introduce the bill without a message. McKinley walked over to a table and wrote on a telegraph blank a single sentence: "For national defense fifty million dollars." Cannon placed the slip of paper in his pocket, returned to his hotel, and prepared a rough draft of the bill. Within two days he piloted the bill through his committee and secured the unanimous vote of 313-0 in the House. A day later the bill passed the Senate and became public law, providing that "for the national defense, and for each and every purpose connected therewith, to be expended at the discretion of the President and to remain available until January first, eighteen hundred and ninety-nine, fifty million dollars."[8]

Emergency relief programs during the Great Depression set aside billions to be spent at the President's discretion. An act of 1934 appropriated $950 million for emergency relief programs and the Civil Works Program, making the money available "for such projects and/or purposes and under such rules and regulations as the President in his discretion may prescribe."[9]

The Emergency Relief Appropriation Act of 1935 appropriated $4,880,000,000 to be used "in the discretion and under the direction of the President." When the proposal was debated on the Senate floor, Senator Arthur Vandenberg noted with disdain and sarcasm the vast amount of authority delegated. The original resolution provided funds for such vague purposes as "relieving economic maladjustments" and "alleviating distress." Vandenberg said the whole proposition could be simplified by merely striking out all the text and substituting two brief sections:

SECTION 1. Congress hereby appropriates $4,880,000,000 to the President of the United States to use as he pleases.

Sec. 2. Anybody who does not like it is fined $1,000.[10]

In order to obtain the funds in lump-sum amounts, the Roosevelt Administration had to consent to a number of compromises: extending assurances to contractors, agreeing to divide the sum among eight categories of expenditure, submitting key appointments to the Senate for confirmation, and a commitment on the part of the President to assume a degree of personal management of the program.[11]

A study published by *Congressional Digest* at the start of FDR's second term estimated that Congress, since March 4, 1933, had given him discretionary authority over $15,428,498,815. That compared to a total of $1.6 billion in discretionary spending power given to all previous Presidents. But the broad delegations of spending power to Roosevelt soon narrowed. Congressional willingness to allow such discretion had been the result of his prestige, political influence, and the novelty and complexity of Federal relief work. In the wake of verified and alleged misuses of authority, Congress became disenchanted with administrative discretion, while Roosevelt's prestige and influence declined after his landslide victory of 1936. After that point Congress began to appropriate relief funds directly to the agencies involved rather than to the President. A study of the relief program by Arthur Macmahon concluded that when a lump-sum request is not accompanied by details as to how the money will be spent, "the legislature will seek to fill the gap."[12]

MANAGEMENT STUDIES

Studies conducted by public commissions during the 20th century have generally supported lump-sum appropriations. Partly that reflects the efficiency-executive orientation of the public administration school. The Taft Commission of 1912 stated that the constant shift toward greater itemization in appropriations and the limiting of discretion for an executive officer was based on "the general theory that he can not be trusted." To the Commission that was at variance with the Constitution; it also operated to produce inefficiency and waste by depriving the Government of the benefits of administrative judgment.[13]

Individual members of the Taft Commission differed on that point. While Frank Goodnow maintained that Federal expenditures had become so specific and detailed that efficient administration was impossible, W. F. Willoughby was more understanding of the need for congressional controls. It was unjustified, he said, to claim that line-item appropriations reflected the wish of Representatives or Senators to "magnify their importance and exercise all the authority they can grasp." What Congress sought was to specify "in the greatest practicable detail how money shall be expended, not because it desires to usurp the functions of the administrator and to deprive the latter of all initiative and discretion, but because it is the only practicable way that it has discovered by which it can exercise its function, which all must agree is its, of supervising and controlling the manner in which the executive performs its duties."[14]

The Budget and Accounting Act of 1921 promised a move toward lump-sum appropriations. During debate on the bill, Congressman French remarked that previous experience with lump-sum funding had exposed these weaknesses:

> Favoritism is shown; unequal and even widely different compensation for the same work is paid; ambitious heads of divisions overreach in extending the activities under them beyond all bounds; these and other evils make dissatisfaction among employees and among division heads. In spite of economies that are disclosed under faithful heads of divisions, the extravagances and overreaching ambitions of unfaithful heads neutralize all good and produce an exceedingly large balance of wrong. To correct these wrongs and protect the public, Congress has been compelled to itemize in large degree the matters for which funds shall be spent.[15]

64

French believed that the proposed budget system, with an independent audit by the General Accounting Office, would allow Congress to institute lump-sum appropriations. The Comptroller General "would be the first to discover abuses, and the budget bureau would have a second check."[16]

The appropriations structure of the 1920s retained some of the line-item quality of previous decades. By the time of his budget message of January 2, 1935, President Roosevelt recommended a "substantial reduction" in the number of appropriation items in order to facilitate budget control and produce departmental economy. He asked Congress to establish a special joint committee to make a detailed study of the appropriation items in each regular appropriation bill "with a view to greatly reducing the number of them, consistent with proper budgetary and accounting requirements." A special unit created by President Roosevelt in 1936 (the Brownlow Committee) suggested that budget-making would be "greatly facilitated by a substantial reduction in the number of appropriation items."[17]

Harold Smith, Budget Director from 1939 to 1946, stressed the need for executive discretion. He argued that effective and economical management may be hindered by line-item appropriation. Although the budget document itself must contain detail for the information of Congress, as well as guidance for executive officials, he said it was desirable to appropriate for broadly defined functions. It would be the responsibility of the executive branch to determine "the precise means of operation to achieve the purposes set forth by law."[18]

Studies by the Hoover Commission in 1949 and 1955 promoted the goal of lump-sum appropriations. In 1949 it recommended that the budgetary concept of the Federal Government should be refashioned by adopting a budget based upon functions, activities, and projects, or what the Commission called a "performance budget." The purpose was to focus attention on work to be done rather than things to be

65

acquired. The concept would require a restructuring of appropriation accounts. The Commission remarked that the

> present appropriation structure underlying the budget is a patchwork affair evolved over a great many years and following no rational pattern. In some areas of the budget, there are entirely too many appropriation items; in others perhaps too few. Some appropriation items are exceedingly broad in scope; others are narrow on account of excessive itemization.[19]

The 1949 Hoover Commission recommended to Congress that a "complete survey of the appropriation structure should be undertaken without delay." Over 200 appropriation items were eliminated from the fiscal 1951 budget, and over 50 others removed the next year. In 1955 the Hoover Commission noted with some satisfaction that the growing use of the performance (or program) budget had been accompanied by broader and more comprehensive appropriation classifications.[20]

UNFORESEEN EXPENDITURES

Since future events cannot be anticipated, or anticipated with great precision, Congress will often provide a separate account to cover contingencies, emergencies, and unexpected expenses. The subsequent use of those funds by executive agencies has often provoked strong criticism from Congress, leading to restrictions in some cases and elimination of the funds in others.

CONTINGENCY FUNDS

An early complaint against contingency funds came from Leonidas Livingston, a Representative from Georgia. During debate in 1906 he declared that all contingency funds were abused by agencies. He did not charge graft or theft, but said that when a contingency fund was put at the mercy of a disbursing officer "it is like giving a child more money than he wants for a trip uptown and back. He will surely spend the balance of it before he gets home."[21] John Rhodes, Republican Representative from Arizona, had this to say in 1961 with regard to the foreign assistance contingency fund:

> Unfortunately, I think it is a matter of public knowledge that in many instances this contingency fund has been used for one contingency only and that contingency is that the House and Senate did not appropriate as much money for this program as the people downtown would like to have appropriated.[22]

A specific illustration occurred in 1959, after the House Appropriations Committee had specifically denied funds for an Incentive Investment Program proposed by the Administration. That denial was not included in the final appropriation bill passed by Congress, at which point the Administration proceeded to use money from the President's contingency fund to initiate the program. The House Appropriations Committee charged that the fund was being used to nullify the actions of Congress and recommended language the next year to curb the practice. This time the denial was spelled out in the appropriation bill, which prohibited the use of any of the funds to finance any of the activities under the Investment Incentive Fund program.[23] That restriction was carried forward in future appropriation bills. Such language, whenever it appears, stands as a reminder that at some earlier period Congress determined that an agency had violated a trust and abused discretionary authority.

The contingency fund in the foreign assistance appropriation bill ranged from $155 million to $275 million from fiscal years 1959 to 1963. During that period President Kennedy issued an Executive Order establishing the Peace Corps. Not until seven months later did Congress appropriate funds for the agency. In the meantime, the President financed Peace Corps activities by using more than a million dollars in contingency funds from the Mutual Security Act. Several years later, during the Johnson Administration, the sum of $450,000 was taken from the Defense Department's contingency fund to pay a portion of the expenses for the President's Commission on Civil Disorders.[24]

The foreign assistance contingency fund encountered spirited criticism from Congress. In 1960 Senator Ellender said that the fund had been used not to meet unforeseen crises but rather to restore funds that Congress had deleted from the Administration's bill.

> During fiscal year 1960, no such crises occurred. However, notwithstanding this, our do-gooders have found a way to rape the contingency fund.
>
> . . . I think it is wrong, both morally and legally, for the executive departments to use a special fund, the contingency fund, to restore congressional cuts in appropriations.[25]

The House Appropriations Committee recommended the following language in 1960 to prohibit executive nullification of specific congressional reductions in the foreign aid bill: ". . . none of the funds appropriated in this paragraph [for the President's Contingency Fund] shall be used for any project or activity for which an estimate has been submitted to Congress." Although the Senate Appropriations Committee eliminated that provision, the enacted bill provided that no part of the contingency fund "shall be used for any project or activity for which an estimate has been submitted to Congress and which estimate has been rejected."[26]

The size of the foreign aid contingency fund began to decline after fiscal 1963. From fiscal 1967 through fiscal 1975 it averaged less than $20 million a year. Even at that reduced rate the Appropriations Committees expressed disapproval with administration of the fund. In 1973 the Senate Appropriations Committee voted to eliminate the budget request of $30 million in contingency funds for foreign assistance. The committee explained that the primary purpose of the fund was supposed to be for disaster relief and situations involving security interests of the United States. Yet of $25 million appropriated for the contingency fund for fiscal 1973, President Nixon utilized $10 million (or 40 percent) for the "Bahamas Livestock and Research project." The project was never presented to the committee for funding, either as a grant or as a loan. A committee inquiry failed to produce evidence that the project was urgent, that it was unforeseen, or (as required by the Foreign Assistance Act) "determined by the President to be important to the national interest." In contrast to the $10 million made available for livestock research in the Bahamas, only $8 million of the contingency fund went for Nicaraguan earthquake relief and only $4,697,000 for the drought plaguing much of the African continent.[27]

House and Senate conferees agreed to a compromise level of $15 million for the foreign assistance contingency fund, but issued this instruction: "The managers agree that the contingency fund should be used to provide assistance for disaster relief purposes as indicated in the authorizing legislation. The managers believe that funds have been too liberally allocated from this fund and should be better controlled."[28]

The reputation of AID's contingency fund suffered another heavy blow in 1974. During a visit to Egypt in June of that year, President Nixon made a gift of a helicopter to President Anwar Sadat. The value of the helicopter and related support, spare parts, and training was $3 million. Many people regarded the idea of an American President giving away Government property, as though it were his own, as extremely offensive. Beyond such matters as appearance and propriety was the question of legal authority and the funding source.

Neither the Defense Department nor the State Department was in a legal or financial position to finance the gift. Defense had the money but not the authority; State had authority but lacked the funds. After exhausting those alternatives the Administration decided that the cost would be borne by AID's contingency fund. The National Security Council directed AID to make an allocation of $1.8 million to the Navy as part of the total package cost. The Navy, which had custody of the helicopter, would carry out the training program for Egyptian pilots and procure the necessary spare parts. The balance of $1.2 million would come from AID's account for security and supporting assistance.

Congress reacted to the gift by establishing a separate account of $40 million for famine or disaster relief and reducing the contingency fund to an authorized level of $5 million. The appropriated amount was cut still further to $1.8 million (to cover the funds already obligated for the helicopter). The fund was subject to the following restriction: "No part of this fund shall be used to pay for any gifts to any officials of any foreign government made heretofore or hereafter."[29] That left in doubt even the legality of the original $1.8 million allocation.

EMERGENCY FUNDS

The Defense Department at one time received a separate Emergency Fund to be used primarily for supporting the exploitation of new scientific developments and technological breakthroughs. The fund was maintained at an annual level of $150 million from fiscal 1959 through fiscal 1964, but criticism soon erupted from both Appropriations Committees. In 1963 the House Appropriations Committee complained that the fund had been resorted to in too many instances when no scientific or technical breakthrough was involved. The fund was being used by some officials "as a general purpose fund from which to finance low priority or unbudgeted programs." Two years later the Senate Appropriations Committee observed that the fund was being tapped frequently in the closing weeks of the fiscal year. To the committee that lent credence to the suspicion that the fund was being used "for other than emergency purposes which would tend to subvert the congressional review and appropriation process."[30]

The level of the Emergency Fund began to decline, dropping to $125 million for fiscal 1965, $100 million for fiscal 1968, and complete elimination in fiscal 1973. In recommending the elimination, the House Appropriations Committee maintained that the expanded transfer authority granted to the Secretary of Defense was adequate to cover all emergency research and development problems.[31]

GENERAL CONGRESSIONAL CONTROLS

Lump-sum figures often exaggerate the scope of executive spending discretion. Administrators are subject to general statutory controls, nonstatutory controls exercised by the committees, and basic good-faith agreements and understanding with Congress.

As an example of general legislation, appropriation bills used to contain a great deal of detail in the salary accounts. For example, the Department of Agriculture appropriation bill in 1923 included the following account for "Office of the Secretary, Salaries":

> Secretary of Agriculture, $12,000; Assistant Secretary, $5,000; director of scientific work, $5,000; director of regulatory work, $5,000; director of extension service, $5,000; solicitor, $5,000; chief clerk, $3,000 and $500 additional as custodian of buildings; private secretary to the Secretary, $2,500; traffic manager, $3,000. . . .[32]

That level of minutiae continued until it described 278 additional positions, including $600 for laborers, $480 for messenger boys, and $240 for charwomen. In all, the account appropriated $382,520 for salaries.

The Classification Act of 1923 was the first systematic effort to achieve a uniform alignment of jobs and salaries among the various Federal agencies. Positions were

71

classified and graded according to their duties and responsibilities. The same pay scale was to be applicable to all positions falling in the same class and grade regardless of department.[33] The effect of the Classification Act was to wash from appropriation bills the mass of detail on different positions. When the agriculture appropriation bill was passed the following year, the account for "Office of the Secretary, Salaries" was now streamlined to read:

> For Secretary of Agriculture, $12,000; Assistant Secretary and other personal services in the District of Columbia, $465,495; and for extra labor and emergency employments, $7,294; in accordance with the Classification Act of 1923; in all $484,789. . . .[34]

In other words, Congress continued to exercise control over individual salary levels, but in a general classification act rather than in individual appropriation bills passed every year. Some Members of Congress objected in 1924 to the "lump-sum" appropriations for salaries, but it was explained that they were not lump-sum in the usual sense, meaning expendable at the discretion of the head of the bureau. Executive officials were required to spend personnel funds in accordance with the terms of the Classification Act.[35]

Administrative discretion is also narrowed by nonstatutory directives that are placed in committee reports, committee hearings, floor debates, and other sources.[36] Another compromise between lump-sums and line-itemization consists of "earmarking." The HUD appropriation act for fiscal 1975 contained $140 million for construction of facilities for the National Aeronautics and Space Administration. However, that amount was earmarked for 19 separate projects identified in the account. The same approach appears in the defense appropriation act for fiscal 1975. The huge sum of $3 billion was provided for the "Shipbuilding and Conversion, Navy" account, but specific dollar amounts were set aside for Trident submarines, nuclear attack submarines, and on down the line, including relatively small amounts of $10.8 million for a fleet ocean tug and $10.4 million for pollution abatement craft.[37]

The public works appropriation act for fiscal 1975 suggests that the Corps of Engineers received a lump sum of $973,681,000 for general construction. But the agency was not at liberty to spend those funds in any way it chose. The two Appropriations Committees had specific projects in mind in arriving at that figure. After the two Houses agreed in conference on the final amount, the projects were listed in the conference report, grouping the individual projects State-by-State.[38] Administrative action is also restricted by legislation in authorization acts, "provisos" in appropriation acts, and general statutory procedures and policies for procurement.

Legislative control is also exercised by holding the President to his itemized budget requests, as amended by Congress. Although those details do not appear in public law, there exists a moral understanding between the agencies and Congress that the money will be spent in accordance with the amended budget requests. This kind of non-statutory control depends on a "keep the faith" attitude among agency officials: a desire to maintain the integrity of the budgetary process and preserve a relationship of trust and confidence with the appropriations subcommittees. If agencies violate that trust and abuse their discretionary powers, they face the prospect the next year of budget cutbacks, restrictive language, and line-item appropriations.

Sometimes this process is formalized by the "committee veto," which obligates an executive agency to submit its program to designated committees before placing the program in operation. A committee-clearance procedure was tied to lump-sum funding in 1951. Congress provided $50 million to the Defense Department to be used to acquire lands and construct depot facilities, subject to the condition that the Secretary of the Army first "come into agreement" with the Armed Services Committees. The same piece of legislation provided a lump sum of $27 million for restoration or replacement of facilities damaged or destroyed and for other urgent construction requirements. The condition of committee approval was not included for that part of the Act, but the Department nevertheless obtained the approval of the Armed Services Committees before using any of the funds.[39]

Dwight Eisenhower and subsequent Presidents objected strongly to the committee-veto procedure, claiming that it invaded administrative responsibilities and violated the separation of power doctrine. Still, the procedure was extended to numerous programs, at times prompting some Members of Congress to complain about the time needed for legislative review. A rider to the 1955 defense appropriations bill authorized the two defense appropriations subcommittees to disapprove the closing of certain military installations and activities. Subcommittee members chafed under the onerous task, finding themselves preoccupied with trifles and minor details. Gerald Ford, at that time a Congressman from Michigan, said that the review of Defense Department proposals "was the greatest and most complete waste of time I have ever experienced on that subcommittee."[40]

Although studies are available on the growth and scope of the committee veto, little is known about a form of committee veto known as "prior-approval reprogramming." Under this procedure the agencies must obtain approval from certain designated committees or subcommittees before shifting funds within an appropriation account. The subject is so complex that it merits a separate chapter.

4

Reprogramming of Funds

THE conflicting needs of administrative flexibility and congressional control are often reconciled by what has come to be known as "reprogramming." This procedure allows executive officials some latitude in shifting funds *within* an appropriation account, moving them from one program to another. It also allows for some participation by the committees and subcommittees of Congress. Although reprogramming involves billions of dollars each year, raising important and fundamental questions about the appropriations process, congressional oversight, administrative discretion, and budget priorities, it remains an esoteric subject.

This chapter concentrates on reprogramming by the Department of Defense. It is in this area that the dollar amounts are large, the procedure highly formalized, and the written material adequate to develop a full perspective. But first a few general observations about reprogramming.

General Principles

Each year executive agencies come before Congress to justify their budget estimates, setting forth in great detail the purposes to which funds are to be applied. Requests are then modified by committee and congressional action, as explained in committee reports and by floor amendments. However, most of the detailed information in agency justification sheets, committee reports, and floor action is omitted from the appropriation bill. The funds are grouped together to form lump-sum accounts.

Judged by the statute itself, the appropriation is lump sum. But the mass of material surrounding and supporting the appropriation—the *non*statutory controls—implies a high degree of line-itemization. Agencies are expected to "keep faith" with Congress by spending the money in accordance with their original departmental justifications, as amended by committee and floor action. Through such actions the integrity of the budget process is preserved.

Appropriations Committees realize that it is often necessary and desirable for agencies to depart from budget justifications. Agencies must estimate many months in advance of the time that they obligate and spend the funds. Often the interval can be a matter of years. As the budget year unfolds, new and better applications of money come to light. Reprogrammings are made for a number of reasons, including unforeseen developments, changing requirements, incorrect price estimates, wage-rate adjustments, and legislation enacted after appropriations.

Executive flexibility to reprogram funds is not the same as budget "transfers," to be discussed in the next chapter. Transfers involve the shifting of funds from one appropriation account to another; reprogramming refers to the shifting of funds *within* an account. Furthermore, the authority to transfer funds is explicitly stated in statutes. In contrast, the basis for reprogramming is generally nonstatutory, to be discovered in committee reports, committee hearings, agency directives, correspondence between subcommittee chairmen and agency officials, and also "gentlemen's agreements" and understandings that are not part of the public record.

The word "reprogramming" does not appear in committee reports and hearings until the mid-1950s. Prior to that time, however, essentially the same kind of practice was carried out under different names, such as "adjustments" or "interchangeability" or even "transfers." The particular context makes it clear whether funds were being shifted between accounts or within an account.

The earliest reference to the *concept* of reprogramming (but not yet the practice) was in an article by W. F. Willoughby in 1912. He recommended that Congress should abandon its custom of appropriating in great detail. But instead of simply advocating lump-sum appropriations, as did many of his colleagues, Willoughby recognized that discretionary spending authority had been abused in the past and that Congress would insist on some means of control. What he proposed was that each official, upon receiving a lump-sum amount, would formulate an administrative budget (a "subappropriation scheme") setting forth in detail how the money would be spent. This specific schedule of allotments would be made in writing; any changes would be in writing. While Willoughby's proposal offered important advantages in visibility, flexibility, and accountability, it did not allow for congressional participation.[1]

Such participation was not long in coming. An article by Arthur Macmahon in 1943 describes a subcommittee process that allowed the Bureau of the Census to spend money that had been appropriated for a somewhat different purpose. A committee report in 1940 contained an understanding that permitted the Forest Service to reallocate appropriations "irrespective of any earmarking that may have been set up in the Budget." Elias Huzar discussed a World War II "gentlemen's agreement," requiring the War Department to notify the military appropriations subcommittees and obtain their approval before effecting important shifts of funds.[2]

Congress tolerated this shifting of funds during the war as a necessary emergency measure. But when the practice continued after the war, members of the Appropriations Committees grew restive and reasserted control. That attitude became pronounced after 1949 when Congress adopted the concept of the performance budget, recommended by the Hoover Commission. The shift toward lump-sum appropriations and the reduction in the number of appropriation accounts resulted in considerable broadening of executive discretion. During the years 1948-50 the number of appropriation accounts for the Department of Defense averaged about 100; within a few years that number was cut in half.[3] Other departments experienced a similar reduction in accounts. Congressional committees began to insist on regular reporting of reprogramming actions, in some cases insisting on prior committee approval.

NONMILITARY REPROGRAMMING

Some of the early references to reprogramming appear in the 1950s with regard to long-term construction projects. In 1956 the House Committee on Appropriations advised the Corps of Engineers not to shift funds to any project in excess of 15 percent of the original amount available. The committee also asked to be advised of all reprogrammings amounting to $100,000 or more.[4]

A conference report the next year discusses reprogramming by the Bureau of Reclamation. The conferees agreed that reprogrammings between projects and units of projects should be limited to 15 percent. They also imposed other restrictions. Reprogramming was not to be used to move projects from the investigation stage to advance planning. Nor should funds be reprogrammed to a project that had not appeared in the budget justification. In other words, reprogramming was not to be used as a vehicle for starting new programs or accelerating a project past the initial investigation stage. Conferees also requested quarterly reprogramming reports to the Appropriations Committees.[5]

A report by House Appropriations in 1958 criticized the use of reprogramming for public works projects. Numerous requests had been made to the committee to allow contractors to accelerate their construction and increase their earnings. The contractors threatened to abandon their project unless Congress supplied the extra funds. The committee issued this sharp warning: "Complete disregard for the limit set on earnings by any contractor coupled with a threat to shut down, can be viewed as an effort to lift fiscal control out of the hands of Congress and place it in the hands of contractors." If it became necessary to reprogram funds to finance accelerated schedules, the committee said it would consider only those requests accompanied by an offer on the part of the contractor to amend his bid figures downwards so that the Government may share in the savings.[6]

There is repeated evidence in committee reports that "understandings" with agencies are not always honored. In 1970 the Senate Appropriations Committee expressed its disappointment that education funds had been shifted without its knowledge. Any program cutbacks or increases were to be cleared with the appropriate committees before final decisions were made. A few months later the committee voiced a similar warning about other programs administered by the Department of Health, Education, and Welfare.[7]

Reprogramming procedures for the District of Columbia were restated and modified by Senate Appropriations in 1969 because of "disregard of and noncompliance with the established guideline . . . ." Funds had been reprogrammed without notifying the committee or seeking its approval. The following year the committee said that budget hearings had revealed that there was still not a full understanding by the D.C. government of reprogramming requirements. And in 1971 the House Appropriations Committee objected that as much as $4 million had been reprogrammed from one purpose to another without the committee's knowledge. In that same year Senate Appropriations charged that the record on D.C. reprogrammings exposed numerous instances in which both the spirit and the letter of requirements were not adhered to.[8]

A 1973 report by the General Accounting Office concluded that the Internal Revenue Service had reprogrammed $42.7 million over a three-year period without the approval of the Appropriations Committees, a violation of prior understandings between the Treasury Department and Congress. In 1974 the House Appropriations Committee had to restate its principles on reprogramming by the Interior Department and 26 other agencies, since the procedure of requesting committee approval and notifying the committee was not "uniformly understood" by the agencies.[9]

A peculiar variant of reprogramming, called "deob-reob," is practiced by the Agency for International Development. Foreign aid administrators deobligate funds for one program and then reobligate them to another. Members of Congress, in the late 1950s, objected to the use of deob-reob to begin projects that had never been justified to Congress. Because of deob-reob, Congressman Passman estimated in 1960 that "it may very well be that perhaps half, or more, of the projects now funded were never approved in the beginning, by any committee of the Congress." Various appropriation accounts included restrictive language to curb the practice. However, a GAO study revealed that over a five-year period (fiscal years 1968 through 1972), the amount of AID deobligations—also called "recoveries"— came to $435 million.[10]

MILITARY REPROGRAMMING

This section explains how reprogramming has developed in the Department of Defense (excluding military construction and the Corps of Engineers). Of special interest are the procedures involved, dollar amounts and frequency, and the irregular uses (or abuses). The end of the chapter discusses efforts to open up the process to make it more visible and to allow for greater participation by Members of Congress.

PROCEDURES

Congressional control over defense reprogramming has progressed through a number of stages. At first the Appropriations Committees required the Defense Department to keep them advised of major reprogrammings; later the Department had to submit semiannual reports; finally the Pentagon was required to obtain prior approval from the Appropriations Committees before implementing certain kinds of reprogramming actions. By 1961 the Armed Services Committees were included in the system of prior approval. The extent of congressional participation has continued to widen.

1. *1950-61.* Hearings by House Appropriations in 1950 indicate that shifting of funds within defense accounts had become commonplace by that time. A representative for the Department of the Army said that funds could not be shifted from one project to another without his direct approval, except in certain areas where the Army allowed 10 percent flexibility or shifts of $100,000, whichever was lower. He also assured the committee:

> As you know, sir, in any change where there is a major factor it is discussed with the committee. I have made a religious practice of that. I have made no shift whatsoever when I figured that they should be brought to your attention.[11]

The essential safeguard was therefore a disposition on the part of the Army to keep faith with the Appropriations Committees and to preserve the integrity of departmental estimates. The committees themselves did not receive regular reports, nor did they spell out for the Defense Department the specific types of reprogramming which

81

should be submitted to the committees prior to implementation.

The first specific legislative guideline appeared in 1954. In reporting out the defense bill, Senate Appropriations identified areas in which economies were believed possible. If reductions could not be made without detrimental effect to programs, the Pentagon should make adjustments. However, the committee directed that in no instance should a project within an appropriation exceed the original budget estimate.[12] The conference report on the bill further defined the Pentagon's authority to shift funds within an appropriation:

> . . . it is agreed by the managers that such transfers [i.e., reprogrammings] shall be effective only with respect to those specific projects which were reduced by the House and made the subject of appeal for restoration to the Senate and only upon prior approval of the Approprations Committees of the Senate and the House of Representatives for the Department of Defense.[13]

In 1955, during hearings before House Appropriations, John Taber (R-N.Y.) explained that defense reprogramming requests were transmitted to the chairman and ranking member of the defense subcommittee for their consideration. Defense Comptroller McNeil said that some diversions took place without committee knowledge, but insisted that committee clearance was obtained on all important matters.[14]

In its committee report on the defense bill in 1955, House Appropriations noted that it was not always practicable to adhere rigidly to budget justifications. However, the mere fact that there was a lessened requirement in one category did not imply either the right or the need for the Defense Department to spend the money elsewhere. Savings were not to be treated as a windfall, as a slush fund to be applied someplace else. The committee also warned that it had never been its intention to permit military departments unrestricted freedom in reprogramming funds without prior notification or consent of the committee.[15]

The committee identified three methods of legislative control. In cases where appropriations had been provided to cover broad categories, the Defense Department should keep faith with the committee and with Congress by adhering to the detailed justifications. Second, when major reprogrammings were necessary, the committee should be notified and given an opportunity for prior approval. The committee now added a third control by requesting semiannual tabulations of all reprogramming actions by the Defense Department. The Pentagon issued a set of instructions to define the scope of reporting requirements and to establish criteria for "major reprogramming" actions.[16]

In 1959 House Appropriations stated that semiannual tabulations, while helpful, had not been sufficiently timely. In anticipation of a phrase made famous by the Watergate affair, the committee said that the practice of advising it of major reprogrammings had become "virtually inoperative." The committee directed the Pentagon to report periodically—but in no case less than 30 days after departmental approval—reprogramming actions involving $1 million or more in the case of operation and maintenance, $1 million or more for research, development, test, and evaluation (RDT&E), and $5 million or more in the case of procurement. New instructions were prepared by the Pentagon to comply with this request.[17]

2. *1961-75.* During hearings in 1961 before House Appropriations, it was revealed that the Navy had preprogrammed $584 million to start construction of five additional Polaris submarines. By the time of the hearings, the Navy had already awarded contracts and projects orders to shipyards for construction. Gerald Ford (R-Mich.) reminded

the Navy officials present in the room that the procedure for major reprogrammings required the Defense Secretary to write to the committee asking for concurrence.[18] Melvin Laird (R-Wis.) asked why the Navy had not sought committee concurrence before shifting the funds. Admiral Morris Hirsch replied:

> Things have moved very fast in the area and this appears to me to have been an attempt to get on with something that the Defense Department felt should be done, and then to make sure that everyone understood exactly what had been done possibly a little bit later.[19]

This kind of after-the-fact notification did not sit well with the committee. Chairman Mahon wrote to Defense Secretary McNamara on March 20, 1961, asking for specific committee approval on the following four categories of reprogramming:

1. Procurement of items omitted or deleted by Congress.
2. Programs for which specific reductions in the original requests were made by Congress.
3. Programs which had not previously been presented to or considered by Congress.
4. Quantitative program increases proposed above the programs originally presented to Congress.[20]

McNamara accepted the first two points, but not the last two. Charles Hitch, Pentagon Comptroller, supported McNamara by expressing concern about additional paperwork, not only for the Pentagon but for the committees. This was couched in terms of economy, but of course the Defense Department does not hesitate to devote manpower and paperwork when informing Congress of its plans and accomplishments. Hitch was worried that prior approval would include the Armed Services Committees as well, because of the trend toward annual authorizations (section 412) begun in 1959.[21]

Mahon agreed to the more modest reprogramming procedure, "at least for a trial period." Roswell Gilpatric, Deputy Defense Secretary, sent the revised understanding to Mahon on May 4, 1961, including review not only by the Appropriations but also the Armed Services Committees. The Gilpatric outline served as guidance until the Pentagon rewrote its reprogramming directive in 1963.[22]

Current DOD directives continue the practice of semi-annual reports, prior approval on selected items, and prompt notification on others. Proposed reprogramming actions must have the personal, specific approval of the Defense Secretary or Deputy Defense Secretary prior to being submitted to the committees. In some cases prior approval must be obtained from the Armed Services and Appropriations Committees; other cases require prior approval only from the Appropriations Committees.[23] Moreover, DOD representatives are to discuss with the committees, prior to taking action, any other cases involving matters known to be of "special interest" to one or more of the committees. Because of different interpretations as to what constitutes an item of "special interest," it may happen that the Pentagon submits a reprogramming in the form of notification rather than prior approval.

A controversy in 1972 publicized the fact that DOD reporting procedures did not permit full compliance with those controls. Despite a requirement that the Defense Secretary and the Appropriations Committees approve any increase in personnel accounts that had been reduced by Congress, the Navy violated the provision. Defense Secretary Laird said it was impossible for him to tell from the reports that the Navy had failed to comply. The DOD instruction was amended to make such actions more visible.[24]

The Defense Department offers this definition of "prior approval": If the Defense Secretary has not been informed of approval or disapproval by the committees within 15 days, "it will be assumed that there is no objection to the implementation of the proposed reprogramming."[25] That may be the assumption, but the Pentagon does not actually *proceed* with the reprogramming. Approval means explicit approval, eventually in writing, whether that takes 15 days, a month, or longer.

Prompt notification (within 48 hours after DOD approval) is required for any reprogramming action, single or cumulative, that exceeds these dollar thresholds:

1. An increase of $5 million or more in a budget activity in the military personnel and operation and maintenance appropriations.
2. An increase of $5 million or more in a procurement line item or the addition to the procurement line item base of a new item in the amount of $2 million or more.
3. An increase of $2 million or more in any budget subactivity line item in an appropriation for RDT&E, including the addition of a new budget subactivity line item of $2 million or more, or the addition of a new budget subactivity line item, the cost of which is estimated to be $10 million or more within a three-year period.[26]

Any reprogramming action to which one or more of the committees concerned takes exception within 15 days of receipt of the notification will be "reconsidered" by the Secretary of Defense.[27] That usually means that the action will be placed on hold until the committees approve.

MAGNITUDES

From statistics made available in committee hearings, committee reports, and committee prints, and by obtaining some material directly from the Defense Department, it is possible to piece together a record of reprogramming actions since 1956. The actions submitted to congressional committees ranged between $1.7 billion and $4.7 billion a year, from fiscal 1956 through 1972, averaging about $2.6 billion a year. For fiscal years 1973 and 1974, the average dollar amount dropped below a billion. Procurement and RDT&E predominate, partly because of the interest of the review committees under prior-approval and notification procedures, but also because of the imprecision of budget estimates for those program activities.[28]

Except for a few years, total dollar amounts are generally in the $2 billion range. A high figure of $3.8 billion for fiscal 1961 coincides with a change in Administrations, suggesting that President Kennedy used reprogramming to modify the budget priorities he inherited. Large figures of $3.4 billion and $4.8 billion were posted for fiscal years 1967 and 1968, a result of the war in Southeast Asia. The military buildup prior to those years was satisfied primarily by budget supplementals. Defense reprogramming in fiscal 1971 totaled $3.3 billion.

Rarely do reprogramming statistics reveal the magnitude of "below-the-threshold" actions, that is, internal actions carried out by the Defense Department without committee notification or approval. Statistics for internal reprogrammings are available for fiscal years 1964 through 1967; for that period they averaged $1.1 billion a year.[29]

There are approximately 100 reprogramming actions a year. The number dropped in recent years, because of congressional impatience, to 56 for fiscal 1973 and 24 for fiscal 1974. Keep in mind that an "action" is often composed of several reprogrammings, with funds reallocated among many projects. A large number of reprogrammings—sometimes as many as 30 to 40—will be bundled together as a single action, given one DOD serial number, and submitted on DD Form 1415. Harold Stoneberger studied the relationship between reprogramming actions and the number of appropriation line-items affected and concluded that each action, on the average, affected eight budget line-items. Fewer line-items have been affected in recent years. For example, the 56 actions in fiscal 1973 involved 129 line-items; the 24 actions in fiscal 1974 involved 37 line-items.[30]

Another crucial statistic is the number of reprogramming actions that are subject to prior approval by the designated committees, compared to those that are merely sent to the committees for notification. Some fragmentary information is available for the portion of fiscal 1968 running from July 1, 1967, to February 19, 1968. During that period the Defense Department sent 97 formal reprogramming actions to the review committees. Of the $3.6 billion involved, prior approval accounted for only $122 million. The balance consisted of submissions for notification. However, that was in the midst of the Vietnam war, at a time of congressional acquiescence. Prior approvals now make up the lion's share of reprogramming actions.[31]

IRREGULAR USES

Substantial differences exist between reprogramming in form and reprogramming in practice. Even the most conscientious reader of committee hearings, committee reports, and DOD directives and instructions may be misled as to actual operations. Without access to reprogramming records in the Pentagon and in the review committees, and without day-to-day practical experience in handling the requests, it is impossible to know the extent to which this spending flexibility is abused. Most reprogrammings appear to be routine and noncontroversial. Yet occasionally the process breaks down, resulting in violations or circumventions of congressional control.

1. *Bypassing the Congress.* It is evident that reprogramming can become a convenient instrument for avoiding the normal authorization and appropriation stages. Instead of obtaining approval from Congress as a whole, executive officials need only obtain approval from certain subcommittees or of subcommittee ranking members.

The opportunity for mischief is substantial. An agency could request money for a popular program, knowing that Congress will provide the funds. Later it can use the money for a program that might not have passed scrutiny of the full Congress. Albert Engel (R-Mich.) recalled in 1950 that the War Department "told us they were going to use money for one purpose and used it for an entirely different purpose for which the committee might not have appropriated the money had it been justified for that purpose." In a 1966 congressional report, three Republican members of the House Appropriations Committee—Glenard Lipscomb of California, Melvin Laird of Wisconsin, and William Minshall of Ohio—characterized reprogramming as essentially "a procedure which bypasses the Congress." They were concerned about the tendency on the part of the Pentagon to use what was an emergency tool "on a more regular and frequent basis than the situations warrant."[32]

Congressional control is also affected when the Pentagon alters the base from which reprogrammings are made. For example, in submitting budget justifications for RDT&E, the Pentagon divides each appropriation account into program elements, which are in turn broken down into separate projects. To illustrate, the account RDT&E/Navy contains the program element "Missiles and Related Equipment," which may contain such projects as the Aegis, Trident, and submarine-launched cruise missile.

This discussion probably strikes the reader as excessively technical, and yet such details go to the heart of reprogramming controls. If funds are to be shifted *between* program elements, committee interest is generally at its highest, requiring either prior approval or notification. If funds are to be shifted *within* a program element, the basic control is exercised by the Pentagon. When the Pentagon presented its budget justifications for fiscal 1973, it reduced the number of program elements. This had the effect of widening Pentagon flexibility and therefore triggered a vigorous protest from the Senate Armed Services Committee. The Pentagon subsequently returned to its earlier budget format.[33]

2. *"Ace in the Hole."* Reprogramming has been used as a remedy for administrative indecisiveness. In the fall of 1964 the House Armed Services Committee approved an emer-

gency request by the Navy to reprogram funds for the TA-4E, a subsonic jet training aircraft. A committee investigation later disclosed that the "emergency" nature of the request resulted from an inability, or unwillingness, on the part of the Pentagon to reach a decision several years earlier. As a consequence, funds had not been included in the regular budget requests for the trainer aircraft. The committee described this kind of reprogramming as an "ace in the hole," used to resolve a situation that had been allowed to deteriorate to the point of emergency.[34]

3. *Undoing the Work of Congress.* The Defense Intelligence Agency (DIA) requested $66.8 million for fiscal 1971 to cover certain operating costs. House Appropriations, convinced that the agency was heavily overstaffed, cut the request by $2 million. DIA reduced its budget by only $700,000, having successfully prevailed upon the Pentagon to request reprogramming of $1.3 million to make up the difference. Incensed, Jamie Whitten (D-Miss.) asked if he was to understand that "after Congress developed the record and made reductions on that basis, we are to have them come in here and ask for restoration, which is what it amounts to, of funds that the Congress saw fit to eliminate?"[35] Of the $1.3 million requested, the Appropriations Committees allowed reprogramming of $700,000.

In 1973 the House Appropriations Committee recommended that the reprogramming process be tightened for the Defense Department. In cases where an item had been presented to Congress, and had been denied, the Pentagon could not resubmit the item under the reprogramming procedure. The committee said that to concur in such actions "would place committees in the position of undoing the work of the Congress. The Committee believes that this is an untenable position and notifies the Department of Defense that henceforth no such requests will be entertained." That restriction was incorporated in the Department of Defense Appropriation Act for fiscal 1974.[36]

4. *Circumventing Thresholds.* For any reprogramming on a new research project of $2 million or more, the Defense Department must present the proposal for committee review. During fiscal 1971, however, the Pentagon wanted to initiate a $4 million research project, to be handled by the Defense Special Projects Group (DSPG). The Pentagon told DSPG to use $1 million to start the project and promised $3 million later from the Emergency Fund. By the time the proposal reached Congress, the project was three months underway. Representative Whitten described the maneuver in these terms:

> You took a million dollars and got it started, and now you come up here and we are caught across the barrel. You have already started with a million dollars, but the million dollars was part of something which cost more than $2 million and clearly comes within the reprogramming agreement.[37]

This particular request was rejected, but it also had further ramifications. DSPG was a new name for the Defense Communications Planning Group (DCPG), which Congress assumed was in the process of being disbanded. Instead, the agency adopted a new name and dreamed up research projects to keep itself alive. House Appropriations called the attempt to perpetuate DSPG a "classic example of bureaucratic empire building and of the bureaucratic tendency to never end an organization even after the work for which it was created has been concluded." Both Appropriations Committees agreed to terminate the agency.[38]

House Appropriations issued a general warning in 1973 against circumvention of thresholds. It said that there had been cases where the Pentagon performed multiple below-the-threshold reprogrammings, the sum of which was above the threshold. That technique was "in violation of the clear agreement the committees have with the Department of Defense." Whenever such cases developed in the future, the request was to be presented to Congress in accordance with the normal reprogramming process.[39]

5. *New Starts.* Reprogramming has been used in several instances to initiate major weapons systems or to move from the research and development stage into production. The electronic battlefield (the "McNamara Line") was started in the fall of 1966 by means of a reprogramming action. Not until years later did Congress as a whole learn of the project. Even Stuart Symington, a ranking member of the Senate Armed Services Committee, said that he first learned about the project when reading a weekly magazine. The cost of the system from fiscal 1967 to fiscal 1971 was $1.68 billion.[40]

Another controversial use of reprogramming involved the F-14 Navy fighter aircraft. In 1969 House Appropriations directed that no funds were to be used for "tooling beyond that needed for fabrication of the test aircraft." The costly experience with the F-111 convinced the committee that technical and developmental problems should be ironed out first before moving to the production stage. But when the Navy requested permission the next year to reprogram $8.5 million for advance procurement items—to allow funds to be obligated toward the production of 26 aircraft—the committee approved the request. The Navy wanted to accelerate the program not because it had resolved the technical problems but because it wanted to keep the production line functioning.[41]

6. *Risk-Taking.* An element of risk accompanies each reprogramming proposal. Whenever the Defense Department requests that funds be shifted from one program to another, it necessarily admits that (1) the original program was overfunded, (2) there has been slippage in the original program, or (3) the original program has been downgraded in priority. Since this is painful to admit, agencies may try to convince the committees that the original program can, with considerable sacrifice, be delayed in order to fund an even

more pressing need. Still, reprogramming alerts the committees to potential areas for retrenchment. For example, in 1969 House Appropriations recommended that the budget for "Aircraft Weaponization" be reduced because about half of the funds appropriated for that program element in the last three years had been reprogrammed for other uses.[42]

Not only may a reprogramming proposal be rejected, the Appropriations Committees might take an additional step and eliminate the program from which the Pentagon was willing to draw funds. In the spring of 1971 the Defense Department announced that it was willing to give up $139.5 million that had been requested for an AOR oil tanker and three ATS rescue and salvage ships. Those funds would then be diverted to a new nuclear-powered aircraft carrier. After strong opposition was voiced by Members of Congress, delaying the carrier until the next year, OMB submitted a budget amendment to delete $52.6 million for two of the salvage ships. Both Appropriations Committees supported that reduction.[43]

CLOSER LEGISLATIVE CONTROL

It is a peculiar fact of the appropriations process that budget estimates are scrutinized by the authorization and appropriation committees, often undergoing intensive review by committees, party study groups, outside professional organizations, and during floor debate. Yet no comparable review exists for the billions of dollars that are reprogrammed after the appropriation bill becomes law.

INDIRECT CONTROLS

Reprogramming may be controlled indirectly by reducing the amount of carryover balances. The availability of unused funds from prior years whets the appetite of administrative officials who want to use the funds for new purposes. The fiscal 1971 appropriation bill for the Defense

Department attempted to bring carryover balances under closer control by changing no-year funds ("available until expended") to multi-year appropriations. (The problem of no-years will be taken up again in Chapter Six, pp. 128-29.) In 1974 the House gave its Appropriations Committee authority to recommend rescissions of appropriations. This authority to cancel existing budget authority stemmed from the hope of the House Select Committee on Committees that the recovery of unused funds from agency accounts "will discourage reprogramming of those funds."[44]

Another indirect approach is to open up the budget process and make reprogramming more visible. In previous years, whenever hearings were held on defense reprogrammings, transcripts were simply filed with the committee. They were not printed in the published hearings (except for brief accounts), nor was there any indication—through deletions or some other notation—that reprogramming hearings had even been held. The House Appropriations Committee, beginning in 1970, has made it a practice to print hundreds of pages of reprogramming deliberations every year.

New rules adopted by the House of Representatives in 1973 provided for open meetings unless the committee or subcommittee, in open session and with a quorum present, determines by roll-call vote that all or part of the remainder of the meeting shall be closed to the public. As a result of that change, the defense subcommittee of House Appropriations began opening up some of its hearings on reprogramming actions.

The heavy volume of defense reprogramming has produced sharp criticism from leading Members of the House and Senate. Chairman Mahon of the House Appropriations Committee remarked in 1971 that "we cannot have double hearings on all programs every year. We are a little irritated—at least I am—that we are confronted with this sort of thing."[45] During hearings that same year by the Senate

Armed Services Committee, chairman John Stennis issued this warning to Defense Secretary Laird:

> I want to refer to reprograming now. It seems to me, and I think others see it about the same way, that this matter of reprograming has gone too far, Mr. Secretary. Someone called my attention to the fact that $42 million of the fiscal year 1971 SAFEGUARD research and development funds are being reprogramed to be used for a variety of personnel purposes. Now we debated 5 or 6 weeks on the floor and told the Members of the Senate who voted for the SAFEGUARD money that it was needed and it was necessary. We had a tie vote in 1969, and we had to go through a battle last year, you remember, and now to come along and say we are going to take $42 million of that because we did not need it after all, looks bad.[46]

The Senate Armed Services Committee set up a separate subcommittee on reprogramming in 1970. The new unit was in response to the growing criticism of the defense budget, the stringency of money, and an insistence on the part of Senate members and the public for greater visibility in budgetary and legislative matters.

COMMITTEES KEEPING FAITH WITH CONGRESS

Just as agencies are to keep faith with the committees, the committees are to keep faith with Congress as a whole. When the Defense Department submitted a reprogramming request in 1964 to use $3.1 million for a new program called STEP (Special Training and Enlistment Program), the action was quickly challenged. During hearings by the defense subcommittee of Senate Appropriations, Leverett Saltonstall (R-Mass.) and Mike Mansfield (D-Mont.) questioned the propriety of using reprogramming to initiate the program. Saltonstall thought the full Congress should be informed, while Mansfield considered it advisable to have the program examined by Senate Armed Services and the full Senate

Appropriations Committee. The request was subsequently turned down by both Appropriations Committees.[47]

Another illustration of committee respect for the prerogatives of Congress occurred in 1971 when Defense Secretary Laird wanted to begin construction of a fourth nuclear-powered aircraft carrier (the CVAN-70, later designated CVN-70). He suggested that funds might be obtained either through reprogramming or by a budget amendment. Senators Walter Mondale, Democrat of Minnesota, and Clifford Case, Republican of New Jersey, wrote to the chairman of the Appropriations Committee to voice their opposition. The chairman, Allen Ellender, assured them that funding would have to follow the regular appropriations process: a budget request from the President followed by congressional authorization and appropriation. John Stennis, chairman of Senate Armed Services, took the same position.[48] Instead of confining legislative approval to the four review committees, the decision was opened up to Congress as a whole.

When the Defense Department submitted a reprogramming request in 1971 for an additional $61.2 million for the Cheyenne helicopter, committee sensitivity was again apparent. Since this weapons system had been the object of severe criticism by Members of Congress, House Appropriations allowed reprogramming of only $35 million to reimburse the contractor for services already rendered. The committee denied the request to reprogram funds for fiscal 1973 development on the ground that "it did not seem proper to anticipate the will of Congress with respect to the Cheyenne program that far in advance." Senate Appropriations noted that Members of the Senate were "opposed to the procedure of providing funds for the continuation of the development program through a reprograming action." With regard to fiscal 1972 development, $9.3 million was placed in the appropriation bill as a separate and identifiable item, allowing the full Congress to work its will.[49] The Army finally canceled the Cheyenne in 1972.

96

SCREENING BY GAO

A more formal and systematic review role for Congress was contemplated in a bill introduced by Senator Lawton Chiles (D-Fla.) in 1971. The bill directed the head of each Federal agency to make an annual report to the Comptroller General, listing the total amount of funds reprogrammed during the year, the specific purposes and amounts for which the funds were reprogrammed, and the specific purposes and amounts for which the funds were originally appropriated. The Comptroller General would then compile the information and furnish it to each committee and to each Member of Congress.[50]

In addition to annual reports, it would seem reasonable to have agencies send an extra copy of reprogramming *requests* to the GAO at the same time they are sent to review committees. GAO and Congress would thus know of reprogramming before, not after, the fact. When committees act on the requests, they could send an extra copy of their actions to the GAO to show which reprogrammings were approved and to what extent. Guidelines and dollar thresholds could be established to provide GAO with greater analytical responsibility. Just as guidelines have been established for the purpose of identifying which reprogrammings can be done internally by the agencies and which require committee notification and approval, so could guidelines be created to indicate the reprogramming actions in need of full congressional attention. While few in number, these could be significant in overall budgetary impact.

With regard to new starts, such as the electronic battlefield or the F-14 aircraft, GAO could have projected the cost over a period of four to five years, as well as checking into developmental and technical problems. Congress could then decide whether to leave the decision in committee or bring it to the floor. Such reprogrammings, initially flagged by GAO, might then be subjected to a "lay on the table" procedure, with the understanding that the actions could not

97

be implemented until a period of 15 to 30 days had elapsed. That would give interested and motivated Members of Congress an opportunity to mobilize support against controversial reprogrammings, drawing support from GAO. With the creation of a Congressional Budget Office in 1974, another central staff agency is available to monitor agency actions—to determine which are routine and which have a significant effect on budget priorities.

The scope of reprogramming helps underscore the highly tentative nature of budget estimates. Although estimates are merely that—*estimates*—there is a tendency to consider them as permanent monuments, chiseled in stone. Defense Secretaries regularly advise the Appropriations Committees that the military budget has been scrutinized and inspected with a fine-tooth comb. The fat has been trimmed; only the muscle remains. To tinker with the budget, Congress is warned, is to risk upsetting the delicate balance of priorities and force levels established by military planners.

The heavy and regular use of reprogramming by the Pentagon, amounting to billions of dollars each year, emphasizes that the defense budget is anything but firm. If more Members of Congress understood how much money is shifted around after passage of the appropriation bill, they might be a little more bold and penetrating when questioning the budget estimates. The prospect of closer legislative review might stimulate the Defense Department to improve its planning operations and procurement policies.

5

Transfers Between Accounts

TRANSFER authority permits agency officials to take funds from one appropriation account and place them in another. The classic justification for transfers was presented by Alexander Hamilton. He offered an example where the condition of roads, worse than expected, exhausted the specific fund that had been appropriated for wagon repairs. At the same time, the consumption of forage by animals turned out to be less than expected. What would be more reasonable, he asked, than to have the public agent transfer the surplus of the latter to the repair of wagons? If this was not allowed, "the motions of the army might, in this way, be suspended, and in the event, famine and ruin produced."[1]

CONGRESSIONAL RESISTANCE

Hamilton found himself at the center of the first major controversy in Congress over transfer authority. In the House of Representatives, in 1793, William Giles of Virginia presented a number of resolutions which charged Hamilton with improper use of funds. The first resolution, implying that Hamilton had transferred funds illegally or improperly, stated that "laws making specific appropriations of money should be strictly observed by the administrator of the finances thereof." William Smith of South Carolina proceeded to refute Giles point by point, arguing that the Administration ought to be free, as a matter of practice, to depart from congressional appropriations whenever the public safety or credit would be improved. Deviations from specific appropriations, instead of being construed automatically as a crime, should be tested by the merits of the executive's judgment. When exercised for the public good, Smith reasoned, executive spending discretion would "always meet the approbation of the National Legislature."[2] The Giles resolutions were subsequently voted down by the House.

This may appear to be a typical collision between the legislative and executive branches, but the dispute was not so much constitutional as it was partisan and personal. It was Hamilton's colleague in the Cabinet, Thomas Jefferson, who had helped draft the resolutions for Giles. The author of Smith's effective rebuttal was none other than Hamilton himself.[3]

Jefferson's strictures against transfers were excessively narrow and failed to halt the practice. During the 1793 debate, it was argued that the discretion to transfer funds had to be lodged somewhere, and it was expedient to entrust that to the executive. It might be found expedient to "mount the militia, or to vary the mode of carrying on the war, and therefore in some cases to apply the money, specifically appropriated for some of the objects which might upon trial be discovered unnecessary, to other objects of real utility."[4]

Precisely that type of situation arose in 1794. Although Congress had authorized the President to call out the militia in order to suppress insurrections, it had neglected to appropriate funds for that purpose. As a result, when President Washington ordered the state militia to march on insurgents in western Pennsylvania, in October 1794, it was necessary to use funds that had been appropriated for something else. Gallatin later insisted that regardless of the necessity for action or the popularity of the move, the President should have convened Congress, "the only competent authority" to resolve the issue. The cost of the expedition was not covered until an appropriation of December 31, 1794.[5]

During Jefferson's own Administration, Congressman Bayard observed that appropriations were unavoidably imperfect in their predictions of future needs. It was therefore necessary to allow expenditures to deviate from appropriations by taking funds from one account and applying them to another. While such transfers were technically illegal, "its being the custom palliates it."[6]

19TH CENTURY RESTRICTIONS

Congress made various efforts to restrict this "custom." An act in 1809 declared that the sums appropriated "shall be solely applied to the objects for which they are respectively appropriated, and to no other." Having proclaimed that general principle, Congress immediately undermined it to some extent by allowing the President to transfer funds while Congress was in recess. During such periods the President was authorized, upon the application of departmental heads, to direct that funds be transferred from one account to another whenever he decided it was "necessary for the public service." He would then report to Congress on such transfers during the first week of the next session.[7]

Proposals to abolish transfers altogether were countered by two arguments. Secretary of the Treasury Crawford told Congress in 1817 that legislators, in receiving reports of transfers, automatically learned where appropriations had been deficient and where redundant, thus providing an instructive guide for future appropriation bills. Furthermore, removal of transfer authority would merely encourage agency officials to submit inflated budget estimates as a means of cushioning against unexpected and unpredictable expenses. Crawford warned Congress that the "idea that economy will be enforced by repealing the provision will, I am confident, be found to be wholly illusory. Withdraw

101

the power of transfer, and the Departments will increase their estimates."[8]

The 1809 transfer act was revised in 1820 to allow transfers by the President throughout the year, whether Congress was in or out of session. But he was restricted to transferring funds only for certain items in the military and naval departments.[9] As described in subsequent pages, statutes over the next few decades permitted other transfers under various circumstances.

Agencies sometimes resorted to transfers in the absence of statutory authority. A Navy official in 1829 explained that toward the close of every year some of the appropriations were found to be deficient. Additional bills were drawn upon the Government for the very appropriation that had a deficiency. To pay the bills, the Secretary of the Navy regularly directed that they be paid out of some of the redundant appropriations.[10]

In that same year, in 1829, Amos Kendall of the Treasury Department informed the Secretary of the Navy that the general practice of transferring funds from one appropriation to another was in violation of law. When Congress appropriated new funds for the deficient account, it had been the custom to refund the amount "borrowed" from the redundant account. Kendall described that as a double violation of law. It contravened the restrictions on transfers; it also violated laws that prohibited funds from being moved from one year to the next (as discussed in Chapter Six). Kendall characterized the system of borrowing from one appropriation to make up deficiencies in another as "nothing more nor less than anticipating the appropriations of the next year." To meet the practical needs of the Navy, in 1832 Congress authorized the President, on application of the Secretary of the Navy, to direct that "a part of the money appropriated for a particular branch of the naval service be applied to another branch."[11]

Illegal transfers were not a simple matter of executive officials flouting the law. Congress itself contributed to the problem by failing to appropriate on time. Secretary of the Navy Southard complained about late appropriations in his report of December 2, 1825. He explained that the Navy appropriation bill was generally passed late in February of the short session and generally not until May of the long session. Since the fiscal year at that time began on January 1, that meant a delay of from two to five months. It was also the practice of Congress to change the "wording and character" of an appropriation, creating an additional delay of from a month to six weeks before legislative instructions were given to and acted upon by Navy agents. Southard concluded that "for nearly one-half of the year, the Department acts in perfect ignorance of the law under which it is bound to act."[12]

In his annual report in 1833, Secretary of the Navy Woodbury said that the naval appropriation bill was about two months late every short session of Congress and about four months late every long session. Without reliance on transfers, it would be necessary to suspend some operations entirely and place in jeopardy the credit of the United States in foreign countries. He suggested two remedies. Prior to the start of the new fiscal year Congress should appropriate for a quarter or a half of the next year for all permanent objects. The second remedy would be to authorize the President to transfer from one account to another whenever the naval appropriation bill was late, and then report to Congress on the amount and causes of such transfers.[13]

Congress chose the latter course. In 1834 it authorized the President to transfer funds during the period between the close of the year and the passage of the new naval appropriation act. Over the next few years he received additional discretion to transfer funds relating to fortification and to the Post Office, while his departmental heads were allowed to use surplus funds from any object to cover deficiencies elsewhere in the same department.[14]

A bill in 1842 to reorganize the Navy Department set the stage for a general revolt against transfer authority. Thomas

King, a Representative from Georgia, attributed most of the "improvidence, waste, and extravagance" in the Navy Department to the practice of transferring funds. With regard to the Navy, Congress repealed all acts, or parts of acts, that had authorized the President or the Navy Secretary to transfer funds from one account to another.[15]

That proved to be too restrictive for administrators during the Mexican War. Consequently, an act in 1846 authorized the President to transfer naval funds upon application of the Navy Secretary and whenever the President decided that the "exigencies of the service require it." The transfer authority did not permit the President to transfer funds that had been appropriated for improvements at naval yards, to transfer funds in such a way that the purposes of an appropriation could not be satisfied, or in such a way as to create the need for a deficiency appropriation.[16]

An 1847 law restricted naval transfers involving the clothing funds, while legislation the next year gave the President transfer authority over $1.5 million of unexpended balances in naval funds. But all of those special transfer authorities over the use of naval and War Department funds were repealed in 1852. The general authorization to departmental heads to use surplus funds to cover deficiencies was removed in 1860. Beginning in 1868, Congress repealed all previous acts authorizing transfers (reaching back to 1809) and stipulated that "no money appropriated for one purpose shall hereafter be used for any other purpose than that for which it is appropriated."[17]

20TH CENTURY PRACTICES

Current law echoes the 1868 principle by declaring that except "as otherwise provided by law, sums appropriated for the various branches of expenditures in the public service shall be applied solely to the objects for which they are respectively made, and for no others."[18] Exceptions to that general rule are fairly common, sometimes supported by statute, sometimes not.

During the 1920s, at a time when neither the President nor the Federal Government was noted for initiative or boldness of action, President Coolidge took funds appropriated for the eradication of animal diseases and used the money to assist storm-stricken farmers in Florida. He acted in the absence of statutory authority. When Congress returned from recess he laid the facts before the legislators and received their approval.[19]

During periods of great emergency, Congress delegates broad transfer authority to the executive branch. The 1932 Economy Act cut Federal spending so hastily, and in such indiscriminate fashion, that Congress permitted the Administration to transfer funds from one agency to another to minimize the damage. As much as 12 percent could be transferred, provided that no appropriation was increased by more than 15 percent.[20]

The Lend Lease Act of 1941 appropriated $7 billion for ordnance, aircraft, tanks, and for other categories of defense articles. The President could transfer as much as 20 percent of the appropriations from one category to another, provided that no appropriation was increased by more than 30 percent. And in 1943 the Budget Director was authorized to transfer 10 percent of military appropriations made available for fiscal 1944, subject to certain conditions. Appropriations in that particular act came to about $59 billion.[21]

In 1945 the Joint Committee on the Organization of Congress held hearings to decide what should be done to preserve and strengthen the powers and responsibilities of Congress. Out of those hearings came a number of recommendations, including the committee's proposal to prohibit the transfer of funds between appropriation accounts or between organization units. When the legislative reform bill was reported out by the Senate, it was noted that Congress had permitted transfers between appropriations, authorized the unlimited use of departmental receipts, and set up credit corporations with separate budgets. Moreover, the executive branch had "mingled appropriations, brought forward and backward unexpended and anticipated balances, incurred coercive deficiencies, and otherwise escaped the rigors of congressional control." But by the time the bill had become law—the Legislative Reorganization Act of 1946—the prohibition on transfers had been removed.[22]

Transfers raise the question as to whether they are "legislative" in nature and therefore under the jurisdiction of authorization committees, or whether the Appropriations Committees can recommend transfers without being subject to a point of order on the floor. The practice has been to treat them as legislative, making it necessary for the Appropriations Committee to obtain a rule that waives points of order. For example, the Second Supplemental Appropriations Bill for fiscal 1973 came onto the floor accompanied by a rule that waived all points of order for failing to comply with the provisions of House Rule xxi, Clause 2 (which prohibits legislation in appropriation bills) and Rule xxi, Clause 5 (which prohibits reappropriations). The bill contained some 109 instances in which the two clauses were violated. Of those, 80 involved transfers.[23] George Mahon, chairman of House Appropriations, offered this perspective:

> I think it might be recited that in prior years, quite a number of years ago, it was in order. It was not held to be in violation of the Rules of the House for the Committee on Appropriations to bring in a bill transferring funds which had previously been approved by Congress.[24]

In 1974 the House Select Committee on Committees agreed that the Appropriations Committee should be able to recommend transfers. However, the select committee added a requirement that transfers of appropriations must be identified under separate headings in all bills and reports issued by the Appropriations Committee.[25]

CAMBODIAN INTERVENTION

On April 30, 1970, President Nixon announced that he was sending U.S. forces into Cambodia to clean out Communist sanctuaries along the border with South Vietnam. The initial financing of that intervention was achieved by the transfer of funds from foreign assistance accounts. Three years later, after a fierce bombing of Cambodia had depleted a number of Defense Department accounts, President Nixon requested additional transfer authority to restore funds to those accounts.

FOREIGN ASSISTANCE TRANSFERS (1970)

After his intervention in Cambodia in the spring of 1970, President Nixon appealed to Congress for $255 million in military and economic assistance. Of that amount, $100 million was to restore funds which the President had *already* diverted to Cambodia from other programs. Section 610 of the Foreign Assistance Act allowed him to transfer up to 10 percent of the funds from one program to another, provided that the second program was not increased by more than 20 percent. Furthermore, Section 614(a) of the Foreign Assistance Act gave the President additional authority to spend funds for mutual security whenever he found it "important to the security of the United States." Also, Section 506 gave the President a $300 million emergency fund for military aid.[26]

Acting under the first two authorities, President Nixon borrowed $40 million from aid programs originally scheduled for Greece, Turkey, Taiwan, and the Philippines; used another $50 million in funds that had been assigned largely to Vietnam; and diverted still other amounts until a total of $108.9 million in military assistance had been given, or committed, to Cambodia.[27] In response to the request for funds for Cambodia, Senator Fulbright remarked:

> Now the administration has well underway a vast program of aid to Cambodia, without having sought any

107

approval by the Congress for such a policy. I have no doubt that the leaders of Cambodia's Government feel confident that the United States is now committed to their survival. And Congress' approval of this bill, as written, will be taken as a ratification of that commitment, both by Cambodia and in the eyes of much of the world. Once again Congress is faced with a proposal to endorse a policy ex post facto.[28]

Similar frustration was expressed by five Democratic members of the House Foreign Affairs Committee: Donald Fraser, Jonathan Bingham, Benjamin Rosenthal, John Culver, and Edward Roybal. They asked, "How long is the Congress going to be asked to give approval to executive actions which commit U.S. forces and resources, particularly in Southeast Asia, on an ex post facto and urgent basis with little or no time to analyze the political and military implications which might follow from that action?"[29]

Not only had the President involved the Government in an obligation for the Cambodian operation itself, but for future expenses as well. As Secretary of State Rogers explained to the Foreign Relations Committee on December 10, 1970: "I think it is true that when we ask for military assistance and economic assistance for Cambodia we do certainly take on some obligation for some continuity." The Cambodian foreign minister said that he felt there was an unwritten treaty between the two countries: "I am convinced that there really is a moral obligation of the United States to help. We are confident that the United States will continue to help us."[30]

In the waning days of the 91st Congress (1969-71), Members of Congress tried to impose two restrictions on Presidential action in Cambodia. The Special Foreign Assistance Act of 1971 barred the use of funds to finance the introduction of U.S. ground troops into Cambodia or to provide U.S. advisers to Cambodian forces in Cambodia. Those restrictions were blunted by the remarks of House conferees, who accepted the restrictions only on the understanding that (1) U.S. troops could be used in border sanctuary operations designed to protect the lives of American soldiers, (2) U.S. military personnel could be provided to supervise the distribution and care of U.S. military supplies and equipment deliveries to Cambodia, and (3) U.S. military advisers could train Cambodian soldiers in South Vietnam.[31] Moreover, in the Administration's bombing operations in Cambodia, air power was interpreted in such broad terms as to circumvent some of the legislative restriction. Helicopter gunships, capable of patrolling at treetop level, blurred the traditional distinction between air power and ground troops.

Another provision in the Special Foreign Assistance Act of 1971 stipulated that military and economic assistance to Cambodia "shall not be construed as a commitment by the United States to Cambodia for its defense."[32] But a commitment, whether legal or moral, did exist in the minds of Administration officials.

Some reporting restrictions were also placed on the President's authority to transfer funds. Legislation in 1971 prohibited the President from exercising certain transfer authorities for the purpose of providing additional assistance to Cambodia unless he first notified the Speaker of the House and the Senate Foreign Relations Committee in writing at least 30 days prior to the date he intends to exercise his authority, or 10 days if he certifies in writing that an emergency exists requiring immediate assistance to Cambodia. The prior notice requirement for the use of these transfer authorities was broadened the next year to cover assistance to any country.[33]

The extent of the commitment to Cambodia was indicated in October 1971 when the Senate debated an amendment which would have limited the total expenditure in Cambodia to $250 million for fiscal 1972. The Administration opposed the restriction, contending that it would threaten the capacity of the Cambodian government to defend itself. John N. Irwin, III, Acting Secretary of State, offered this appraisal: "We believe that with continued United States assistance at the levels requested by the Administration, the Cambodians with some external logistics and maintenance support will continue to make progress in defending their country from foreign invasion."[34]

On October 29, 1971, the Senate voted to increase the ceiling on expenditures in Cambodia from $250 million to $341 million, which was the figure requested by the Administration. While the Senate agreed to give the Administration the funds it wanted, it also asserted the right of Congress to set limits on expenditures. The ceiling could not be circumvented by special powers and authorities, such as the ability of the Pentagon to declare defense articles "excess" and give them to Cambodia, or the broad authority of the Defense Department and the Central Intelligence Agency to transfer funds from one area to another. If it turned out that more than $341 million was required, the ceiling would force the Administration to return to Congress for additional authorization.[35]

The $341 million ceiling did not apply to combat air operations. Moreover, it was weakened by the fact that House conferees, in accepting the ceiling, did so only with amendments which specifically excluded the obligation or expenditure of funds attributable to South Vietnamese operations in Cambodia. President Nixon signed the foreign assistance act, containing this ceiling, on February 7, 1972.[36]

DEFENSE TRANSFERS (1973)

After his intervention in Cambodia in 1970, President Nixon announced in a television report to the nation that the "only remaining American activity in Cambodia after July 1 [1970] will be air missions to interdict the movement of enemy troops and material where I find that is necessary to protect the lives and security of our men in South Vietnam."[37] The basis for military action appeared to have disappeared with the signing of a cease-fire agreement in Paris, on January 27, 1973, and the withdrawal of all American troops from Vietnam by March 28, 1973. And yet the Nixon Administration continued to let run a massive bombing operation in Cambodia.

The State Department submitted a statement which discussed the President's authority to continue U.S. air combat operations in Cambodia. Part of the justification rested on Congress' "cooperation" with the President in bringing about the cease-fire agreement: "This cooperation has been shown through consultations and through the authorization and appropriation process." The statement pointed out that Congress had rejected proposals by some Members to cut off appropriations for necessary military expenditures and foreign assistance.[38]

A number of Federal judges had also endorsed the theory that Congress could indirectly assent to a war by appropriating the necessary funds. Some of those judges, however, began to have second thoughts about the proposition. As Judge Wyzanski of the U.S. Court of Appeals for the District of Columbia noted, in a 1973 decision concerning the war power:

> This court cannot be unmindful of what every schoolboy knows: that in voting to appropriate money or to draft men a Congressman is not necessarily approving of the continuation of a war no matter how specifically the appropriation or draft act refers to that war. A Congressman wholly opposed to the war's commencement and continuation might vote for the military appropriations and for the draft measures because he was unwilling to abandon without support men already fighting. An honorable, decent, compassionate act of aiding those already in peril is no proof of consent to the actions that placed and continued them in that dangerous posture. We should not construe votes cast in pity and piety as though they were votes freely given to express consent.[39]

The financing of the Cambodian war in 1972-73 was facilitated by the existence of large transfer authority made

111

available to the Pentagon, amounting to $750 million for fiscal 1973. The exercise of that authority was supposedly subject to congressional approval. The understanding was that transfer proposals would be forwarded to the Appropriations Committees under prior-approval reprogramming procedures, requiring the explicit approval of those committees prior to implementation.[40]

Whether "committee approval" would be decisive and controlling, or merely perfunctory and after-the-fact, depended on the timeliness of Defense reporting. As it turned out, although the Pentagon obligated funds for the bombing in Cambodia during the months of November and December 1972, it was not until February and March of the following year that the Appropriations Committees were permitted to act on the bulk of transfer requests. Technically the transfers would be made with committee approval, but the crucial administrative decisions had been made months before.

This dispute was complicated by the existence of other statutory authority. Legislation in 1972 required the Secretary of Defense to "immediately advise" Congress whenever the President waives the apportionment process, which is the principal means by which Congress avoids deficiencies. Although President Nixon invoked the authority on November 24, 1972—for the fiscal 1973 Operation and Maintenance accounts for the Army, Navy, and Air Force—the Appropriations Committees were not notified until a letter of March 16, 1973. Throughout that period of almost four months the Defense Department was spending at a deficiency rate for certain accounts.[41]

The Pentagon had already programmed the entire amount of $750 million transfer authority; $492 million was for Southeast Asia. The large items were for three Operation and Maintenance accounts: $319.7 million for the Air Force, $92.6 million for the Navy, and $33.6 million for the Army.[42] By the time hearings were held before House Appropriations, on April 12, 1973, the $492 million had been obligated and most of it spent. This development sparked the following dialogue between committee members Sikes and Minshall and the Acting Assistant Secretary of Defense (Comptroller) Don R. Brazier:

MR. SIKES. What authority does the Department of Defense have to expend the $492 million for Southeast Asia in view of the fact that prior approval reprogramings associated with the transfer authority must be approved by the appropriate committees of Congress before funds are committed?

MR. BRAZIER. Sir, the decision with respect to financing the Southeast Asia operations was a decision of the Secretary of the Defense and the President. It was the judgment of the Department that this was the only course of action available to us during the period Congress was not in session and when we were not able to actually submit a supplemental.

MR. MINSHALL. When was that decision made?

MR. BRAZIER. It was made during the development of the 1974 budget, and specifically during the month of November.

MR. SIKES. Were you unable to submit reprograming requests because Congress was not then in session?

MR. BRAZIER. Yes, sir. That was also true.

MR. SIKES. We have been in session since early January. Could you not have come to us subsequent to the reconvening of Congress?

MR. BRAZIER. Yes, sir. The reprogramings were submitted just as quickly as we could process them subsequently to the submission of the President's budget in late January.

MR. SIKES. Are you going to say you ran out of money and you had to get the ox out of the ditch the best way you could? Is that what you are saying?

MR. BRAZIER. Yes, sir. That is what I am saying.[43]

113

After Congressman Sikes had reviewed the established procedure for defense transfers, noting with dissatisfaction that funds had been obligated and spent without committee prior approval, Brazier offered this justification: "Mr. Chairman, while those moneys and those expenses have indeed been incurred, we have not literally transferred the moneys into those appropriations. We are now operating in those accounts at a deficiency rate. We have not in fact transferred the dollars into the appropriations, and would not until this committee acted."[44] In other words, the substantive decision to commit the funds was made unilaterally by the Pentagon; the technical and routine operation of transferring the funds would be shared with Congress.

On March 21, 1973, President Nixon asked Congress to increase the transfer authority for the Defense Department from $750 million to $1.25 billion. OMB Director Ash explained that the $500 million increase was needed in part because "combat activity rates during January and February were above budgeted levels. . . ."[45] In the event that Congress failed to provide this additional transfer authority, Defense Secretary Richardson warned that a number of "drastic actions" would have to be considered.

> These would include standing down forces; curtailment of flying hours and steaming hours programs; reduction or elimination of scheduled training operations; cancellation of supply procurements, leading to gaps in operational support; deferral or cancellation of maintenance; and a freeze on promotions, military enlistments, and civilian and military personnel accessions.[46]

When John McClellan, chairman of the Senate Appropriations Committee, asked whether it was correct to say that even if Congress denied the requested $500 million transfer authority "the Cambodian proceedings and operations will go on anyway, that the administration feels it has the authority to continue these operations and incur the cost involved irrespective of whether the Congress grants this transfer authority. . . ," Richardson replied "Yes; that is correct. . . ."[47]

The House Appropriations Committee reduced the transfer authority to $430 million. Eight Democratic members of the committee joined in a separate statement expressing strong opposition to the committee's decision. They felt it amounted to a "Congressional blank check approving combat activities of the Defense Department which have already taken place and giving Congressional approval to any future combat activities which may be deemed necessary to preserve our flexibility." The grant of transfer authority reminded them of the Gulf of Tonkin Resolution and the erosion of congressional influence in decisions affecting Southeast Asia. To approve the transfer request would start the "entire sordid chain of events in motion once again."[48]

The supplemental appropriation bill reached the House floor on May 10. An amendment by Joseph Addabbo of New York, to strike out the additional transfer authority for the Pentagon, carried 219 to 188, thus overturning the recommendation of House Appropriations. In addition, the House adopted an amendment by Clarence Long of Maryland to prohibit the use of any funds in the supplemental bill to support directly or indirectly U.S. combat activities in, over, or from off the shores of Cambodia. That amendment passed 224-172.[49]

The Senate Appropriations Committees voted to recommend only $170 million in increased transfer authority for the Pentagon, prohibiting any transfers for the purpose of supporting combat activities in Cambodia or Laos.[50] By the time the Senate committee acted, however, it was apparent that new legislative restrictions would be needed to prevent the Administration from continuing to bomb Cambodia. Even if denied transfer authority or access to funds in the supplemental bill, executive officials could finance the bombing with funds that had been appropriated in prior years.

To close that door, Senate Appropriations adopted a more comprehensive amendment to forbid the use of *any* funds to support U.S. combat activities in Cambodia or Laos—a restriction that covered funds contained in the supplemental bill as well as all funds made available by previous appropriations. Senator Roman Hruska (R-Neb.) challenged this blanket prohibition (known as the Eagleton amendment) on a parliamentary point; he made the point of order that it was not germane to the supplemental bill. The Senate decided 55-21 that it *was* germane and later reinforced that procedural step by voting 63-19 to adopt the Eagleton amendment.[51]

The two Houses reached a compromise on the amount of additional transfer authority for the Pentagon: $75 million, provided that none of the funds transferred could be used in support of U.S. combat activities in Cambodia or Laos. More troublesome was the choice between the Long amendment (prohibiting the use of funds in the supplemental bill for combat activity in Cambodia or Laos) and the Eagleton amendment (prohibiting the use of any funds for those purposes). Mahon appealed to House pride by saying that the Eagleton amendment infringed upon the fiscal prerogatives of the House of Representatives; the House should not "capitulate to the Senate." Long responded that in normal times he would have preferred his own amendment, and would have fought to uphold the preeminence of the House in appropriation matters, but the immediate issue was of such constitutional importance that he regarded the Eagleton amendment as stronger and therefore deserving of support.[52]

A motion by Robert Giaimo (D-Conn.), to have the House recede from its disagreement with the Senate and to concur in the Eagleton amendment, passed 235 to 172. At that point Mahon offered a motion for the purpose of delaying by 60 days the effective date of the Eagleton amendment. His motion failed on a tie vote, 204-204.[53]

The matter was now in the hands of the President. On June 27 President Nixon vetoed the bill because of the "Cambodian rider," which he said would "cripple or destroy the chances for an effective negotiated settlement in Cambodia and the withdrawal of all North Vietnamese troops. . . ." He also warned that the bill contained a number of appropriations which were essential for the continuation of governmental operations. Within a day, he said, nine agencies would have exhausted their authority to pay the salaries and expenses of their employees. In its attempt to override the veto, the House of Representatives failed on a vote on 241-173, short of the necessary two-thirds.[54]

A stalemate, a deadlock, beckoned as the issue boiled to its climax. If Congress continued to press its point, inserting restrictive language in the supplemental bill, the President could blame Congress for stopping the machinery of Government. On the other hand, Congress could have argued that the language represented a legitimate and constitutional effort to restrict the President's freedom to wage war and to commit the Nation to unauthorized expenditures. If the President refused to acknowledge Congress' pre-eminence in matters of the purse, he could have been held responsible for the paralysis of agency operations.

On this confrontation it was Congress that chose to back off. A revised supplemental bill was drafted to delay the effect of the Eagleton amendment until August 15, thereby allowing the President to bomb Cambodia for another 45 days. The compromise threw many members in a moral quandary. Don Riegle of Michigan protested that the President was basically saying, "If you will withdraw your objection to my bombing—and help me bomb for 45 more days—then I will stop." To Riegle that meant that "we must join the lawbreaking and killing in order to finally stop it. It is a shameful suggestion—Executive blackmail."[55]

The supplemental appropriation bill which Nixon finally signed contained the August 15 deadline. It also retained the substance of the Long amendment by prohibiting the use of any funds in the bill for combat activities in Southeast Asia. Lastly, the additional $75 million in transfer authority for the Defense Department was stricken from

117

the bill. That led some legislators to conclude that the request for transfer authority, from the very beginning, was a bogus issue, an attempt by the Pentagon to obtain Congress' stamp of approval for the Cambodia operation.[56]

The relationship between transfer authority and litigation-impeachment efforts is so close that it may be useful to take a few pages to complete the story.

LITIGATION

The August 15 compromise affected litigation that had been progressing in the Federal courts. Robert Drinan and three other Members of the House asked that the 1973 bombing of Cambodia be declared a violation of domestic and international law. Judge Tauro of the U.S. District Court in Massachusetts ruled that only in situations where a conflict between the executive and legislative branches appeared to be incapable of resolution should the courts intervene. Adoption of the August 15 compromise, he said, "demonstrates clearly and objectively that the branches were not in resolute conflict." Had Congress indicated an unwillingness to compromise, "we would have a clear issue of conflict before us that would have required judicial determination."[57]

Congresswoman Elizabeth Holtzman filed a separate suit to have the courts determine that the President could not engage in combat operations in Cambodia and elsewhere in Indochina in the absence of congressional authorization. Judge Judd of the U.S. District Court in the Eastern District of New York, in a decision of July 25, 1973, held that Congress had not authorized the bombing of Cambodia. Its inability to override the veto and its subsequent adoption of the August 15 deadline could not be taken as an affirmative grant of authority: "It cannot be the rule that the President needs a vote of only one-third plus one of either House in order to conduct a war, but this would be the consequence of holding that Congress must override a Presidential veto in order to terminate hostilities which it has not authorized."

Judd enjoined the President from engaging in combat operations in Cambodia, but postponed the injunction for 48 hours to permit the Administration to apply for a stay from the Court of Appeals.[58]

When the circuit court ordered a stay of the injunction until August 13, Holtzman appealed to the Supreme Court. Justice Marshall, assigned to oversee the proceedings of the second circuit, denied the Holtzman motion to vacate the stay. Marshall noted that once the August 15 date was reached "the contours of this dispute will then be irrevocably altered. Hence, it is difficult to justify a stay for the purpose of preserving the status quo, since no action by this Court can freeze the issues in their present form."[59]

The Judd order was reversed on August 8 by the Court of Appeals. Judge Mulligan treated the dispute as basically a political question, to be resolved by the executive and legislative branches, but did note that the August 15 date constituted congressional approval of the Cambodian bombing.[60]

IMPEACHMENT

Cambodia developed into a potential article of impeachment against President Nixon. Hearings by the Senate Armed Services Committee in 1973 disclosed that there had been secret bombings in Cambodia beginning on March 18, 1969, continuing in secret until American ground forces invaded Cambodia on April 30, 1970. This prior bombing was concealed from most Members of Congress until July 13, 1973. At least three classified reports to the Senate Armed Services Committee in 1971 and 1973 failed to mention that the raids had taken place. Prior to the April 30, 1970 intervention, American B-52s flew 3,630 sorties into Cambodia and dropped approximately 104,000 tons of munitions at a cost of nearly $150 million.[61]

The Pentagon created a system of false reporting of Cambodian bombings so that it would appear they had taken place in South Vietnam. After this deception was reported in the *New York Times*, and after hearings had been held by the Senate Armed Services Committee, the Defense Department issued a report on B-52 bombing operations in Cambodia during the period from March 18, 1969 to May 26, 1970. A B-52 strike on a target in South Vietnam would be requested through normal communication and command channels. Through a highly classified separate channel, a strike on the Cambodian target nearest the requested target in South Vietnam would be proposed. Upon approval, the aircraft would fly its mission in such a way that on its final run it would pass over or near the South Vietnam target before releasing its bombs in Cambodia. Routine reports would then be filed showing the strike to have been in South Vietnam.[62]

On July 30, 1974, the House Judiciary Committee considered a proposed article of impeachment dealing with the unauthorized bombing of Cambodia and the concealment from Congress of that fact.

> In his conduct of the office of President of the United States, Richard M. Nixon, in violation of his constitutional oath faithfully to execute the office of President of the United States and, to the best of his ability, preserve, protect, and defend the Constitution of the United States, and in disregard of his constitutional duty to take care that the laws be faithfully executed, on and subsequent to March 17, 1969, authorized, ordered, and ratified the concealment from the Congress of the facts and the submission to the Congress of false and misleading statements concerning the existence, scope and nature of American bombing operations in Cambodia in derogation of the power of the Congress to declare war, to make appropriations and to raise and support armies, and by such conduct warrants impeachment and trial and removal from office.[63]

The committee, voting 26-12, decided not to report that article to the House. Opponents of the article argued that

President Nixon was performing his constitutional duty in ordering the bombing, particularly to protect American troops, and that Congress had been sufficiently notified. Opponents also maintained that Congress shared the blame because of its acquiescence or ratification of President Nixon's actions.[64]

That transfer authority has been abused in the past is plain enough. Equally clear is the need to resist efforts to abolish transfers altogether. The objective should be to keep transfer authority in the proper channels by singling out the areas of abuse. It is one thing to transfer funds while carrying out the policies and programs of Congress. Wholly different is the use of transfer authority to initiate long-term financial commitments (as in Cambodia) that deprive Congress of its freedom to act and to choose. Members of Congress become locked in to paying for policies and programs set in motion by the executive branch.

Transfer authority is also abused when invoked to circumvent Congress as a whole. If an agency has submitted a program to Congress, and been rejected, it may try to accomplish the same purpose by transferring other funds to that program. To the extent that this occurs, it represents an unwarranted defiance of the Congress that can result only in legislative mistrust and lack of confidence in executive officials. As a consequence, the legislative process becomes increasingly encumbered with many peripheral details in an effort to check, restrain, or overturn irresponsible actions.

Beginning with fiscal 1974, and continuing the next year, Congress prohibited that kind of diversion by the Defense Department. The House Appropriations Committee explained that to concur in such actions "would place committees in the position of undoing the work of the Congress. The Committee believes that this is an untenable position. . . ." Because of this restriction, the Pentagon can no longer use transfer authority "where the item for which funds are requested has been denied by Congress."[65]

The spotlight has been directed on the Pentagon in recent years. Much less is known about discretionary spending actions in the domestic agencies. Monitoring by committees seems less intense. There may be cases where transfer authority is used to achieve what could not be accomplished by the regular appropriations process. Two abuses are possible. One is to come to Congress, be rebuffed, and then resort to transfers. The other is to rely on transfers without coming to Congress at all. We know little about either area.

6

Timing of Obligations

In addition to transferring funds from one project to another, executive officials have broad discretion in deciding when to obligate and spend funds. In some cases that involves delays or "impoundments" of funds, to be discussed in Chapters Seven and Eight. Here I focus on different issues: the transfer of funds from one year to the next; agency efforts to prevent unobligated funds from reverting to the Treasury; and a variety of other agency practices that determine when funds shall be obligated and, in some instances, what Congress will have to appropriate.

UNEXPENDED FUNDS

An early dispute during the Washington Administration concerned the practice of transferring funds from one year to the next. Alexander Hamilton, in his final report on public credit, proposed that any sum unexpended for more than two years after the end of the calendar year in which the appropriation was made should be carried over into a "surplus fund." There it would cease to be available for the original purpose. Hamilton permitted two exceptions: payment of interest on the debt and for purposes of the sinking fund. He objected to leaving other appropriations indefinite as to time, since that could tie up funds no longer needed for the intended purpose.[1]

Congress translated Hamilton's recommendations into law in 1795. With certain exceptions, such as payment of interest on the national debt, any unexpended funds remaining in the Treasury for more than two years were to be transferred to a surplus fund. There the appropriation would lapse.[2]

An incident in 1819 served notice that Congress still had difficulties in controlling unexpended funds. Congress passed legislation to suppress the slave trade and to punish crimes of piracy, but in assigning those new responsibilities to the executive branch Congress failed to appropriate the required funds. President Monroe supplied the necessary vessels by using old balances remaining on the books of the Navy Department. When legislators protested that this violated the two-year limit, they were advised that the balances were exempt from the law because they had been in the hands of the *Treasurer* (who acted as agent for the military departments) rather than in the Treasury itself.[3]

Congress responded with legislation in 1820, directing the Secretary of the Treasury to carry to the surplus fund any Army or Navy funds that remained unexpended "in the treasury, or in the hands of the treasurer, as agent for those departments. . . ." Implementation of the statute depended on a statement from the Secretary of the Department that "the object for which the appropriation was made has been effected." By failing to make such a declaration, the Department could retain access to those funds in future years. However, a decision by the Attorney General in 1831 actually tightened the application of the law. Moneys appropriated to the War Department, and unexpended after the expiration of two years from the calendar year in which they were appropriated, could be carried to the surplus fund without a report from the Secretary of War that such moneys were no longer required. Such moneys became liable to the transfer "by the mere efflux of time." The report of the Secretary of War would be necessary only when moneys remained unexpended for a period less than two years, and the object of the appropriation had been effected.[4]

More stringent legislation appeared in 1852. Congress directed that any moneys unexpended after two years be carried immediately to the surplus fund, with the appropriation regarded as having ceased. Again, there were certain exceptions: interest on the debt, payment of interest and reimbursement according to contract of any loan made on account of the United States, and any moneys appropriated for a purpose where a statute assigned a longer duration than two years.[5]

Decisions by the Attorney General quickly diluted the force of that statute. In cases of contracted items, personal service, or other claims on the Government, appropriations would remain available from year to year until the obligation was fully discharged. Under that interpretation, where "unexpended" actually meant "unobligated," the appropriation did not lapse into the surplus fund. In a second decision, the Attorney General held that it was proper for a department to begin a year by first expending old balances. Since old money would be used first (the rule of "first in-first out"), the Attorney General said it would be impossible for a balance of two or more years to exist "unless the balance of a previous year exceed in amount the whole expenditure of the present year. . . ."[6]

At the conclusion of the Civil War, agencies held large balances of funds with no immediate need to spend them. By June 30, 1869, unexpended appropriations reached a level of $102 million, in effect doubling the budgets of the various departments. Senator Sherman wanted to carry into the surplus fund the bulk of those balances.[7]

Legislation in 1870 placed new restrictions on the use of unexpended balances. Section 5 of the act reduced from

125

two years to one year the availability of unexpended balances. All balances of appropriations contained in the annual appropriation bills and made specifically for the service of any fiscal year, and remaining unexpended at the end of that fiscal year, "shall only be applied to the payment of expenses properly incurred during that year, or to the fulfillment of contracts properly made within that year. . . ." Balances not needed were to be carried to the surplus fund. Section 5 did not apply to appropriations known as "permanent" (made for an unlimited period) or "indefinite" (where no amount was specified). Section 6 required the Secretary of the Treasury to report to the auditor of the Treasury all balances remaining on the books which had not been drawn against for two years. If such balances were not needed in the settlement of accounts, they could be carried into the general treasury. Finally, the act stipulated in section 7 that it would be unlawful for any department to spend in any one fiscal year any sum in excess of appropriations for that year, or to involve the Government in any contract for the future payment of money in excess of such appropriation.[8]

Within a matter of weeks the Attorney General issued an opinion that narrowed the application of section 6. The opinion held that the "fact that a balance has been drawn against within two years since the last appropriation, reserves it from the operation of this section, no matter how large the balance may be, or how small the amount may be which has been drawn against it." Even with that construction, however, the act brought into the Treasury over $174 million of accumulated unexpended balances. A single bureau, over the past quarter century, had managed to squirrel away $36 million.[9]

Additional restrictions were placed on unexpended balances in 1874. The act provided that beginning on July 1, 1874, the Secretary of the Treasury "shall cause all unexpended balances of appropriations which shall have remained upon the books of the Treasury for two fiscal years

126

to be carried to the surplus fund and covered into the Treasury. . . ." That provision did not apply to permanent specific appropriations, appropriations for rivers and harbors, lighthouses, fortifications, public buildings, or the pay of the Navy and Marine Corps. Also exempted were unexpended balances required for a treaty with Great Britain or to fulfill contracts existing at the date of the passage of the act. This law was interpreted more strictly by the Administration.[10]

TWO-YEAR CONSTITUTIONAL LIMIT

According to Article I, Section 8 of the Constitution, appropriations to raise and support armies shall not be for a longer term than two years. Yet no-year funding of military procurement (where funds "remain available until expended") has been upheld in several opinions by the Attorney General.

A 1904 opinion argued that to raise and support an army was one thing; to equip it was another. The constitutional prohibition applied only to the former. This appears to be mere playing with words, but the early drafts of the Constitution offer some support for this interpretation. The word "equip" was used initially in reference to the Navy, as in "raise armies. ⟨& equip Fleets.⟩"; "raising a military Land Force—and of equiping a Navy—"; or "raise Armies; to build and equip Fleets."[11]

The delegates later agreed to insert the words "and support" after "raise," and they also adopted "provide and maintain" in place of "build and equip."[12] The two-year limit applied to armies, not to naval forces. Thus, whereas the Constitution empowers Congress to "raise and support armies, but no appropriation of money to that use shall be for a longer term than two years," it merely empowers Congress to "provide and maintain a navy." The Framers appeared to be concerned chiefly about a standing army, not the availability of funds over a period of years for the construction of vessels. Carried a step farther, one could argue that the same reasoning applies to long lead-time construction items for the Army, Air Force, and Marine Corps.

That, in any event, was the interpretation adhered to by Congress and the Department of Defense. For many years the appropriation accounts for defense procurement and for defense research, development, test, and evaluation (RDT&E) were made available on a no-year basis. The amount of no-year funds appropriated for those accounts in 1969 came to $25.5 billion. In an effort to bring carryover balances under closer legislative control, the House Appropriations Committee recommended a change from no-year to multi-year: allowing funds to remain available for two years in the case of RDT&E and for three years in the case of procurement (except five years for shipbuilding). The Senate Appropriations Committee had a different solution. The Administration should review its accounts and propose rescissions of unobligated balances that remained available for three or more fiscal years in the case of procurement (except shipbuilding, which required five years) and two or more years for RDT&E. The Senate approach was enacted into law.[13]

House Appropriations was not satisfied with the results of the rescission experiment. In 1970 it offered this objection to the availability of unobligated and unexpended balances in the Defense Department:

> When funds remain available until expenditure, financial managers can recoup sums when contracts are cancelled, contingency funds are not utilized, programs slip or are changed in scope, or in other ways. Such funds are held and are applied to other programs as required in subsequent years. A recent example is in a reprograming request submitted to the Committee on September 24th which "found" unexpended funds from fiscal years 1961, 1962, 1963, 1964, 1965, and 1966, primarily from the

construction of POLARIS submarines, as a source of funding. The availability of these funds makes defense planners, to a limited extent, immune from tight Congressional fiscal control.[14]

House Appropriations again recommended that no-year funds be replaced by multi-year accounts.

The Defense Department objected to multi-year appropriations partly on the ground that they would entail a "major administrative burden, and great confusion in future budgetary development and presentation." The Department predicted that abandonment of no-years would create a year-end buying psychology, encouraging agencies to obligate all of their funds so they would not lapse. Moreover, enactment of multi-years would increase the Pentagon's budget requests by $500 million to $1 billion, unless old balances remained available. If Congress allowed that money to remain available (by "reappropriating" the unobligated amounts), the effect would be to have no-year money plus new administrative burdens.[15] As explained in the next section, that has partly come about.

The defense appropriation act for fiscal 1971 adopted the multi-year approach. A few years later the Senate Armed Services Committee commented on the implementation of this new funding cycle. With regard to two-year funding of RDT&E, the committee said that most witnesses agreed that the provision had caused no significant problems in the execution of the programs. On the positive side, two-year funding had "instilled a measure of discipline throughout the DOD research and development organizations which is accomplishing a more timely and effective use of funds authorized and appropriated. The committee is satisfied that this provision of law has been constructive and that it should continue in effect."[16]

The shift to multi-year funding for the Defense Department does not mean that unobligated balances will lapse and that carryover amounts will be reduced. Congress prevented that from happening in many instances by reappropriating the unused amounts.

REAPPROPRIATION

When funds are made available for a specified period of time (either for one year or a multiple of years), any funds not obligated by that time will lapse. To prevent the return of those funds to the Treasury, Congress will sometimes "reappropriate" part or all of the unobligated balance.

Reappropriation has been a source of dispute for at least a century. During debate in 1876, Senator Morrill of Maine challenged a claim by the House of Representatives that it had reduced appropriations by $39 million. What the House had done was to reappropriate some old balances and exclude them from the total for new appropriations.[17] The agency received the funds it needed, while Congress received credit for appropriating a "smaller" amount.

Various precedents were established over the next few decades to decide which reappropriations were permissible and which were subject to a point of order. The practice of carrying funds forward from one year to the next, when they would otherwise have lapsed, was studied in 1945 by the Joint Committee on the Organization of Congress. Of particular concern was the failure to include reappropriations as part of new appropriations. In this way Congress could understate the amount of money made available to an agency. Situations arose where it appeared that Congress had cut an agency's budget by $100 million. However, after taking into account reappropriations, there was not a dime's worth of difference between the Administration's request and the congressional action.[18]

To eliminate deception and confusion, the joint committee recommended that the practice of reappropriating unobligated balances be discontinued, except in the case of appropriations for public works. Appropriations each year would represent the total amount of money available to an agency. That restriction was incorporated into the Legislative Reorganization Act of 1946. It is repeated in the Rules of the House of Representatives and is referred to in the standard compilation of Senate procedures and in the Senate Manual.[19]

Nevertheless, reappropriations are still used on occasion, either because no one raises a point of order or because points of order have been specifically waived in the resolution that accompanies an appropriation bill to the House floor. In some cases the word "reappropriated" is used where funds are in no danger of lapsing. For example, in 1972 the House Committee on Appropriations said that it was reappropriating $58 million in Farmers Home Administration water and sewer grants and $500 million in Department of Housing and Urban Development water and sewer grants.[20] However, those funds were no-year and would not have lapsed. The committee was simply using "reappropriate" to underscore its intention that the funds impounded by the Administration be released for obligation and expenditure.

Other than foreign assistance, to be discussed later, the major area of reappropriation is the Department of Defense. The fiscal 1973 defense appropriation act, in order to prevent the lapsing of some procurement and RDT&E funds, "transferred" (actually, reappropriated) a total of $746.2 million. To take the case of "Aircraft Procurement, Army," only $33.5 million was appropriated, but that amount was augmented by $95 million in old funds.[21] The appropriation account in question was adequately funded, drawing on a mixture of new money and old money.

Here the reader can appreciate some of the conceptual difficulties that obscure the area of reappropriation. Certain agriculture funds are called reappropriations, but they are not; other funds, as in defense, are not called reappropriations, but they are.

Foreign assistance reappropriation is complicated, in a legal sense, by legislation that authorizes the continued availability of unexpended balances. Moreover, each year

131

the appropriation act for foreign assistance provides language that permits unobligated balances to be carried forward for an additional year. This language is challenged from time to time by points of order, sometimes successfully, sometimes not. A point of order by Congressman Passman in 1955 was sustained by the Chair on the basis of the 1946 prohibition on reappropriation. A point of order by Congressman Gross in 1960 was also sustained. Although a mutual security act, passed in 1955, had authorized the reappropriation of unexpended balances, Gross argued successfully that when the House adopted its rules in January 1959, the rules included the 1946 prohibition. The latter action by the House took precedence.[22]

The parliamentary situation was reversed in 1961. After the House adopted its rules, Congress passed new legislation authorizing the reappropriation of foreign assistance funds. This time a point of order by Gross was rejected on the ground that the most recent expression by Congress was in support of reappropriation.[23] Presumably a point of order in 1975, after the House adopted its rules for the 94th Congress, would be successful, for the rules would be a reaffirmation of the 1946 prohibition on reappropriation.

In recent years the Senate Committee on Appropriations has expressed concern about the scope of spending discretion that is available to administrators in the Agency for International Development. The committee requested the General Accounting Office and the Congressional Research Service to study the reappropriation of foreign assistance funds. The committee also directed AID, in 1973, to take "immediate steps to thoroughly review the pipeline and to purge it of those obligations which are no longer valid." And in 1974 Congress passed legislation to restrict AID's access to loan receipts. Previously AID was able to extend loans to foreign countries and then later, after the loans were repaid, use the receipts to extend new loans. The effect of the "loan reflow" procedure was to bypass the appropriation process. The 1974 legislation requires that after

July 1, 1975, the loan receipts will be deposited in the Treasury.[24]

OBLIGATIONS

A crucial step in the spending process consists in the obligation of funds. If agencies fail to obligate by a certain time, the funding authority lapses and reverts to the Treasury. Prior to 1954, administrators managed to retain access to funds by including them within a fluid concept called "obligated balances." The term meant different things to different people. The General Accounting Office and the Budget Bureau developed their own definitions, but there was no agreement.

In 1949 the Hoover Commission said that agency reports on available balances were often' misleading, "since the spending agencies may report their obligations as they see fit." Studies by GAO in 1953 and 1954, in conjunction with the staff of the House Appropriations Committee, concluded that various agencies were recording obligations where no real obligation existed. Senator Harry F. Byrd noted in 1953 that the term "obligated" had no uniform meaning. A number of agencies reported funds as obligated even though no contract had been entered into.[25]

During floor debate in 1954, Congressman Vorys drew upon his experience with the foreign aid program to make this observation:

> Department and agency people, in their determination to hold on to leftover funds, unused funds, to prevent their reverting to the Treasury; to tie the hands of Congress in considering whether the agency needs these funds, have adopted the device of pasting the labels obligation or obligated balance all over such funds.[26]

Congress finally established, in 1954, legal criteria for obligation, requiring documentary evidence of binding agreements and other liabilities on the Government. In that same year, however, Congress authorized the Defense

133

Department to place in reserve certain funds in order to make reimbursements. Considerable confusion existed over the next few years as to the distinction between obligation and reservation.[27]

For example, the Administration was prevented by law from obligating more than 25 percent of mutual security funds during the last 60 days of the fiscal year. But in 1955 Congressman Passman said that the Foreign Operations Administration, in the last hour of the last day of the fiscal year, had placed hundreds of millions of dollars in the reservation category. Passman estimated that agency officials had either obligated or reserved in excess of 42 percent of the entire fiscal year's appropriation in the final 60 days.[28]

The Administration maintained that a reservation need not be the same as an obligation. Yet the terms appeared to be identical in the sense of carrying balances forward. A report by House Appropriations in 1955 stated that $614 million had been reserved on the final day of the fiscal year, "which has the effect of continuing these funds available in fiscal year 1956."[29] The report also voiced concern about agency practices of obligating, deobligating, and reobligating funds. Appropriations which had been certified as obligations were later deobligated and then reobligated to entirely different projects. There was reason to believe, said the committee, that

> funds are frequently obligated late in the fiscal year in order to carry them forward, even though the obligations are not based on firm agreements or commitments. Further, the Committee has developed numerous instances where funds for projects initiated as far back as 1952 and 1953 are still being carried as obligations despite the fact that little or no activity has taken place on such projects.[30]

A 1955 act tightened congressional control; not more than 20 percent of any funds made available in a mutual security appropriation act could be "obligated and/or reserved" during the last two months of a fiscal year. Reservation appears to be something short of an actual obligation. A glossary prepared by the Agency for International Development distinguishes reservation as a step prior to a legally binding obligation. It is the step that occurs "before a signed agreement (obligation) is consummated. As such, it is not binding on the U.S. Government to pay out money." Additional confusion results when the military services try to understate the size of unobligated balances by "committing" funds—at times making the commitments in June and then "decommitting" the funds the following month.[31]

ACCRUED EXPENDITURES

The system of granting agencies obligational authority, resulting in large carryover balances, has been criticized by those who want a direct relationship between congressional appropriations and agency expenditures. George Galloway, long-time student of congressional reform, recommended in 1948 that Congress should appropriate each year only the funds needed for actual cash payments within the fiscal year. It should also ban all carryovers of appropriations from one year to the next, "so as to equate appropriations and expenditures in the law."[32]

The Hoover Commission, in 1955, also criticized the system of carryovers and the process by which agencies entered into obligations. It was to an agency's advantage to use all available funds to prevent them from lapsing. Congress had no effective control over the annual budget surplus or deficit, since there was no direct relationship between what was appropriated for one year and what was actually obligated or spent. Funds appropriated one year might not be obligated until the next, with expenditures occurring a year or two after that. The practice of appropriating on a no-year or multiple-year basis had created large carryover balances, making it impossible for Congress to exercise control over expenditures.[33]

135

To remedy this, the Hoover Commission advanced the idea of an "Annual Accrued Expenditure Budget." Instead of giving agencies authority to obligate money, they would receive whatever was necessary to cover goods and services estimated to be received during the year. "Accrued expenditures" represented the charges incurred for goods and services received and for assets required, whether or not payment was made. (The term "accrued expenditures" is not synonymous with cash disbursements.) How could Congress meet the needs of long lead-time programs, such as construction of an aircraft carrier? The Hoover Commission recommended that Congress give the Navy contracting authority for the full amount. But Congress would appropriate only what was needed to cover estimated accrued expenditures required for the year under consideration. Any unexpended balances would be rescinded.[34]

In an effort to mobilize public and congressional support for its recommendations, the Commission decided to translate into dollar terms the potential improvements in financial management. No precise means of measurement was available. One member of the task force on budgeting ventured that he would never go into an improvement project in the private sector unless he expected to save 10 percent. The task force seized upon that figure and applied it against the controllable part of the Federal budget, which at that time was approximately $48 billion. From that they estimated $4.8 billion in savings, rounded off to an even $4 billion. Before long the public had the impression that $4 billion could be saved simply by changing the accounting methods and adopting the accrued expenditure proposal.[35]

This claim, which the Commission never intended, was subject to a good deal of ridicule. Also objectionable to many Members of Congress was the heavy reliance on contract authority—giving agencies authority to enter into contracts in advance of appropriations. Chairman Mahon of House Appropriations objected to the idea of appropriating on a piecemeal basis, such as giving the Navy contract authority to begin a $310 million aircraft carrier and then appropriating $10 million to do preliminary work, $20 million the next year for initial construction, and so forth. It was better to appropriate the full amount ("full funding"), even if that meant a large carryover balance for future years. Responsible action by Congress required a vote on the full amount through an appropriation bill. Said Mahon: "If the billboard says $310 million for a Navy carrier, we will snap wide awake. If it is a small downpayment it doesn't seem so important." He dismissed the accrued expenditure idea as an accountant's dream and a legislator's nightmare.[36]

The House Appropriations Committee had already gone on record as vigorously opposed to contract authority:

> Contract authority is a workable device but not the most economical. . . . Far from contributing to economy and retrenchment, it tends to the opposite effect. It ties the hands of the President and the Congress in making up and considering future appropriation budgets by introducing undesirable rigidities into the budget picture. It is a snare and a delusion. Its "appeal" is one of its principal defects. It is often viewed as "merely an authorization," with the consequent tendency to pass over it more lightly, to fail to give it the same thorough examination as a direct appropriation. Psychologically, the situation can be likened to a charge account at the store—relatively easy to open because it is not necessary to have the cash in hand.[37]

Congress took several steps toward maintaining agency accounts on an accrual basis. Legislation in 1956 directed the agencies, in accordance with principles and standards prescribed by the Comptroller General, to maintain their accounts on an accrual basis. Another statute, enacted in 1958, authorized the President to include in his budget a proposed limitation on annual accrued expenditures. At the end of the fiscal year concerned, any unused balances of the limitation would lapse, except for amounts needed to cover liabilities. President Eisenhower recommended accrued expenditure limitations on a number of appropriations, but Congress rejected all of his proposals.[38] It should be noted that with the exception of Eisenhower's first Budget Director, Joseph M. Dodge, the next three had been accountants by profession: Rowland R. Hughes, Percival F. Brundage, and Maurice H. Stans.

No attempt has been made to implement the major Hoover Commission proposals: rescission of all carryover balances and the adoption of contract authority for long lead-time items. The magnitude of carryover balances increases from year to year. The budget for fiscal 1976 showed $493.9 billion in unspent authority available from prior years. Only $111.6 billion was expected to be spent in fiscal 1976; $354.3 billion would be spent in future years ($27.9 billion was scheduled to expire). By the end of fiscal 1976 the total amount of carryover balances was expected to reach $502.4 billion. In terms of sheer magnitude, those are frightening figures. But $165 billion of the latter amount consists of trust funds (Social Security and other accounts). Of the balance ($337 billion), budget projections showed $247 billion to be obligated but not spent. That would leave $90 billion in non-trust funds (Federal funds) both unspent and unobligated.[39]

ACCELERATED SPENDING

The Eisenhower Administration used accelerated procurement in 1958 as an anti-recession device. Public works were accelerated, Housing and Home Finance programs speeded up, and Government supply levels raised, all in an effort to pump more money into the economy and to stimulate recovery. This technique was not without its drawbacks. Advance procurement adds to the cost of storage space and inventory checks. It also creates administrative complications by forcing agencies to depart from prior schedules and long-term contractual commitments. Moreover, if a fixed amount is appropriated for those programs, acceleration must at some point be followed by deceleration. That retards the economy at the very moment the recovery phase needs reinforcement—a serious matter since the automatic stabilizers (such as unemployment compensation and the individual income tax) reverse direction in the recovery phase and have a retarding effect of their own.[40]

In 1961 President Kennedy also relied on accelerated procurement to combat recession. He directed the Veterans Administration to speed up the payment of $258 million in life insurance dividends, making the amount available in the first quarter instead of spread over the entire year. A special dividend payment of $218 million was made later, thereby reinforcing the speed-up with new funds and contributing a permanent boost to the economy. Kennedy also directed the heads of each department to accelerate procurement and construction wherever possible. He hastened payments to farmers under the price support program, increased the annual rate of free food distribution to needy families from about $60 million to more than $200 million, and made immediately available to the States the balance of Federal-aid Highway funds ($724 million) that had been scheduled for the entire fiscal year.[41]

AGENCY TACTICS

Many of the decisions regarding the timing of obligations occur at the agency level. To Congress, the accumulation of large unobligated balances may imply poor agency planning and a threat to legislative control. Large balances give agencies some independence from annual legislative action. Consequently, the Appropriations Committees will take into account carryover balances when providing new funds.

Robert Moot, Comptroller of the Pentagon for many years, said there was "nothing as difficult as going asking for money when you've already got a pile of unused money." That was underscored in 1967 when House Appropriations ordered a decrease in weapons procurement funds (primarily Navy) because the military services were maintain-

139

ing excessively large carryover balances. In 1974, because of large unobligated balances in planning grants for the Airport and Airway Trust Fund, Congress refused to appropriate any new funds.[42]

It is to the advantage of an agency to report a low figure for carryover balances. Several techniques have been tried, not always with success. Large obligations are especially suspicious when they occur in the closing month of a fiscal year ("June buying"), or when emergency and contingency funds are depleted in the final weeks. A circular by Budget Director Dawes in 1921 noted that agencies were entering into contracts and obligations in June, "with the possible purpose and inevitable result of there being no unobligated balance to their credit at the close of the fiscal year." If agencies play it too close and obligate down to the last dollar, Congress is apt to conclude that agency officials are spending funds without due regard for economy. A modest balance makes a better appearance.[43]

Hasty obligation is likely to draw criticism in the case of complicated weapons systems. The Defense Department obligated funds for the Cheyenne helicopter and the Sheridan armored vehicle before testing or developmental work had been completed. House Appropriations remarked in 1969 that budgetary considerations based on "fear of losing funding authority have often dictated such decisions rather than sound technical judgment." However, agencies that accelerate the rate of obligation in the last half or last quarter of the year have argued that efficiency is served. In 1972, in response to criticism that the Navy had intentionally stepped up the pace of obligations and expenditures, Admiral Zumwalt told the Senate Committee on Armed Services that

> Congress has asked that the funds be spent in an orderly and efficient manner. That is what the Navy is seeking to do, to conduct its business briskly, to let contracts without delay after the Congress acts, and to go

about the business of defending the country with dispatch, and seriousness in the 6 months that generally remain after we get the money.[44]

This last comment was a reference to late passage of the defense appropriation bill. His observation would be valid if the Pentagon had to spend and obligate at a slow pace while funded by a continuing resolution, but generally the picture has been exactly the opposite. Disproportionate amounts are obligated in the first two quarters. The next section (and also Chapter Ten) explores this in greater detail.

In an attempt to curb last-minute obligations, various appropriation bills prohibit the obligation of more than a certain percent of funds during the closing months of a fiscal year. For example, the Defense Department is prohibited from obligating more than 20 percent of annual appropriations during the last two months. Instead of heavy buying on June 30, the rush date shifts to April 30. April buying replaces June buying.[45]

Agencies can minimize the size of carryover balances by underestimating the amount of unobligated funds to be carried forward. During fiscal 1961 the Army estimated that $30.1 million in unobligated funds for RDT&E would be carried forward to the next year; the actual amount turned out to be $89.3 million. For that same period, the comparable figures for the RDT&E/Navy account were $26.7 million estimated and $134.3 million actual. Where there is a pattern of underestimating unobligated balances, the Appropriations Committees will often cut the current budget requests to avoid overfunding.[46] In some cases underestimates stem from overzealous and unrealistic planning. Agencies think they can accomplish more in a year than they actually can. Here the action is good faith, however misguided, without ulterior motive.

Agencies also have access to other funds as the fiscal year unfolds. Such funds are called "deobligations," "recoveries,"

141

or "recoupments." They represent funds that had been tied up but, because of various factors, are later made available for agency use. In 1962 House Appropriations noted with displeasure that the Navy's budget for fiscal 1962 had estimated $30 million in recoveries from prior appropriations. Afterwards the Navy discovered that recoveries would come to approximately $227 million. With errors of that magnitude the Appropriations Committees are inclined to cut the current budget estimates.[47] GAO studied recoveries in the foreign assistance area over a five-year period—from fiscal 1968 through fiscal 1972—and found that actual recoveries for that period came to $435.3 million, rather than the estimated $253.5 million.[48] In other words, AID had access to an additional $181.2 million that Congress had not anticipated.

In order to determine which agencies habitually underestimate unobligated balances, deobligations, recoveries, and recoupments, congressional committees could require officials to present a table comparing estimated amounts and actual amounts over the past five years, listed year by year. If a pattern of underestimating is apparent, the committees would be in a position to authorize and appropriate less new money.

Agencies sometimes resort to extraordinary means to hold on to funds. A spectacular example occurred in 1972. The Office of Education discovered that the fiscal year had ended before it had time to award the full amount of contracts and awards. Rather than lose the funds, OE officials proceeded to backdate 755 actions (totaling $55 million) to make it appear that the obligations had taken place during fiscal 1972. When the illegal transactions were uncovered, OE had to charge the $55 million to fiscal 1973. That created a new complication, since other program levels might have to be reduced to make room for the $55 million. The "overage" included $26 million for education to the handicapped and $17 million for educational renewal programs.[49]

The Appropriations Committees were faced with a nasty choice. They could refuse to appropriate supplemental funds, thereby holding OE officials responsible for their mistakes and protecting Congress from any complicity in the illegal practices. But would the penalty fall more heavily on the officials or on the groups awaiting Federal services? David Obey, Democrat of Wisconsin, did not condone the backdating and did not want Congress to ignore the illegal activities, but "neither do I believe that handicapped children ought to pay for the bungling of anonymous bureaucrats."[50]

House Appropriations did not provide additional funds for the Office of Education. Instead, it requested the Secretary of HEW to submit a reprogramming plan showing how the extra costs would be absorbed from fiscal 1973 appropriations. Senate Appropriations provided $26.3 million in supplemental funds to cover education of the handicapped. House and Senate conferees agreed on the $26.3 million figure, but financed it with $13.8 million in new money and $12.8 million available from previous appropriations. President Nixon vetoed the bill because it contained the "Cambodian rider." A revised supplemental bill was later signed into law, providing the $26.3 million as proposed by the conferees.[51]

CONTINUING RESOLUTIONS

Continuing resolutions are generally regarded as routine pieces of legislation needed to take care of late appropriations. Whenever Congress fails to complete action on appropriation bills by the beginning of the fiscal year, it enacts a "continuing resolution" to provide stop-gap funding authority for the affected agencies. When the resolution expires after a few months, and Congress has still failed to enact the necessary appropriation bills, a new resolution is passed. During fiscal 1973, because of Presidential-congressional disputes over foreign assistance and Labor-HEW,

143

some agencies had to operate under a continuing resolution for an entire year.

It is tempting to simplify the subject by saying that agencies are funded at the "current rate" (or at last year's level). In actual fact the situation is much more complex. Some projects and activities are funded at the amount passed by the House or the Senate, whichever is lower. If the Senate has yet to act, funding is at the lesser rate of the House or the current rate. If neither chamber has acted, agency operations are conducted at a rate not in excess of the current rate or the rate provided in the budget estimate, whichever is lower. For operations not covered by a budget estimate, or where the budget request has been deferred for later consideration, the rate of operations is not to exceed the current rate.

Matters are made more confusing by a lack of agreement on what is meant by "the current rate." Although the general thrust of a continuing resolution is clearly in the direction of modest funding levels, there is sufficient ambiguity for an agency to launch more ambitious plans. If it anticipates heavy cuts by Congress on its budget requests, it may try to obligate funds at a fast pace while under the continuing resolution. A disproportionate rate of spending is possible since OMB's apportionment process is waived for agencies funded by a continuing resolution.

The two problem areas for Congress have been military assistance and foreign assistance. In recent years the Administration has asked for more in each area than Congress has been likely to appropriate. During debate in 1972, Senator Proxmire pointed out that the Pentagon had used its authority under a continuing resolution of the previous year to obligate in excess of what it would have received from Congress. Five days after receiving its stop-gap funding authority, the Defense Department went to the Treasury and applied for warrants to obligate $374 million for the military assistance program. It continued to apply for warrants until it reached a level of $499.4 million, which was far in excess of the $350 million eventually allowed by the Senate. But by that time funds had been obligated and the Senate's option eliminated.[52]

To prevent a recurrence, Proxmire proposed to limit the Pentagon to obligations of no more than one-fourth of the current rate during the first quarter of the fiscal year. That would have imposed a type of apportionment control while the Pentagon operated under a continuing resolution. He withdrew the amendment after receiving from OMB Director Weinberger a pledge to advise all departments and agencies of the importance of obligating funds under a continuing resolution at rates "which will not tend to close off the Congress's options in acting on the regular appropriation bills." Weinberger subsequently issued OMB Bulletin 73-1, stating the policy for obligating funds while on a continuing resolution. He directed each agency to conduct its operations "in such a manner as to permit the Congress to maintain its Constitutional prerogatives." Agencies were to make every effort to identify projects or activities that faced a possibility of reduced appropriations. In such instances agencies "must establish controls so that future congressional action is not preempted by a high (even though legal at the time) rate of obligation under the Continuing Resolution."[53]

Congress opted for statutory protection a year later by enacting a one-fourth rate for foreign assistance funds (in the continuing resolution for fiscal 1974). It discontinued that pacing scheme the following year, but warned agencies involved in the administration of foreign aid activities not to obligate funds at an accelerated rate. Activities were to be funded at a rate not to exceed one quarter of the annual rate "except in cases of extreme importance or in cases of dire emergencies." In such cases the Appropriations Committees were to be notified in advance of the obligation.[54]

At the same time that Congress discontinued the statutory one-fourth rate for foreign assistance, it imposed it on the Defense Department for support to South Vietnam. The annual rate was set at $1 billion in the continuing resolution for fiscal 1975, with the stipulation that none of the activities for support of South Vietnamese military forces should be funded at a rate exceeding one quarter of the annual rate.[55]

It would be impractical to attempt a summary of a chapter containing such diverse elements. More so than reprogramming and transfers, the issue "timing of obligations" is peculiarly technical and many-sided. The complexity should not obscure the importance of the subject or discourage congressional investigation and control. Far more familiar to the public, as a result of controversies during the Nixon Administration, is the problem of impoundment. But as the next two chapters will demonstrate, familiarity is not a substitute for understanding.

7

Impoundment: Politics and the Law

FROM the 1930s through the 1960s the issue of impoundment was of sporadic interest. Franklin Roosevelt held back funds from public works projects; Harry Truman impounded Air Force funds and cancelled a supercarrier; impoundments took place during the Eisenhower, Kennedy, and Johnson Administrations. In each case the political system made the necessary adjustments to accommodate the actions. A constitutional crisis did not emerge.

During the Nixon years, however, the issue of impoundment ripened into a genuine confrontation between the two branches. Congressional hearings were held, Members of Congress delivered protests and denunciations, and legislation was eventually enacted that placed general controls on impoundment. The Federal courts intervened to issue dozens of decisions against the Administration. Like a top official in the Nixon Administration, who resigned under rather hasty and unattractive circumstances, impoundment had become a household word.

Some officials in the Nixon Administration complained of discrimination. Had not impoundment been used in the past without creating such a stir? Indeed it had, but impoundment is an omnibus term covering many types of actions. They come in many shapes and colors. Some are routine managerial functions, in no sense representing a threat to legislative prerogatives. Other impoundments encroach upon the ability of Congress to make policy and decide budget priorities. As House Appropriations chairman Mahon once remarked: "Economy is one thing, and the abandonment of a policy and program of the Congress another thing."[1] Distinctions must also be drawn between deferrals and outright terminations, between domestic and military impoundments, between actions that have a statutory basis and those that rely on the Constitution.

This chapter describes four basic types of impoundment: (1) routine actions taken for purposes of efficient management, (2) withholdings that have statutory support, (3) withholdings that depend on constitutional arguments, particularly the Commander-in-Chief clause, and (4) the impoundment of domestic funds as part of policy-making and priority-setting by the Administration. The latter type, in particular, involves policy decisions "with prejudice" toward the affected programs.

Efficient Management

It has long been the practice of the executive branch to regard appropriations as permissive rather than mandatory. From the days of George Washington, then, impoundments occurred whenever expenditures fell short of appropriations. Routine withholdings occur to effect savings, because of changing events, and for basic managerial reasons.

to effect savings

Attorney General Harmon declared in 1896 that an appropriation was not mandatory "to the extent that you are bound to expend the full amount if the work can be done for less. . . ."[2] As noted in Chapter Two, the same point was made by Budget Director Dawes and by President Harding. It was repeated again in 1942 by President Roosevelt, who defended the setting aside of budgetary reserves as sound fiscal practice when done for the purpose of preventing deficiencies or for effecting savings. To mandate the full expenditure of all funds, he said, "would take from the Chief Executive every incentive for good management and the practice of commonsense economy. . . ."[3] In 1950 the House Appropriations Committee emphasized that economy "neither begins nor ends in the Halls of Congress." An appropriation of a given amount for a particular activity constituted

> only a ceiling upon the amount which should be expended for that activity. The administrative officials responsible for administration of an activity for which appropriation is made bear the final burden for rendering all necessary service with the smallest amount possible within the ceiling figure fixed by the Congress.[4]

In each case those grants of power were limited and circumscribed. President Roosevelt, in his same remarks in 1942, said that budgetary reserves to prevent deficiencies or to effect savings were not "a substitute for item or blanket veto power, and should not be used to set aside or nullify the expressed will of Congress. . . ." The 1950 statement by House Appropriations warned that while it was "perfectly justifiable and proper for all possible economies to be effected and savings to be made," there was no justification to use impoundment to thwart a major policy of Congress.[5]

CHANGING EVENTS

If Congress provides funds for a purpose, and later events make the expenditure unnecessary, administrators are expected to withhold the funds and return them to the Treasury. Harry Truman, during his service with the United States Senate, supported impoundment powers for the President in two situations: a change in conditions that might require a project to be deferred for a short period, and a change in conditions that might eliminate the need of part or all of a program. Since Congress had to appropriate far in advance of agency obligation and expenditure, some discretion was needed. In Truman's words: "What looks like a good program one day may be completely unnecessary 6 months later."[6]

Jefferson found it unnecessary on repeated occasions to use all of the money provided in a contingency fund. He regularly returned the unexpended balance to the Treasury. A more publicized impoundment by Jefferson concerned his withholding of $50,000 for gunboats in 1803. Officials in the Nixon Administration took special delight in citing this as a "precedent." When HUD Secretary Romney was questioned by a Senate committee on impoundment, he replied: "I guess Thomas Jefferson started this." OMB Director Weinberger told another Senate committee that it all started "in the days of Thomas Jefferson. Every President since Thomas Jefferson has done precisely the same thing. . . ." After sharing some statistics with the committee, Weinberger claimed that "we are doing not only nothing different than any other President since Thomas Jefferson has done; we are doing it in no greater degree."[7]

If we descend from the abstract plane of "impoundment" to the specific incidents involved, we find that the Nixon impoundments have little in common with the Jefferson event. When Jefferson notified Congress that the funds appropriated for gunboats would remain unexpended, he explained that the "favorable and peaceable turn of affairs on the Mississippi rendered an immediate execution of that law unnecessary. . . ." The emergency contemplated by Congress failed to materialize (because of the Louisiana Purchase) and Jefferson saw no reason to spend the money. Neither did Congress. A year later, having taken the time to study the most recent models of gunboats, he informed Congress that he was proceeding with the program.[8]

His action was temporary, in contrast to decisions by the Nixon Administration to terminate programs. His action was routine, in contrast to efforts by President Nixon that directly challenged the right of Congress to make policies and decide priorities. Furthermore, Jefferson acted in response to a genuine change in events. The critical issues facing the country during the Nixon years—such as housing shortages and water pollution—did not disappear; yet funds were impounded nonetheless.

MANAGERIAL RESPONSIBILITIES

An administrator may have a number of other valid reasons for suspending a program or payment. In 1840 the Supreme Court supported a decision by the Secretary of the Navy, who had withheld payment from a widow although her claim was based on a resolution passed by Congress. Had the Secretary mechanically followed the direction of Congress, without exercising judgment or discretion, the widow would have received two pensions: one from the specific resolution adopted on her behalf, a second from a general pension bill. The Secretary properly concluded that Congress could not have intended double benefits. In a number of cases the Federal courts have distinguished between ministerial duties (where no discretion exists) and executive duties (where judgment and discretion are needed). Only in the first situation, involving basically clerical duties, do courts feel empowered to direct an executive official to spend money.[9]

After World War II, President Truman temporarily withheld funds from a program to build hospitals for veterans. The Administration decided it would be better to wait until the returning servicemen had settled, and in that way achieve the most effective placement of medical facilities.[10]

In January 1971, the Department of Housing and Urban Development interrupted a mortgage-subsidy program designed to help poor families buy their own homes. HUD Secretary Romney suspended part of the program when it became apparent that abuses by real estate speculators were "more prevalent and widespread than had previously been evident." After the abuses were corrected, Romney ordered the program reinstated. Several months later HUD suspended a low-income housing program in New Jersey because of inadequate administration by the Newark Housing Authority. The money was released after the Authority complied with HUD's request for organizational changes.[11]

In 1971 HEW withheld Federal funds from black nationalist Col. Hassan Jeru-Ahmed's drug rehabilitation program. Inadequate bookkeeping was cited as the reason. A GAO report disclosed that at least $171,533 in Federal drug treatment funds had been paid to a relative and to friends of Hassan, were spent for automobiles and real estate, or could not be accounted for.[12]

Statutory Authority

In many cases the President is authorized or directed by law to withhold funds. Chapter Two discussed some of the Economy and Reorganization Acts that were passed during the Hoover and Roosevelt Administrations. Another general grant of impoundment power appeared in the single-package ("omnibus") appropriation bill of 1950, which directed the President to cut the budget by not less than $550 million without impairing national defense. No other legislative guidelines were provided. Truman fulfilled the statutory directive by placing $572 million in reserve, including $343 million in appropriations, $119 million in contract authority, and $110 million in authorizations to borrow from the Treasury.[13]

SPENDING CEILINGS

In 1967 Congress directed a spending cut of $4.3 billion. Legislative action reduced spending by $1.8 billion, leaving $2.5 billion to be trimmed by the President. The budget-cutting formula required each civilian agency to reduce its budgeted obligations by an amount equal to 2 percent of payroll, plus 10 percent of other controllable obligations.

Defense Department obligations were to be reduced by an amount equal to 10 percent of non-Vietnam programs.[14]

In 1968, 1969, and 1970, Congress enacted ceilings on expenditures, thereby giving the Nixon Administration additional statutory authority to impound funds. Policy-making was an inevitable result, since the Administration could unilaterally select the programs to be sacrificed. In retaliation, Congress refused to adopt a spending ceiling in 1971. Rep. Joe L. Evins told an executive official that Congress did not want to give the Nixon Administration "a flexible ceiling which you could use as a tool to freeze and impound funds as you did in the past." A spending ceiling proposed by President Nixon in 1972 was eventually rejected when the two Houses of Congress could not agree on a formula to limit executive discretion.[15]

PUBLIC DEBT LIMIT

Several Administrations have relied on the debt ceiling as statutory authority to withhold funds. In 1957, in order to keep within the statutory debt limit, the Eisenhower Administration issued a series of orders and announcements for cutbacks and stretchouts in defense programs. When Congress later raised the debt limit, the money was released. The debt ceiling argument was invoked frequently by the Nixon Administration.[16]

Adherence to a debt limit appears to be deference to congressional authority. But in "protecting the debt limit" the Administration may give preference to its own programs and priorities at the expense of those enacted by Congress. When the Nixon Administration distributed revenue sharing funds (a program it supported), it did not feel constrained by the debt limit. Yet it withheld funds from other programs on the pretext that the debt limit could not accommodate them. Nothing prevented the Administration from asking that the ceiling be raised; nothing prevented the Administration from requesting an increase in tax revenues. In fact, if estimated revenues and carryover balances are less than projected expenditures, the law requires the President to make recommendations in his budget for new taxes, loans, or other appropriate action to meet the estimated deficiency.[17]

EMPLOYMENT ACT OF 1946

OMB Director Weinberger told a Senate committee in 1973 that the Employment Act of 1946 "requires the President to maintain policies that guard against inflation."[18] It does no such thing. The Act merely requires the President to present an economic report each year to Congress; independent powers are not conferred upon him. The development of policies to satisfy the statutory goals of "maximum employment, production, and purchasing power" is a joint responsibility of Congress and the President.

The obvious thrust of the Act, which was to serve as an instrument for countering a postwar depression, was on employment. While it is possible to interpret the goal of "maximum purchasing power" as an implied goal for combating inflation, purchasing power was to be promoted by increasing employment and production. Impoundment of funds has precisely the opposite effect. Moreover, it is significant that discretionary spending power for the President, included in the early drafts of the legislation, was stripped from the bill as enacted.[19]

ANTIDEFICIENCY ACT

As amended in 1950, the Antideficiency Act authorized the President to establish budgetary reserves "to provide for contingencies, or to effect savings whenever savings are made possible by or through changes in requirements, greater efficiency of operations, or other developments subsequent to the date on which such appropriation was made available." To OMB Director Ash, inflationary pressures could be considered an "other development" and therefore a reason for placing funds in reserve.[20] Nothing in the language of the Act or in its legislative history supports that proposition.

The 1950 language grew out of a dispute with the Post Office in the spring of 1947. Instead of apportioning its funds to avoid a deficiency situation, the Post Office allotted $370 million for the first quarter of the fiscal year, $409 million for the second, and $364 million for the third. That left only $9.5 million (less than 1 percent) for the final quarter. Congress found itself across a barrel. If it did not provide supplemental funds for the last quarter, the Post Office threatened to curtail activities.[21]

Members of Congress were outraged by the circumstances. After hearing the Post Office interpret the Antideficiency Act, Senator Ball of Minnesota exclaimed: "You might as well repeal the act. It has no effect." Senate Appropriations vigorously condemned what it called the "false propaganda disseminated by certain postmasters throughout the country blaming Congress for the lack of sufficient funds to meet their expenditures."[22]

Other than issuing fulminations, what was to be done? Senate Appropriations directed the Budget Bureau and the General Accounting Office to recommend ways to improve the Antideficiency Act. Their joint report began with the assumption that it was impossible to completely eliminate deficiencies. Changing conditions would always require certain deficiency or supplemental appropriations. However, changing conditions should also produce some *surpluses*. It should work both ways. In order to prevent the agencies from spending the surplus funds on low-priority or frivolous items, reserves should be established to pay for unanticipated expenses. The BOB-GAO report suggested this language:

> In apportioning any appropriation, reserves may be established to provide for contingencies or to effect savings whenever savings are made possible by or through

changes in quantitative or personnel requirements, greater efficiency of operations, or other developments subsequent to the date on which such appropriation was made available.[23]

With very little change, that language was adopted by Congress in 1950 when it amended the Antideficiency Act.

This legislative history clearly demonstrates that the purpose of the language was to build up surpluses in some accounts in order to balance deficiencies that developed elsewhere. Nowhere was there an implied authority to set aside reserves to cancel or curtail a program. At no time was the Antideficiency Act conceived of as a tool for stabilizing the economy. If an administrator could execute a program by spending fewer dollars than appropriated, all well and good. But the purpose of the appropriation itself was not to be denied.

That was a well-established policy. The BOB-GAO report had cautioned that the authority to set aside reserves "must be exercised with considerable care in order to avoid usurping the powers of Congress." The same position was taken two years later by the Hoover Commission when it recommended that the President "should have authority to reduce expenditures under appropriations, if the purposes intended by the Congress are still carried out." In reporting out the antideficiency language in 1950, House Appropriations explained that the grant of authority to set aside reserves was not to be taken as "justification for the thwarting of a major policy of Congress by the impounding of funds." BOB amplified that policy in its Examiners Handbook in 1952 by stating that reserves "must not be used to nullify the intent of Congress with respect to specific projects or level of programs."[24]

The language of the Antideficiency Act was tightened in 1974 by deleting the "other development" clause. The objective was to remove from the act any excuse for withholding funds for such policy reasons as combating inflation.

156

Reserves were to be set aside "solely" to provide for contingencies or to effect savings.[25]

OTHER STATUTORY PROVISIONS

Individual appropriation bills will often provide for some measure of impoundment authority. The Labor-HEW appropriation bill for fiscal 1970, after encountering a Nixon veto, was modified to limit expenditures to 98 percent of appropriations. No amount specified in the appropriation could be cut by more than 15 percent. The Labor-HEW appropriation bill for fiscal 1974 authorized the President to withhold up to $400 million, provided that no activity, program, or project be reduced by more than 5 percent.[26]

The President has been directed to withhold economic assistance in an amount equivalent to that spent by an underdeveloped country for the purchase of sophisticated weapons systems, unless he informed Congress that the withholding of such assistance would have a detrimental effect on national security. The "Hickenlooper amendment," applied against Ceylon in 1963, requires the President to suspend assistance to any government that seizes any property from U.S. corporations and fails to compensate them within a reasonable time.[27]

The 1964 Civil Rights Act empowers the President to withhold funds from federally financed programs in which there is discrimination by race, color, or national origin. States that fail to enact billboard control legislation, as required by law, have been threatened with a loss of Federal aid for highway improvement. A 1968 act required States to update their welfare payments standards in order to reflect cost-of-living increases. Failure to comply can lead to a cutoff of Federal welfare assistance. When the Nixon Administration relied on the Economic Stabilization Act Amendments of 1971, as authority to impound funds for general fiscal reasons, Senator Eagleton introduced an amendment (later enacted into law) to provide that nothing in the Act "may be construed to authorize or require the withholding or reservation of any obligational authority provided by law, or of any funds appropriated under such authority."[28]

CONSTITUTIONAL POWERS

During a news conference on January 31, 1973, President Nixon asserted that the constitutional right of a President to impound funds—for the purpose of combating inflation or avoiding a tax increase—was "absolutely clear." Officials in his Administration maintained that impoundment was consistent with the President's constitutional duty to "take care that the laws be faithfully executed" and "was authorized by the constitutional provisions that vest the executive power with the President."[29]

The constitutional claim is difficult to analyze. Statements from the Nixon Administration used "impoundment" as a blanket term, rarely attempting to isolate certain categories or types of impoundment. The statements did not suggest limits to the impoundment power; the Administration appeared to have unfettered discretion. Also, the claim is troublesome since it opens the door to the shadowy area of inherent and implied powers.

Nevertheless, to deny the President any discretion and judgment over the expenditure of funds, other than what Congress specifically delegates to him, would reduce his office from that of Chief Executive to Chief Clerk. It would prevent executive officials from making even the routine kinds of decisions previously described as "efficient management." It would carry to impractical extremes the Brandeis dictum that the doctrine of separated powers was adopted "not to promote efficiency but to preclude the exercise of arbitrary power." The period from 1774 to 1787 contains ample evidence that the framers wanted a separate executive to impart efficiency and accountability to government.[30]

The Supreme Court has acknowledged the need for some discretion and judgment on the part of executive officials in the handling of public funds. *Kendall* v. *Stokes* (1838) appears to bear directly on the issue of impoundment. The Court declared that to contend that "the obligation imposed on the President to see the laws faithfully executed, implies a power to forbid their execution, is a novel construction of the constitution, and entirely inadmissible."[31] But this case involved the refusal of the Postmaster General under the Jackson Administration to pay the claim of an individual who had contracted to carry the mails and now sought compensation for his services. The Court held that the Postmaster General could not refuse payment. In contrast, impoundment generally does not entail a claim for services performed. Such services would not be rendered until the funds were made available for obligation, a step which impoundment prevents.

Moreover, the Court was careful to circumscribe its jurisdiction to avoid a collision with a coequal branch. Payment of the claim in this instance was a "purely ministerial" act, for which there could be no discretion. The question of judicial intervention in an *executive* act, requiring discretion and judgment, was carefully distinguished. The Court explained that the mandamus to pay the amount did not seek "to direct or control the postmaster-general in the discharge of any official duty, partaking in any respect of an executive character; . . ." In *Reeside* v. *Walker* (1850), the Court again drew a distinction between ministerial and executive actions. A mandamus was "only to compel the performance of some ministerial, as well as legal duty. . . . When the duty is not strictly ministerial, but involves discretion and judgment, like the general doings of a head of a department . . . no mandamus lies."[32]

If a degree of discretion and judgment regarding the spending of funds inheres in the executive power, the difficult task is to establish boundaries. Limits can be spelled out in law, but that is easier said than done. Still other boundaries are of a nonstatutory form, relying on good-faith efforts and the integrity of administrative officials.

159

FOREIGN AFFAIRS

Officials in the Nixon Administration argued that the President's discretion to withhold funds is especially broad in the area of foreign affairs. Deputy Attorney General Sneed maintained that the President had "substantial authority" to control spending in national defense and foreign relations: "Such authority flows from the President's constitutional role as Commander-in-Chief of the Armed Forces and from his relatively broad constitutional authority in the field of foreign affairs." Sneed suggested that congressional directives to spend in those areas "may intrude impermissibly into matters reserved by the Constitution to the President." He also thought it noteworthy that Congress "has never successfully challenged an impounding action in the foreign relations and national defense fields."[33]

This position, while correct in its essentials, needs some qualification. With regard to foreign affairs (national defense is treated in the next section), numerous statutes authorize the withholding of funds. When the President acts under such authority, it is in support of congressional policy, not antagonistic to it. Furthermore, the practice in foreign assistance—far from impounding funds—had been to spend every available dollar. In 1971, after it was learned that a number of domestic programs had been affected by impoundment, congressional hearings revealed that not one dime had been withheld from projects overseas. That led to a provision in the Foreign Assistance Act of 1971 which prohibited the obligation or expenditure of funds available under that Act and the Foreign Military Sales Act unless certain funds withheld from the Departments of Agriculture, HEW, and HUD were released.[34]

NATIONAL DEFENSE

The scope of the Commander-in-Chief clause remains a source of dispute. Justice Jackson said in the Steel Seizure Case that the phrase implies "something more than an empty title. But just what authority goes with the name has plagued presidential advisers who would not waive or narrow it by nonassertion yet cannot say where it begins or ends."[35] An aggressive use of the Commander-in-Chief clause to impound funds could infringe directly on Congress' own constitutional responsibility to raise and support armies and to provide and maintain a navy.

To protect its prerogatives, Congress has resorted to "floors" (minimum levels) for military forces. In 1958 the Eisenhower Administration wanted to keep the strength of the Army Reserves at 270,000 and reduce the Army National Guard from 400,000 to 360,000. In a countermove, Congress inserted in the defense appropriation bill a higher level for personnel strengths. A proviso for Army Reserve specified that personnel "shall be maintained at an end strength of not less than three hundred thousand for the fiscal year 1959." A similar proviso directed that the Army National Guard shall be maintained at an average strength of not less than 400,000 for the fiscal year 1959. Subsequent authorization acts for the Defense Department also contained minimum force levels for reserve components.[36]

Surrender of the Axis powers left the Government with tens of billions of dollars in excess of military needs. That balance was brought under control by Congress (rescinding funds) and by the President (impounding funds). In response to a directive by Congress, President Truman submitted a list of proposed reductions in the civilian war agencies and in the naval and military establishments. When Congress passed the rescission bill, it included a rider to require decentralization of public employment offices. Truman opposed the provision both in substance and procedure, insisting that such issues "should not be dealt with as riders to appropriations." Although he refused to sign the bill into law, he told Congress that he would heed the sections that dealt with rescissions. He then directed the Budget Bureau to designate those amounts as nonexpendable.[37]

161

Prior to the Nixon Administration, the most controversial impoundment actions involved weapons systems. Two examples are presented here to illustrate the complicated political context in which such actions occur: the withholding of Air Force funds by Truman, and Kennedy's refusal to release funds for large-scale production of the B-70 bomber.

Air Force Funds. In 1949 Congress voted to increase President Truman's Air Force request from 48 to 58 groups. He countered by placing the unwanted funds in reserve. A number of factors produced this collision between the two branches. First, Louis Johnson replaced James Forrestal as the new Defense Secretary and proceeded to subject the military budget to fresh scrutiny. He concluded that larger defense appropriations, because of waste within the Pentagon, would be like throwing money "down a rat hole."[38]

It was widely believed at that time that Soviet Russia intended to bankrupt the American economy by forcing the United States to spend massive amounts for defense. Skepticism of defense spending increased when the Eberstadt task force of the Hoover Commission released its findings on the Pentagon. In December 1948 the task force criticized the military services for lacking a "sense of cost consciousness" and being "far too prodigal" with public funds. The following April former President Hoover advised Congress that $1.5 billion could be cut from the military budget without impairing national security. In June, Franz Schneider, who had headed the Eberstadt study of the fiscal 1950 budget, told a Senate committee that defense savings could run as high as $2 billion.[39]

Still another factor was Truman's fiscal policy of relying on budget surpluses and debt retirement to restrain inflation. Twice in 1947 he vetoed tax-reduction bills. In 1948, when he again vetoed a tax-reduction bill, Democrats joined with Republicans to override him. With revenues lost to tax relief, and tax receipts down because of the 1948-49 recession, Truman redoubled his efforts to control expenditures.[40]

The Senate joined with Truman in opposing the Air Force funds added by the House. But as the matter lay deadlocked in conference committee, the House rejected a Senate motion to vote continuing appropriations. With adjournment close at hand and the military services in need of funds to meet payrolls, the Senate reluctantly agreed to the 58 groups. It did so, however, on the understanding that the money might not be spent. Senator Elmer Thomas, a ranking Democrat on the Appropriations Committee, left the impression that "if the money is appropriated it may not be used."[41]

Truman signed the bill, after announcing that he was directing the Secretary of Defense to place the extra $735 million in reserve. He justified the impoundment on the need to maintain a balance between national security and a sound economy, the importance of preserving the elements of a unified strategic concept among the military services, and the President's authority as Commander-in-Chief. Neither Senator McKellar nor Representative Cannon—chairmen of the Appropriations Committees—questioned Truman's authority to withhold the money.[42]

B-70 Bomber. The Kennedy Administration was embroiled in the controversy over the B-70 bomber, a long-range aircraft billed as successor to the B-52. President Eisenhower had restricted the program to production of prototype aircraft, to be made available for flight testing in 1963. Concluding that an increasing part of strategic forces would be composed of fixed-based and mobile ballistic missiles, he doubted the value of B-70s in an age of ICBMs and Polaris submarines.[43]

In 1961 Congress added $180 million to the $200 million requested by the Kennedy Administration for development of the B-70. Defense Secretary McNamara, who stressed America's advantage over the Soviets in bombers and in deterrent capability with missiles, refused to release the unwanted funds. In March 1962 the House Armed Services

163

Committee, under the leadership of Carl Vinson, voted to direct the Secretary of the Air Force to spend not less than $491 million during fiscal 1963 toward production of the aircraft (now redesignated RS-70). The committee figure was $320 million above the Administration's budget request. To remove any doubts about its intentions, the committee said that the Secretary was "directed, ordered, mandated, and required" to spend the full amount.[44]

In a letter to Vinson, President Kennedy urged that the word "authorized" be used in place of "directed." Kennedy contended that the change in language would be more suitable for an authorization bill, since funds had yet to be appropriated. He also thought the wording would be "more clearly in line with the spirit of the Constitution" and its separation of powers. Kennedy insisted on "the full powers and discretions essential to the faithful execution of my responsibilities as President and Commander in Chief, under article II, sections 2 and 3, of the Constitution."[45]

Vinson had miscalculated. Among the military, he was supported only by the Air Force. The rest of the Joint Chiefs sided with McNamara. Vinson also encountered stiff resistance from the House Appropriations Committee. Chairman Mahon said that it was improper and impractical to direct the President to spend money before it was appropriated; the Armed Services Committee should not direct his committee to appropriate money. Gerald Ford, ranking minority member on House Appropriations, was "unalterably opposed" to the use of the word "directed." According to Ford, the language invaded the responsibilities of the President, usurped the authority of the Appropriations Committee, and created inflexibility in the program. Opposition to the mandatory language also came from Charles Halleck, House Minority Leader, John McCormack, Speaker of the House, and Carl Albert, House Majority Leader.[46]

To ease Vinson's embarrassment, Kennedy announced that McNamara would initiate "a new study" of the aircraft. Vinson took the floor to claim that Congress had "caused

the Department of Defense to see the error of their ways."
Interpretations from other Members of the House were less
charitable. The Administration proceeded with its original
plan to build two prototypes of the RS-70 before considering full-scale production. One prototype crashed in June
1966; the second ended up in the Air Force Museum at Day-
ton, Ohio.[47]

ADMINISTRATIVE POLICY-MAKING

Any impoundment action by an executive official represents policy-making to some degree, even when in compliance with statutory language. Policy is part of every budget
and fiscal decision. Several types of impoundment, however, illustrate policy-making in such pure form—taken
without statutory authority and unrelated to Commander-
in-Chief functions—that they are included here as a separate category.

UNWANTED PROJECTS

Prior to the 1960s several Presidents practiced a form of
"item veto" on public works legislation; they agreed to execute certain projects while ignoring others. Senator Stephen
Douglas of Illinois recalled that an appropriation act of
1857 had failed to benefit his State. The President, who had
quarreled with Representatives from Illinois, penalized
them by withholding funds from their districts. The funds
were scheduled for post offices and other public buildings.
In 1876, in signing a river and harbor bill, President Grant
objected to particular projects and announced that he would
refuse to spend funds on projects that were "of purely private or local interest. . . ."[48]

This selective enforcement of the laws received support
from influential legislators. In 1896 Senator John Sherman,
second-ranking Republican on the Finance Committee, expressed regret that Cleveland had chosen to veto a river
and harbor bill. Sherman regarded the appropriation bill as
permissive:

If the President of the United States should see proper to say, "That object of appropriation is not a wise one; I do not concur that the money ought to be expended," that is the end of it. There is no occasion for the veto power in a case of that kind.[49]

In 1923 President Harding threatened to use his impoundment power to curb river and harbor spending. Whether he could have won that particular confrontation with Congress is an academic question. Within a matter of months he was dead; there is no evidence that his successor impounded the funds.[50]

An impoundment dispute in the 1940s concerned the Kings River Project in California's Central Valley Basin. In this case the protagonists were two executive agencies competing for control: the Corps of Engineers and the Bureau of Reclamation. President Roosevelt instructed his Secretary of War not to allocate any funds or submit any estimates for appropriations without review by the Budget Bureau and the President. When Congress funded the project in 1946, President Truman announced that he would submit his own plan for developing water resources in that area. He then impounded the funds pending a determination of prospective costs. In February 1947, after submitting his report to Congress, Truman released the money.[51]

In 1965 a dispute over legislative procedures led to the impoundment of funds for small watershed projects. Instead of vetoing a river and harbor bill, President Johnson noted his opposition to a committee-veto provision and asked that it be repealed in the next session. Congress refused and the funds for small watershed projects remained impounded. The funds were later released by President Nixon, who advised his Secretary of Agriculture that he would not object to this particular committee-veto procedure.[52]

In a fiscal 1966 appropriation, Congress provided $9.2 million for construction of a national aquarium. The Johnson and Nixon Administrations impounded practically the entire amount. In 1971 President Nixon halted construction of the $180 million Cross Florida Barge Canal, a project that was years in the making and more than one-third complete. The President said the project was suspended "to prevent potentially serious environmental damages." Later some of the funds were released as a result of litigation in the Federal courts.[53]

During December 1972 and January 1973, the Nixon Administration announced the termination or postponement of numerous agricultural, environmental, and housing programs. So crucial are those issues that I devote a large part of the next chapter to them.

ANTI-INFLATION POLICY

Truman's impoundment of Air Force funds, as discussed earlier, was motivated partly out of efforts to restrain inflation and to effect a balance between national security and a stable economy. Other Presidents have withheld funds for general fiscal reasons. In signing an agricultural appropriation bill in 1966, President Johnson expressed dissatisfaction with the $312.5 million that Congress had added to his budget request. "During a period," he said, "when we are making every effort to moderate inflationary pressures, this degree of increase is, I believe, most unwise." He proceeded to reduce expenditures for certain items "in an attempt to avert expending more in the coming year than provided in the budget."[54]

President Johnson's economic message to Congress, on September 8, 1966, estimated that spending had to be cut by $3 billion to protect the economy. Wherever possible, appropriations that exceeded the President's budget would be withheld. After the November elections, Johnson announced a $5.3 billion reduction in Federal programs, requiring more than a $3 billion cut for the remaining seven months of the fiscal year. However, sensitive to criticism from the States, Johnson began releasing large sums of money early the next year.[55]

The Nixon Administration's anti-inflation policy was buttressed by congressionally enacted spending ceilings for fiscal years 1969, 1970, and 1971. Apart from those statutory grants of power, Nixon also relied on general executive authority to impound funds. During the fall of 1970, while allowing a sewer and water authorization bill to become law without his signature, he warned that appropriations could not match the authorized levels without producing a "disastrous fiscal effect." In the event that Congress refused to exercise restraint, "I must and will act to avoid the harmful fiscal consequences of this legislation. I will be compelled to withhold any overfunding." The following day, upon signing a public works appropriation bill, Nixon stated his intention to consider all means possible "to minimize the impact of these inflationary and unnecessary appropriations, including the deferment of the proposed starts and the withholding of funds."[56]

The Nixon Administration went ahead with the public works projects that it had recommended in the budget. It also deferred, without exception, all of the projects that Congress had added. OMB Deputy Director Weinberger offered this explanation to a House appropriations subcommittee: "Given the necessity for retrenchment in some areas, I think it is inevitable that the President would feel that the items he included were items that should be released first."[57] Why inevitable? Why only the President's items? Did executive officials enjoy some special technical or professional advantage that gave them the edge in selecting top-priority projects? Apparently not. The Administration made no effort to justify its choices in terms of project merit, cost-benefit ratios, or any other criteria. Weinberger even acknowledged that congressional committees explored in "much greater depth" than OMB the technical merits of public works projects:

> The point I made is that the discretion we exercise is done on a single basis, the idea that the President's bud-

get should stand and that all of the congressional add-ons be deferred, when a deferral is necessary in this amount, rather than exercising a cavalier or an independent judgment on individual projects. We don't feel qualified to do that.[58]

OMB depended on advice from the Corps of Engineers and the Bureau of Reclamation to decide which projects had lower priority—"by definition those projects that are not included in the budget. . . ."[59] In other words, instead of treating the budget as a mere set of recommendations, to be acted upon at the discretion of Congress, OMB decided that the President's budget conferred on certain projects a superior status.

CHANGING PRIORITIES

After inheriting the "Great Society" programs of the Johnson years, President Nixon relied on impoundment to move toward his own priorities. In this respect he parted company from earlier precedents. President Harding inherited "New Freedom" programs; President Eisenhower found himself saddled with a host of "New Deal" and "Fair Deal" programs. But in neither case did they attempt to use impoundment to wipe Democratic programs from the books.

In contrast, after less than a year in office President Nixon announced plans to reduce research health grants, Model Cities funds, and grants for urban renewal.[60] Critics noted that the cutbacks were made at the same time that the Administration was sponsoring such costly projects as the supersonic transport, a manned landing on Mars, general revenue sharing, a larger Merchant Marine fleet, and the Safeguard ABM system. While the cutbacks were made in the name of fiscal integrity, in actual fact they were part of a redistribution of Federal funds from Democratic programs to those supported by the Nixon Administration.

That was evident in the spring of 1971, when the Nixon Administration reported the withholding of more than $12

169

billion, much of it in highway money and funds for various urban programs. Part of that withholding was tied to the Administration's desire to drop the system of categorical grant-in-aid programs and replace them with consolidated grants and revenue sharing. After Congressman Clement Zablocki (D-Wis.) complained about the impoundment of water and sewer funds, an Administration official said that he shared the concern over urban public facility needs, but "the President firmly believes that revenue sharing represents a much more effective way of helping local governments provide for local needs than the narrowly-focused categorical grant programs which now exist."[61] The effect of this was to announce that the Administration intended to implement a program not yet enacted, but would not implement a program already authorized and funded.

The withholding of water and sewer grants was defended by OMB Director George Shultz, in 1972, in these terms:

> I might say that this is one area where there are some funds in reserve that are restrictive [i.e., not routine] in nature. I think it reflects our feelings that while other funds will be released by the end of the fiscal year, we can appropriately drag our feet just a little bit while the Congress examines the extent to which it wants to transfer to the Federal Government what has historically been a function of local government, usually financed by the people who benefit directly.[62]

That was essentially a States rights argument, compatible perhaps with the political philosophy of John Calhoun and John Taylor but not even remotely supported by statutory authority, constitutional grants of power, or even the present distribution of power between the Federal Government and the States.[63] The argument is not consistent with the reality of Federal financing of health, education, welfare, and transportation—areas which at one time were "a function of local government." Adherence to the Shultz position would have required the Nixon Administration to withhold from local governments still other funds for programs which the President strongly supported, such as law-enforcement grants.

STATISTICAL GAMES

The categories used in this chapter need not be accepted by the reader. But categories of impoundment, of one sort or another, must be constructed. It is of little value to speak of impoundment in a general sense. Unless we discriminate between different types of actions, and try to separate the routine from the significant, we fall prey to beguiling statistical claims.

OMB Director Ash told Congress in 1973 that "budgetary reserves" (the term OMB used for impoundment), when measured as a percent of total outlays, averaged 6 percent under President Kennedy, 5.4 percent under President Johnson, and only 3.5 percent under President Nixon. Ash told the House Committee on Rules: "Mr. Chairman, I review these statistics in order to drive home one fundamental point: the 'impoundment crisis' is fiction."[64]

Those words were directed at a committee which had so many impoundment control bills referred to it that hearings were required. Comparable legislative activity was underway on the Senate side. Dozens of cases had been filed in the Federal courts. Of what meaning were the aggregate statistics compiled by OMB?

Before introducing some details and specifics, let me underscore the point that aggregate statistics on impoundment, whether by percentages or overall dollar figures, are not useful. This can be seen by a simple comparison. Suppose that one Administration impounds $10 billion—$8 billion of it routine and $2 billion of a policy nature. The latter would be prejudicial to the programs and a clear sign of disagreement between President and Congress on budget priorities. Much more serious, however, would be the Administration that impounds only $8 billion, half of it of a policy nature. The total amount would be less, but the policy and priority impact would be twice as great.

Second, OMB seriously understated even the aggregate amount of funds impounded by the Nixon Administration. When it reported $8.7 billion in "budgetary reserves" as of January 29, 1973, it managed to omit approximately $9 billion in other funds that had been impounded.[65] It did so by adhering to a narrow, technical definition of impoundment.

The largest omitted item was $6 billion in contract authority withheld from the States for the water-pollution control program. The reason for the omission lay in the definition of contract authority: budget authority "which permits obligations, but requires an appropriation or receipts 'to liquidate' (pay) these obligations." Since States could not enter into obligations until the President allotted the authority to them, the $6 billion (unallotted) never satisfied the technical definition of either contract authority or budget authority. By that reasoning, nothing existed to impound or place in reserve. But Congress did not ask for reports on budgetary reserves. It asked for reports on impoundment, and no one could deny that the $6 billion had been impounded. To argue otherwise would assume that the Federal courts were entertaining themselves with imaginary issues.[66] (The introductory text of OMB reports, beginning in 1974, cited the withholding of clean-water funds, but did not include those amounts in summary tables or individual agency accounts.)

Another large chunk of money withheld, but not reported by OMB, was $1.9 billion for the Departments of Labor and Health, Education, and Welfare. The Administration decided to keep programs at the President's revised 1973 budget requests, rather than the higher level permitted under a continuing resolution. The amount of $1.9 billion was not technically in "budgetary reserves," since the apportionment process is waived for continuing appropriations, but the effect was identical to impoundment.[67]

Other amounts withheld, but not included in the OMB impoundment report, consist of $441 million in contract authority withheld because of the housing moratorium, $382.8 million in proposed rescissions, and approximately $300 million withheld from the emergency loan program of the Farmers Home Administration.[68] Adding these five omitted items to the OMB list of $8.7 billion brings the impoundment total up to $17.7 billion.

A third failing of aggregate figures is that they fail to show program impact. OMB reported $1.899 billion withheld from the Defense Department (military functions), $1.497 billion from the Department of Agriculture, and $529 million from the Department of Housing and Urban Development. As percentages of total available budget authority for fiscal 1973 these translate to 2.4 percent for Defense, 13.0 percent for Agriculture, and 10.5 percent for HUD. When Defense is underrepresented, the main burden of impoundment obviously falls on the domestic sector.

Those percentages actually understate the full extent of the burden. Two other calculations are needed. The first involves OMB's omission of $300 million in FmHA disaster loan funds and $441 million in HUD contract authority. A more accurate comparison would therefore be 2.4 percent for Defense, 15.6 percent for Agriculture, and 19.2 percent for HUD.

A second calculation focuses on the amount of unobligated funds which would lapse at the end of the fiscal year. In other words, here we are interested in deferrals versus the outright loss of funds. Of the Defense Department, all of the impounded funds were scheduled to be available except for $7.5 million in annual accounts. Less than one-half of 1.0 percent of Defense impoundments were scheduled to lapse. The actions represented routine deferrals.

That was in stark contrast to the $207 million of Agriculture money not available beyond fiscal 1973. Moreover, additional funds were technically or legally "available" after

173

fiscal 1973, but the Administration had no plans to spend the money: $300 million for the FmHA disaster loan program, $210 million for the Rural Environmental Assistance Program (REAP), $11 million for the Water Bank Program, $456 million for rural electrification loans, and $120 million for rural water and waste disposal grants. In a practical sense, then, 72.6 percent of Agriculture impoundments would have been lost without legal and legislative efforts to restrain the Administration.

All of the $970 million withheld from HUD was technically available after fiscal 1973. But with the single exception of $6.6 million in housing production and mortgage credit, the Administration had no intention to spend the money. Thus, a comparison of the three Departments in terms of the percent of impoundments that would lapse—either legally or politically—reveals: Defense, 0.4 percent; Agriculture, 72.6 percent; and HUD, 99.3 percent.[69]

The most controversial impoundments by the Nixon Administration occurred in agriculture, housing, and water-pollution control. The following chapter discusses those actions and the legislation that resulted: the Impoundment Control Act of 1974.

8

Impoundment: The Nixon Legacy

In 1972, as President Nixon made his bid for reelection, the character of impoundment took a decisive turn. A series of announcements attempted to portray Congress as profligate and irresponsible in money matters. Nixon's message of July 26, calling for a spending ceiling, claimed that the budget crisis resulted from the "hoary and traditional procedure of the Congress, which now permits action on the various spending programs as if they were unrelated and independent actions." In a nationwide radio address on October 7 he warned that "excessive spending by the Congress might cause a Congressional tax increase in 1973." John Ehrlichman, the President's domestic adviser, castigated the "credit-card Congress" for adding billions to the budget. He likened the lawmakers to a spendthrift brother-in-law "who has gotten hold of the family credit card and is running up big bills" with no thought of paying them.[1]

It was a bold move, calculated to put Congress on the defensive. If Senators and Representatives subscribed to the goal of fiscal restraint, and acknowledged the need for legislative reform, the President could use that as a justification for impounding funds. That is precisely what happened. Most Members even outdid the President in decrying the irresponsibility of Congress. They told their constituents that fiscal sanity could not be restored until Congress altered its procedures and organization. The facts did not support such a simplistic picture, but legislators seemed to derive some satisfaction by downgrading their own institution. As Richard Fenno observed: "Members run for Congress by running against Congress."[2]

Although both Houses supported the President's request for a \$250 billion spending ceiling for fiscal 1973, they could not agree on a formula to limit executive discretion. But, Phoenix-like, the spending ceiling emerged from the ashes, this time in the form of an administratively imposed ceiling. Nixon announced his determination to stay within \$250 billion, using that as one reason for withholding funds from numerous domestic programs. It was an extraordinary performance. Congress went through the legislative exercise of rejecting the President's request and then discovered that he would act without Congress' consent. If the President believed he had unilateral authority to establish a spending limit, why ask for a statutory ceiling? Speaker Albert remarked that Nixon's action made "a monkey out of the legislative process."[3]

At the same time that President Nixon was accusing Congress of going on a spending binge, he nevertheless sought passage of the five-year, \$30 billion General Revenue Sharing Act. The Administration had promised the States and localities that such funds would be supplemental—not a substitute—to what they were presently receiving in the form of Federal categorical programs. That promise was breached. The Administration soon advised the communities to rely on revenue sharing funds if they wanted to continue programs eliminated or curtailed by impoundment.[4]

The Nixon impoundments were unprecedented in their scope and severity. Never before had congressional priorities and prerogatives been so altered and jeopardized. During December 1972 and January 1973, the Administration announced major cancellations and cutbacks. Frequently the actions were defended on the superficial theory that Congress had failed to enact mandatory language for the programs. In other words, the mere existence of discretionary authority, which had been granted by Congress to enable executive officials to administer the programs more effectively, was used as an excuse to deny the programs in their entirety.

In past years, executive officials were expected to operate on a good-faith basis, using authority with restraint and circumspection and preserving a foundation of trust with Congress and its committees. That nonstatutory system of controls collapsed during the Nixon years. In self-defense, Congress began to delete from legislation various forms of executive spending discretion. A general impoundment control act was passed in 1974. Federal courts were brought into the dispute in dozens of cases, for the most part deciding against the Administration. Several case studies are presented here to illustrate the extraordinary character of the Nixon impoundments.

AGRICULTURE

During December 1972 the Nixon Administration made wholesale reductions in farm programs. The first two casualties were the $225.5 million Rural Environmental Assistance Program (REAP) and the $10 million Water Bank Program. Subsequently the Administration terminated the disaster loan program of the Farmers Home Administration, the rural electrification program, and the water and sewer grant program.

In each of those cases the Department of Agriculture advanced the following theory: since legislation for the programs authorized but did not require the Secretary to carry them out, they could be completely suspended or canceled at any time. If substantive legislation and appropriation acts did not compel the obligation and expenditure of funds, it was the Department's opinion that the programs could be legally terminated.[5]

That was an absurd position, a strained effort to import some semblance of legality to the actions. It conveniently

177

ignored the fact that congressional committees had held hearings on the programs, prepared committee reports, and recommended positive action on the floor. Members of Congress debated the programs and passed the necessary authorizations. The entire process was repeated to appropriate the funds or budget authority. As a means of facilitating the operation and implementation of the programs, Congress delegated to administrators a measure of discretion and flexibility.

Instead of using that discretion to carry out the programs, the Nixon Administration seized upon the discretionary language to terminate them. That totally negated the efforts of Congress. Discretion was used for precisely the wrong objective. As the Comptroller General later observed: "We do not believe it follows that by employing permissive language the Congress envisions the bulk of appropriation acts as carrying with them the seeds of their own destruction in the form of an unrestricted license to impound."[6]

REAP AND WATER BANK

The Rural Environmental Assistance Program, based on legislation dating back to 1936, was a cost-sharing program (usually on a 50-50 basis) in which the Federal Government and farmers carried out conservation and environment measures. The Water Bank Program was established to preserve wetlands for waterfowl. As late as September 29, 1972, the Department of Agriculture announced the continuation of REAP, naming the following features as high priority goals during fiscal 1973: establishing or improving permanent vegetative cover; developing facilities for livestock water; building water impoundment reservoirs; constructing terrace systems and sediment or chemical runoff measures; and a number of other objectives.[7]

Both programs were terminated on December 26, 1972. In addition to the argument that termination was necessary to protect the President's budget ceiling of $250 billion, a legal opinion prepared by the Department of Agriculture

178

observed that the legislation for REAP and Water Bank authorized programs but did not require that they be carried out. Congressional action did not constitute "a mandate to the Department to approve all qualifying projects for which funds are available."[8] From that narrow foothold, permitting some discretion as to the level of the program, the Department managed to justify complete cancellation.

The response from Congress was predictable. The House Committee on Agriculture said that while it normally sought to give the Secretary "maximum discretion in administering the programs assigned him by the Congress as a contribution toward sound administration, the REAP termination signals an abuse of that discretion." In place of discretionary language, Congress inserted mandatory provisions. Instead of saying that the Secretary "shall have power" to carry out REAP, the committee proposed that he "shall" carry it out. Rather than letting the Secretary make payments "in amounts determined by the Secretary to be fair and reasonable," he was directed to make payments "in an aggregate amount equal to the sums appropriated therefor. . . ."[9]

The Senate added mandatory language for the Water Bank Program. But because of differences between the two Houses, and doubts as to whether either House had the necessary two-thirds majority to override a veto, the bill was never presented to the President. A modified REAP program, entitled "Rural Environmental Conservation Program," was later enacted into law. The Water Bank Program was also revived.[10]

FmHA DISASTER LOANS

The emergency loan program of the Farmers Home Administration was established to provide a source of loan funds for farmers and ranchers in areas designated as disaster areas. In a press release dated December 27, 1972, the Department of Agriculture announced that funds were being cut off to counteract inflationary pressures and to adhere

179

to the President's $250 billion spending limit. Subsequently the Department offered additional justifications: the debt ceiling limit, the need to avoid a tax increase, and projections that the program might cost $1 billion or more. The higher costs were the result of exceptionally bad growing and harvesting weather and also because of a $5,000 forgiveness feature which had been used earlier in disaster relief acts. Critics of the Administration observed that when unexpectedly high costs affect other programs, such as the B-1 bomber or the C-5A cargo plane ("crop failures in weapons systems"), the programs are not canceled.[11]

Secretary Butz terminated the FmHA program after designating 15 Minnesota counties as eligible for emergency loans. Farmers in those areas were told that applications would be accepted and processed through June 30, 1973. They were further advised to file after the harvest (late November or early December) to ensure that all eligible losses would be included in the applications. Because of the large number of applications after the harvest, many farmers were told that appointments for review could not be made until early 1973. Then, on December 27, Secretary Butz directed the Minnesota State FmHA office not to accept any applications for the 15 counties.[12]

The dispute was taken to a U.S. District Court in Minnesota. Judge Lord distinguished between two types of secretarial actions: discretionary (declaring which areas were entitled to disaster assistance) and ministerial (processing applications after a designation was made). After a designation, it was the duty of the Secretary to accept loan applications and consider them. Judge Lord declared that Butz had acted in excess of his authority and in an arbitrary, capricious manner. Furthermore, Butz had violated several regulations promulgated by the Department of Agriculture. The termination violated regulations providing for prior notice of rule-making, an invitation to the public to participate in rule-making, and publication of an adopted rule in the Federal Register not less than 30 days before its effective date. Failure to give notice prior to the termination also violated the Administrative Procedure Act.[13]

Congress rewrote the FmHA emergency loan program to eliminate the $5,000 forgiveness feature and to raise the interest rate on loans from 1 percent to 5 percent. The new law also eliminated some discretionary authority for the Secretary of Agriculture. Instead of "authorizing" him to make loans, the law states that he "shall" make them. And whereas previous law provided that the Secretary "may" designate any area as an emergency area when he finds that a need exists, it now provides that he "shall" make the designation. Finally, the law includes an 18-day grace period for eligible applicants in areas designated by the Secretary of Agriculture after January 1, 1972 but prior to December 27, 1972.[14]

REA PROGRAM

On December 29, 1972, the Department of Agriculture terminated the program of direct loans to rural electric and telephone borrowers of the Rural Electrification Administration. Instead of offering direct loans at a 2 percent interest rate, the Administration planned to insure or guarantee private loans at 5 percent.[15] The next month, at a news conference, President Nixon resorted to ridicule in an effort to justify the decision:

> ... what I have found is that when I first voted for REA, 80 percent of the loans went for the purpose of rural development and getting electricity to farms. Now 80 percent of this 2 percent money goes for country clubs and dilettantes, for example, and others who can afford living in the country. I am not for 2 percent money for people who can afford 5 percent or 7.[16]

Several days later, at hearings before a Senate committee, Secretary Butz was asked whether he agreed with the President's statement that most REA loans were going to

181

dilettantes and country clubs. Butz replied: "No, not most of them. There are some going like that, of course, in rural areas. I think the choice of the use of the word 'most' was probably unfortunate and not premeditated on his part. There are some going like that, Mr. Chairman, but surely not most of them."[17]

Legislation was introduced in each House to reactivate the program. A Senate report stated that the characterization of REA as "2 percent money" was an exaggeration. Most loans combined 2 percent REA money with supplemental funds from the Rural Utilities Cooperative Finance Corporation (CFC), a private credit cooperative. Fewer than 10 percent of the borrowers were eligible for 2 percent loans. The rest relied on blended loans, with about 54 percent eligible for 70 percent REA/30 percent supplemental funds, 20 percent for 80/20 loans, and 17-18 percent for 90/10 loans.[18]

The Senate bill replaced discretionary language with mandatory provisions. Instead of providing that the Administrator is "authorized and empowered" to make loans, with discretion as to the amount, the bill "authorized and directed" loans to be made "in the full amount determined to be necessary by the Congress or appropriated by the Congress. . . ." The House version, which also contained mandatory clauses, proposed a compromise to meet some of the Administration's objections. For example, the House incorporated a new revolving fund for two types of insured loans, one at a "special rate" of 2 percent and the other at a "standard rate" of 5 percent.[19]

Secretary Butz pledged to carry out the REA program if Congress deleted mandatory language from Section 305, which "authorized and directed" the Administrator to make insured loans. The conference committee went along with his request, as did the enacted bill. When the Administration failed to implement the program, Congress threatened to prevent payment of certain salaries and expenses for persons responsible for the delay. The threat was withdrawn after Congress received assurance from OMB Director Ash that he would recommend and support implementation of the program. On November 29, 1973, a U.S. District Court in South Dakota held that the Secretary of Agriculture did not have congressionally delegated authority to terminate the 2 percent direct loan program and to rechannel those funds into a 5 percent loan program.[20]

RURAL WATER AND SEWER GRANTS

On January 10, 1973, the Department of Agriculture announced that it was "terminating" planning and development grants in the water and waste disposal programs of Farmers Home Administration. The effect was to impound $120 million for fiscal 1973. The impoundment was justified on the ground that alternative sources of funds were being made available, either through the Clean Water Act administered by the Environmental Protection Agency or from General Revenue Sharing. Members of Congress challenged both arguments. They doubted whether rural communities could obtain the necessary funds from EPA or General Revenue Sharing. Moreover, the Clean Water Act could assist only waste disposal programs, not water systems. And finally, as to the proposition that General Revenue Sharing would allow local decision-making, Members pointed out that decentralization was already satisfied by administration through the county FmHA offices.[21]

The House Agriculture Committee reported a bill to restore the program. It said that the grant of discretion by Congress, and the subsequent abuse of that discretion, made the remedy apparent: "The Committee has little choice but to act to remove the discretionary features of the original Poage-Aiken Act, and reinstate the program as originally established by law." The House bill, substituting the word "shall" for the words "is authorized to" and "may," passed by a vote of 297-54. The Senate passed the bill 66-22. Despite the generous margins of those votes, Congress was unable to override the President's veto. The House could muster only a vote of 225-189 on its override attempt.[22]

CLEAN-WATER FUNDS

The Federal Water Pollution Control Act Amendments of 1972 were enacted into law when both Houses overrode a Presidential veto, the Senate 52-12 and the House 247-23. A month later President Nixon instructed the head of the Environmental Protection Agency (EPA) to withhold from the States more than half of the waste treatment allotments. Instead of following the statutory ceilings of $5 billion for fiscal 1973 and $6 billion for fiscal 1974, the amount of $3 billion was held back from each year.[23] Later President Nixon released only $4 billion of the $7 billion scheduled for fiscal 1975. Thus, he withheld exactly half of the $18 billion provided for the three years.

STATUTORY LANGUAGE

The statute provided contract authority to be alloted to the States. On the basis of that authority, and Administration approval of plans and projects, the States could enter into obligations with contractors. In order to liquidate those obligations, Congress would have to appropriate funds at a later stage. If the Administration wanted to limit the level of spending, it had two potential means of control: by withholding the initial allotments of contract authority from the States, or by withholding the obligation and expenditure of funds at a later date.

On its face, the statute appeared to make the allotment step mandatory. Section 205 directed that sums "shall" be allotted. However, the mandatory nature of that language was weakened by two changes made to the bill while in conference. The original language of the House bill had directed that *all* sums shall be allotted. The word "all" was eliminated in conference. Moreover, administrative flexibility seemed to be enhanced by another change made in conference. The phrase "not to exceed" was inserted in Section 207, which authorized the dollar amounts to be appropriated. The amounts of ("not to exceed") $5 billion, $6 billion, and $7 billion were authorized for fiscal years 1973, 1974, and 1975, suggesting that those amounts were ceilings rather than mandatory levels for obligation and expenditure.

There was little dispute that the statute contained spending flexibility, but two difficult questions remained: Was there any flexibility at the *allotment* stage? What was the *extent* of discretion over obligations and expenditures? On neither point was the legislative history conclusive. The conference report, which would normally provide some guidance and narrative as to legislative intent, was silent. It merely indicated that the word "all" had been deleted from Section 205 and that the phrase "not to exceed" had been added to Section 207.[24]

The next place to look is House and Senate action on the conference report. Edmund Muskie, leading Senate sponsor of the bill, explained that the two changes had been made in conference to reduce the possibility of a veto. Clearly a concession was made, but the nature of that concession was in doubt. Muskie did note that all of the sums authorized

> need not be committed, though they must be allocated [i.e., allotted]. These two provisions were suggested to give the administration some flexibility concerning the obligation of construction grant funds.[25]

According to this interpretation, the allotment step was mandatory but some flexibility was available for obligations and expenditures. The scope of the latter discretion appeared to be modest. Muskie emphasized that the two changes made in conference were not to be used "as an excuse in not making the commitments necessary to achieve the goals set forth in the act." Thus, only in such situations in which the obligation of funds might be contrary to other

185

public policies (as the National Environmental Policy Act) would the Administration be expected to refuse to enter into contracts for construction.[26]

The House discussed the conference committee's changes in some detail, but ambiguities remained. William Harsha, ranking Republican on the conference committee, stated that elimination of the word "all" and insertion of the phrase "not to exceed" were intended to "emphasize the President's flexibility to control the rate of spending." But could "flexibility" also determine the *scope* of the program? And what was the relationship between "rate of spending" and the specific statutory step of allotting contract authority to the States? An exchange between Harsha, Robert Jones (chairman of the House conferees), and Minority Leader Gerald Ford merely underscored that there was some discretion at the obligation and expenditure stages. The extent of that discretion was not discussed, nor was it clear whether the President had any discretion over allotments.[27]

When he vetoed the bill, President Nixon recognized the existence of discretionary spending authority. Certain provisions, he said, "confer a measure of spending discretion and flexibility upon the President, and if forced to administer this legislation I mean to use those provisions to put the brakes on budget-wrecking expenditures as much as possible." Not much light was shed on the issue when both Houses overrode the veto. Muskie continued to say that the President had some flexibility concerning the obligation of funds. Harsha spoke of the President's flexibility to control the "rate of spending" and the "rate of expenditures."[28]

COMMITMENT AND TIMETABLE

The statutory language of Sections 205 and 207 must be read in concert with another central feature of the bill: the commitment on the part of Congress to combat water pollution within a scheduled period of time. The objective of the bill, as stated in the declaration of goals and policy, was "to restore and maintain the chemical, physical, and biological integrity of the Nation's waters." The timetable called for the elimination of the discharge of pollutants into navigable waters by 1985. A second national goal declared that "wherever attainable, an interim goal of water quality which provides for the protection and propagation of fish, shelllife, and wildlife and provides for recreation in and on the water be achieved by July 1, 1983." Additional goals were to be attained by July 1, 1977.[29]

Conflicting statements were made regarding the nature of the commitment. During action on the conference report, Muskie admitted that $18 billion was "a great deal of money," but insisted it would cost that much to "begin to achieve the requirements set forth in the legislation." That amount was the "minimum amount needed to finance the construction of waste treatment facilities which will meet the standards imposed by this legislation." Robert Jones, manager of the bill on the House side, characterized the 1985 target date as a "goal, not a national policy." While he hoped that the date could be met, he said that the conference report recognized that "too many imponderables exist, some still beyond our horizons, to prescribe this goal today as a legal requirement." The chairman of the full House Committee on Public Works, John Blatnik, offered this answer to those who called the bill "enormously costly": "We must act now, and must be willing to pay the bill now —or face the task of paying later when, perhaps, no amount of money will be enough." Harsha, in agreeing that the committee had "accurately assessed the need for such a large sum of money," said that spending flexibility had been added because of the many competing national priorities.[30]

Those statements were made in the hope of averting a veto, but after Nixon's disapproval the congressional tone switched more firmly to the concept of a commitment. Representative Jones was now to say that everyone knew the program was a costly undertaking: "But we know also that the people who are this greatest Nation on earth are prepared to pay the price of this undertaking. . . ."[31] Harsha

187

added that Congress had "an overriding environmental commitment to the people of this Nation. We must keep it." Would overturning of the veto, Harsha asked, mean a vote for higher taxes? He gave this counsel: "So be it, the public is prepared to pay for it. To say we can't afford this sum of money is to say we can't afford to support life on earth."[32] In voting with the Senate to override the veto, Muskie stressed that the "whole intent of this bill is to make a national commitment." The bill was asking of Congress "a commitment that these people in other levels of government and the private sector could rely upon. Of course there is a commitment."[33]

Administration spokesmen claimed that it was impossible to use the full amount of contract authority provided by Congress. John Ehrlichman, in his capacity as Director of the Domestic Council, said that there are "only so many contractors who can build sewer plants. There is only a certain amount of sewer equipment that can be purchased. It becomes obvious that there is no point in going out and tacking dollar bills to the trees. That isn't going to get the water clean."[34]

Why should the Administration assume a static size to the environmental industry—an inability to respond and to increase its capacity? It would have been more realistic to expect industry to gear up to meet the clean-water commitment, provided the Government committed itself financially to the goal and established target dates. When President Eisenhower and Congress joined in a commitment for 41,000 miles of interstate highways, or when President Kennedy set the goal of putting a man on the moon by the end of the 1960s, no one argued that those commitments could not be met because of a lack of contractor capability. The commitment came first; the capability followed.

After the President's veto, EPA Administrator Ruckelshaus argued that it was economically unwise to allot the full amounts authorized by Congress: "The fastest way to increase inflation is to pour more money into the community than the construction industry can absorb." That contradicts what he wrote *prior* to the veto, when he strongly recommended that the President sign the bill. He said the near-term construction costs would correspond closely to what would have been initiated under the Administration bill. Thus, the "potential inflationary impact upon the entire construction sector would be minimized."[35]

As to the total costs resulting from the $18 billion figure, Ruckelshaus pointed out that the additional spending authority provided by Congress was "largely the result of the Congress adopting a later EPA needs survey than the one that provided the basis for the Administration's request." Moreover, the EPA estimate did not allow for inflation nor did it include funds for combined, storm, and collection sewers, or for recycled water supplies, which were responsibilities under the bill passed by Congress. During Senate debate on the override, Muskie offered several other reasons for the $18 billion figure. The EPA estimate was based on existing standards and requirements. The Clean Water Act, in making those standards more stringent, would make it more expensive to meet them. Also, the older estimates did not take into account the statutory deadlines, which accelerated the construction timetables and required more money in less time.[36]

IN THE COURTS

How could the conflicting concepts of spending flexibility and goal commitment be reconciled? If a commitment existed, why would Congress give the President unbridled discretion in releasing the funds? Did the Administration use its discretion to undermine the commitment? Those were some of the complex issues injected into the Federal courts.

The first decision handed down was by Judge Oliver Gasch of the U.S. District Court for the District of Columbia. He concluded that the discretion implied by "not to exceed" and the deletion of "all" referred to the obligation and expenditure stages, not to allotment. He held that the act required the Administration to allot the full sums authorized to be appropriated by Section 207. The Gasch decision was affirmed the next year by the U.S. Court of Appeals for the District of Columbia. That court read the legislative history as a commitment by Congress—a recognition that the States needed to be assured of Federal funds. If discretion at the allotment stages would make the achievement of the legislative goal more difficult, "it must be assumed that Congress intended no such authorization."[37]

A number of other district courts agreed that full allotment was mandatory. Judge Lord of Minnesota emphasized the commitment given by Congress to environmental protection:

> Any such exercise of discretion must be consistent with the policy and provisions included in the Act itself. Congress has clearly given the highest priority to the cleaning up of the nation's waters. Nothing in the Act grants the Administrator the authority to substitute his sense of national priorities for that of the Congress.[38]

Similar decisions were handed down by district courts in Florida and Texas. In each case the courts determined that the Act required full allotment (although discretion might be exercised at the obligation and expenditure stages) and that Congress had adopted the contract authority and allotment procedure to enable the States to make long-range plans in their fight against water pollution. It would be illogical, said Judge Roberts of Texas, to think that Congress would inject uncertainty back into the system by giving the Administration discretion to choose how much should be made available. District courts in Illinois, Ohio, and Maine also decided against the Administration. In a Los Angeles decision—the nearest the Administration came to a "victory" —Judge Hauk dismissed the case for reasons of standing. But in his *dicta* he maintained that the plaintiff would not have prevailed on the merits, for the legislative history of the Clean Water Act "supports our conclusion that the statute simply does not require that the EPA allot every authorized dollar."[39]

A wholly different type of interpretation was handed down by Judge Robert Merhige of the U.S. District Court for the Eastern District of Virginia. Although he ruled that the impoundment of 55 percent of the contract authority ($6 billion out of $11 billion for fiscal years 1973 and 1974) constituted a violation of the Clean Water Act and a "flagrant abuse" of executive discretion, he concluded that Congress did intend for the executive branch to exercise some discretion with respect to allotment. However, the withholding of $6 billion conflicted with the commitment on the part of Congress to environmental protection and "the willingness to incur vast expenses in achieving that commitment." The U.S. Court of Appeals for the Fourth Circuit remanded the Merhige decision for further proceedings. The Court of Appeals questioned the holding of a district court to find an executive action arbitrary, on its face, in a *per se* ruling, without any other evidentiary support.[40] The circuit court wanted to know why the withholding of 55 percent constituted a "flagrant abuse." What if the Administration had withheld 40 percent of the allotments? 30 percent? At what point would withholding no longer be in conflict with the policy and provisions of the Clean Water Act?

The Supreme Court avoided that issue by deciding, on February 18, 1975, that the Clean Water Act required *full* allotment. The addition of "not to exceed" in Section 207 and the deletion of "all" from Section 205 was of interest to the Court, but a unanimous decision by Justice White rejected the view that those changes in conference altered the "entire complexion and thrust of the Act." The legislation was intended to provide a firm commitment of substantial sums within a fixed period of time. "We cannot believe," wrote Justice White, "that Congress at the last

191

minute scuttled the entire effort by providing the Executive with the seemingly limitless power to withhold funds from allotment and obligation."[41]

It was not a full-fledged victory for Congress. The Court dealt with the issue only in terms of statutory construction, not of inherent constitutional authority to impound. The language of the Clean Water Act and its legislative history were so peculiar that the Court's decision has scant bearing on other impoundment disputes. Moreover, litigation had lasted for two years. The program had been stretched out; the deadlines established by Congress were now impossible to meet. The Administration achieved its purposes even while losing in court.

HOUSING AND URBAN DEVELOPMENT

COMMUNITY DEVELOPMENT

In a 1971 appearance before a Senate committee, Secretary Romney announced that funds were being held back from various urban programs in anticipation of the President's revenue sharing proposal. He remarked that there was no point in accelerating programs that were "scheduled for termination."[42] It was a familiar doctrine by the Nixon Administration: a proposal by the President enjoyed a status superior to a public law enacted by Congress.

Two years later Senator Ervin cited this example as the type of impoundment that Congress found offensive. He was assured by OMB Director Ash that the Romney episode "dealt not with this year but earlier activities. This year the reasons are very compelling ones and different ones." And yet matters had not changed. Impoundment was still very much a part of the Administration's strategy to replace categorical grant programs with urban special revenue sharing. Less than a month before the Ash assurance, Romney stated that HUD had ordered a "temporary holding action on new commitments for water and sewer grants, open space grants, and public facility loans until these activities are folded into the Special Revenue Sharing program."[43]

To impound funds in this prospective sense—holding on to money in anticipation that Congress would enact an Administration proposal—was a new departure for the impoundment technique. Money was not being withheld to avoid deficiencies, to effect savings, or even to fight inflation, but rather to shift budget priorities from one Administration to the next, all prior to congressional action. It gave precedence to an Administration recommendation, not yet enacted, over a public law already on the books and funded by Congress.

Communities were caught in a dilemma. They could look forward to Federal assistance from special revenue sharing or bloc grants (provided Congress eventually went along), but in the meantime they were denied funds for existing categorical programs. In the words of the National Association of Counties: "In some respects, county officials find themselves in the position of a man watching his mother-in-law drive over a cliff in his Cadillac."[44]

A number of legislative efforts were made to pry loose the funds for community development, but none survived conference committee action. In 1974, however, a U.S. District Court ruled that the Secretary of HUD had an "affirmative obligation" to administer the water and sewer grant program. While discretion existed, there was no statutory authority to suspend the program in its entirety. The Secretary's failure to carry out the program marked an "abuse of discretion."[45]

Several weeks after the court decision, Congress enacted the Housing and Community Development Act of 1974. This legislation provided new bloc grants for community development, thereby replacing several categorical assistance programs that had been in operation for a number of years. The following programs were terminated: public facility loans, open space grants, water and sewer, neighborhood facilities, urban renewal, model cities, and neighborhood development program (NDP) grants.[46]

The Administration had succeeded in its effort to convert categorical grants into bloc grants, but the abrupt action in 1973 was accompanied by heavy costs: hardship on disadvantaged people who found social services interrupted for a long period without interim relief; economic waste and loss of momentum as the programs lay idle; demoralization among Federal and local agency personnel responsible for operating the programs; and the appearance of bad faith and deceit on the part of local elected officials who put their reputations on the line in supporting and sponsoring the programs.

HOUSING MORATORIUM

On January 5, 1973, the Nixon Administration placed an 18-month moratorium on the following subsidized programs: low-rent public housing, rent supplements (Section 236), homeownership assistance (Section 235), and rental housing assistance. In a speech three days later, HUD Secretary Romney claimed that the accumulation of housing programs over a period of decades had created a "statutory and administrative monstrosity that could not possibly yield effective results even with the wisest and most professional management systems." The same position was repeated a week later by the Director of the Domestic Council, Kenneth R. Cole, Jr. He cited "mounting evidence that the present programs, for the most part, have proved inequitable, wasteful, and ineffective in meeting housing needs."[47]

Members of Congress pressed the Administration for the analyses and studies that justified the moratorium. Senator Proxmire, a senior member of the Housing Subcommittee, wanted to know if the Cole statement was true and what documentation or evidence he had to support it. As it turned out, the moratorium was imposed *prior* to the availability of such documentation. William Lilley, HUD's Deputy Assistant Secretary for Policy Development, expressed dismay that "no sophisticated analytical work" had been done prior to the Administration's announcement. Only after the subsidized housing program was suspended did HUD devote a day and a half to an initial rationalization, which Lilley called "paper thin, highly subjective and totally unsupported by any back-up data."[48]

That lent weight to the suspicion that the Nixon Administration had merely contrived an excuse to suspend the program. The fact that the housing moratorium came on the heels of the December bombing in Southeast Asia did not go unnoticed. Proxmire made the observation that President Nixon had decided to spend several billion dollars more in bombing Asia, and to spend several billion dollars less on housing: "The effect is to increase the housing shortage both in Asia and the United States. That is reorganizing priorities with a vengeance."[49]

What was wrong with the subsidized housing program? Did it "fail to work" because of defects in the law or because of mismanagement and a deep-seated policy objection by the Nixon Administration? Anthony Downs, in a lengthy study, described the homeownership and rental housing programs as "effective instruments for meeting the key objectives of housing subsidies." He considered the basic design as sound, while the

> major inadequacies so far encountered in the execution of these programs have stemmed mainly from either poor administration by HUD or the inherently higher risks of investing capital in housing for relatively low-income households in relatively deteriorated areas. Such higher risks are inescapable in any meaningful attempts to achieve the basic objectives of housing subsidies.[50]

As for public housing leasing and rent supplements, Downs stated that the programs had "major advantages that indicate they should be significantly expanded." After identifying and analyzing the major criticisms of housing subsidies, he maintained that the "widely expressed conclusion that current housing subsidy programs 'have failed' or are generally ineffective is false."[51]

The Joint Economic Committee reached a similar view. Most of the scandals and abuses in the housing program were due to "faulty administration" by HUD rather than to any inherent defects in the legislation. "Shoddy construction, poor inspection procedures, almost no tenant counseling, no careful analysis of the cause of high default rates, excessive land costs, and excessive legal and organizational fees" were examples the Committee found where HUD did not do its job.[52] Part of the administrative misjudgments came from Romney's desire to produce housing. Ironically, some field directors who earned citations from Romney for productivity were later suspended because of their zeal in processing applications prior to the moratorium.

The Nixon Administration had four years to study the housing programs—four years to alert Congress to alleged defects. If the programs were faulty in design and contained fundamental flaws, there was adequate time to recommend changes in the statute. Nothing was proposed except for a consolidation and simplification bill. To wait four years and then impose the drastic medicine of a moratorium, without adequate evidence that the program was structually unsound or administratively unworkable, and without offering constructive amendments to the housing laws, was an act of Presidential bad faith.[53]

The process by which the decision was made underscores the bad faith. The decision to terminate the housing and community development programs probably was made in late November or during the first week in December 1972. Up to that point Romney had recommended a continuation of the subsidized housing program, holding it to a minimum level until more was known about its effectiveness. OMB's proposal for a complete moratorium was furnished to James Lynn, Romney's eventual successor, early in December. Romney received official word of the pending action shortly before Christmas. He opposed the action, even to the point of not announcing the termination at a Houston speech scheduled for January 8, 1973, but eventually he went ahead with the announcement. The housing suspension was not the result of a long and deliberate evaluation of the programs. It was a precipitate action, without benefit of analysis or study worthy of the name.

Judge Richey of the U.S. District Court for the District of Columbia called the housing moratorium unlawful. He said it was not within the discretion of the President "to refuse to execute laws passed by Congress but with which the Executive presently disagrees." He was later reversed by the U.S. Court of Appeals for the District of Columbia. The decision, although in support of the Administration, was not a rousing affirmation of executive discretion. The court confined itself to the question whether the HUD Secretary had discretion to withhold "exercise of contract authority, given him by Congress for a specific purpose, in order to determine whether that purpose would be achieved or frustrated by its continued exercise under existing circumstances." Did the Secretary have the discretion, and even the obligation, to suspend a program when he believes that its implementation is "not serving Congress's purpose of aiding specific groups in specific ways . . ."? But in determining whether the congressional purpose had been satisfied, the court relied on HUD's own after-the-fact study of the housing moratorium. The possibility of the study being a self-serving document was not admitted. Nor did the court attempt to determine whether the original suspension decision was an abuse of discretion when made. In what appeared to be half-hearted language the court upheld the Administration: "We hold that, in the circumstances revealed by this record, the Secretary is not without authority to suspend" the housing programs; "we are unable to say that the Secretary acted unreasonably in terminating rather than continuing" the Section 235 program; "we have no basis for saying the Secretary acted unreasonably in terminating" the Section 236 program.[54]

Impoundment Control Act of 1974

In addition to ad hoc efforts to restore individual programs, Congress developed a more general control for impoundment. Congressman Mahon, who had previously supported limited powers of withholding funds in the interest of good management and economy, introduced legislation to curb the policy type of impoundment. His bill gave Congress 60 days to disapprove an impoundment. By the time the bill came out of committee it had been liberalized to allow disapproval by only one House. The House of Representatives passed the bill on June 25, 1973.[55]

The Senate also passed an impoundment control bill, but it posed a more stringent test for the Administration. Unless both Houses *supported* an impoundment within 60 days, the funds would have to be released for obligation.[56] Whereas the House bill placed upon either the House or the Senate the responsibility of disapproving an impoundment action, the Senate bill required the Administration to gain the support of both Houses. The difference between the two bills was so substantial, with neither House willing to make concessions, that the legislation remained in a dormant state in conference committee.

In the meantime, Congress made progress with budget reform legislation. The general idea was to establish budget committees in each House with responsibility for reporting out a budget resolution in the spring. The resolution would establish tentative targets for outlays, budget authority, and revenues, including an appropriate surplus or deficit in light of economic conditions. Budget totals would also be broken down into large functional categories, such as National Defense, Commerce and Transportation, and Income Security. Passage of that resolution would signal Congress' effort to establish control over budget totals and budget priorities. Subsequent action on individual appropriation bills and other legislation creating budget authority would take place within the general contours of the initial budget resolution.

In the final month prior to the start of the new fiscal year (now changed by this legislation to begin October 1 rather than July 1), Congress would pass a second budget resolution to fix binding totals and complete a reconciliation process if there was any discrepancy between the second budget resolution and action on other bills.[57]

A major thrust of the legislation was to strengthen Congress' control over budget priorities. Members began to realize that what they had done at budget resolution time could be undone by impoundment. Both Houses therefore agreed to add to the budget reform legislation a separate title dealing with impoundment. They faced the prospect of two entirely different, seemingly irreconcilable, approaches. The impasse was broken by devising two types of impoundment: "deferral" (to be governed by the one-House veto) and "rescission" (requiring the support of both Houses). In a very general sense, deferrals meant the delay or stretch-out of a program while rescission represented the actual cancellation of budget authority. In practice, however, the two terms could not be so easily distinguished. Congress recognized that by authorizing the Comptroller General to reclassify actions reported by the Administration, changing a rescission to a deferral or vice versa.

Another difficulty with the legislation was the decision by Congress to have *all* impoundments reported—the routine as well as the policy-making variety, even those that were pursuant to statutory authority. The failure to discriminate between the significant and the unimportant was partly the result of congressional experience with the impoundment reporting act of 1972. The Administration consistently underreported, often leaving out the most controversial impoundments. To play it safe, Congress asked for literally every type of withholding. That placed an enormous burden on the Office of Management and Budget and the agencies, complicated the review role of the General Accounting Office, and subjected Congress to an avalanche of reports. A more selective approach was available, for if the

Administration attempted to conceal impoundments under the 1974 legislation, the Comptroller General was authorized to report to Congress on such actions. His report would be received just as though it had come from the President.

The Impoundment Control Act had another unexpected consequence. Instead of performing as a restriction on Presidential power, it was interpreted by the Administration as a new source of authority for withholding funds. Such a reading was possible because of ambiguities in the Act, ambiguities resulting from the decision in conference committee to ram together disparate elements of previous House and Senate bills. Usually the two Houses can split the difference without harmful effects; in this case fusion spawned confusion. Little attention was devoted to satisfying standards of clarity or coherence. The "legislative history" in the conference report was practically silent. Members of Congress, under the impression that they had curbed impoundment, awoke months later to find that the number of policy impoundments under President Ford had actually increased.

What the Ford Administration did was to send back to Congress—in the form of proposed rescissions and deferrals—much of what Congress had added to the President's budget. In the case of public works projects for the Corps of Engineers and the Bureau of Reclamation, the Administration deferred one-half of the amount added by Congress. With regard to Labor-HEW, House Appropriations found that in almost every instance the proposals represented a return to the President's budget; the Administration had merely singled out for rescission the congressional add-ons. The picture for Defense and other departments was much the same.[58] The effect was to recreate the very condition that had precipitated the impoundment crisis under Nixon. Recommendations in the President's budget were being accorded a higher status than programs and activities funded by public law.

Legislation on impoundment control had contemplated a process whereby the President could review programs throughout the year and recommend to Congress any delays or terminations. He would have to document his case fully. Congress would then judge the merits of his recommendations. Senator Ervin anticipated a few dozen policy actions a year—the record under President Nixon.[59] But the Act was interpreted by the Ford Administration to allow more than a hundred policy impoundments a year, generally directed against congressional initiatives. The sheer volume of the requests, together with the fact that they were prejudicial to programs added or augmented by Congress, undermined the prospect for careful congressional review and deliberation. Rescission proposals came up in a bushel; wholesale they were rejected. The new impoundment procedure was off to a very disappointing start.

Used with restraint and circumspection, impoundment had been used for decades without precipitating a major crisis. But during the Nixon years restraint was replaced by abandon, precedent stretched past the breaking point, and statutory authority pushed beyond legislative intent. For all its trappings of conservatism and "strict constructionism," the Nixon Administration never demonstrated an understanding of what lies at the heart of the political system: a respect for procedure, a sense of comity and trust between the branches, an appreciation of limits and boundaries. Without good-faith efforts and integrity on the part of administrative officials, the delicate system of nonstatutory controls, informal understandings, and discretionary authority could not last. At a time when public programs could have benefited from flexibility and executive judgment, Congress was forced to pass legislation with mandatory language and greater rigidities. That part of the Nixon legacy will cast a shadow over future Administrations.

9

Covert Financing

In a democratic society, budgeting is expected to satisfy such fundamental standards as visibility, clarity, explicitness, and comprehensiveness. Without adherence to those standards the public is unable to judge and hold accountable the actions of governmental officials.

It was in the interest of accountability that the Framers included in the Constitution the following clause: "A regular Statement and Account of the Receipts and Expenditures of all public Money shall be published from time to time." Various statutes buttress that constitutional principle. The Budget and Accounting Procedures Act of 1950 stated that the Federal Government shall provide "full disclosure of the results of financial operations. . . ." The Secretary of the Treasury is directed by law to prepare reports on the results of financial operations "for the information of the President, the Congress, and the public. . . ."[1]

The force of those constitutional and statutory injunctions has been diluted over the years. Although a statement of receipts and expenditures is published each year by the Treasury Department, billions of dollars in Federal funds remain hidden from public view. They undergo no audit by the General Accounting Office. They are concealed even from most Members of Congress.

The Statement and Account Clause was first breached by the use of confidential funds for diplomatic purposes, as authorized by Congress in 1790. Building on that precedent, confidential funds began to appear in other appropriation accounts with little or no relationship to diplomatic activities. Entirely separate is the area of secret funds, notably for the Central Intelligence Agency and other elements of the U.S. intelligence community. In 1974 the Supreme Court decided a case in which CIA funding was challenged as a violation of the Statement and Account Clause. Beyond the areas of confidential and secret funds are other dark corners of the budget, where congressional knowledge and GAO auditing are slight or nonexistent.

STATEMENT AND ACCOUNT CLAUSE

The requirement for a public statement of receipts and expenditures did not appear in the early drafts of the Constitution. Not until September 14, 1787, when the Philadelphia Convention was drawing to a close, did George Mason propose that "an Account of the public expenditures should be annually published."[2] Debate on the motion was brief and confusing.

Gouverneur Morris objected that publication would be "impossible in many cases." Was that an allusion to the need for secrecy in diplomatic and military matters? Given the war with England and the operations of the Continental Congress, surely the delegates appreciated the need for confidentiality. Rufus King remarked that it would be "impracticable" to publish the expenditures of "every minute shilling," suggesting monthly statements of a more general character.[3] His objection appears to be aimed not at the need for secrecy but rather the pragmatic issue of how much detail to include and with what frequency.

James Madison proposed that statements be made "from time to time" instead of annually. While it would be the

203

objective to publish on a frequent basis, adoption of general language in the Constitution would "leave enough to the discretion of the Legislature." James Wilson, supporting Madison, added that many operations of finance "cannot be properly published at certain times." Both of those statements could be read as oblique references to the need for secrecy. At any rate, Madison's phrase "from time to time" was adopted without a dissenting vote. The Mason amendment was rewritten to include an accounting for receipts as well as expenditures. Moreover, the requirement for publication was applied to "all public Money."[4]

The issue was muddied somewhat at the Virginia ratifying convention, June 17, 1788. Mason objected to the phrase "from time to time" as being too loose an expression. He claimed that the "reasons urged in favor of this ambiguous expression, was, that there might be some matters which might require secrecy." How does *timing* relate to *coverage*? Perhaps he was referring to delays in the publication of sensitive material. Mason offered this elaboration:

> In matters relative to military operations, and foreign negotiations, secrecy was necessary sometimes. But he did not conceive that the receipts and expenditures of the public money ought ever to be concealed. The people, he affirmed, had a right to know the expenditure of their money.[5]

Of course it makes no sense at all to argue both for secrecy and full disclosure. His statement would be consistent only by assuming that the cost of secret operations, after a brief period of time, would be made available to the public.

It would be too doctrinaire to assert that secret funding is totally incompatible with representative government. The Framers were not innocents in this matter. John Jay, who had served as minister to Spain and as Secretary for Foreign Affairs prior to the Philadelphia Convention, justified secrecy in the diplomatic area. As he observed in Federalist

64: "It seldom happens in the negotiation of treaties, of whichever nature, but that perfect *secrecy* and immediate *dispatch* are sometimes requisite. There are cases where the most useful intelligence may be obtained, if the persons possessing it can be relieved from apprehension of discovery." To reveal the parties involved, or the purposes for which the funds were to be used, might have compromised negotiators and embarrassed the participating nations.

CONFIDENTIAL FUNDS

From the very start, then, it was the practice of Congress to provide the President with a fund over which he had complete control. He could exercise his own judgment in concealing the purposes to which funds were applied. The appropriation was public, but the expenditure could remain confidential.

An act of July 1, 1790 provided $40,000 to the President to pay for special diplomatic agents. It was left to the President to decide the degree to which such expenditures should be made public. In 1793 Congress continued that fund for the purposes of intercourse or treaty with other nations. The President was allowed to make a certificate of such expenditures, with each certificate "deemed a sufficient voucher for the sum or sums therein expressed to have been expended." Certificates simply state that funds have been spent, without supplying invoices or other documentary evidence on the details of the expenditure. Reliance on certificates, as a substitute for vouchers, is a departure from standard auditing and accounting practices. The 1793 authority has been carried forward and remains part of contemporary law.[6]

President Polk and Congress confronted one another on this subject of confidential funds. In 1846 the House of Representatives asked Polk to furnish an account of all payments made on Presidential certificates for the contingent expenses of foreign intercourse, spanning the period from

March 4, 1841 to the retirement of Daniel Webster from the Department of State. Polk reminded the legislators that the President had statutory authority to decide whether such expenditures should be made public. While he himself had settled all expenditures for contingent expenses of foreign intercourse by regular vouchers, he refused to surrender certificates made by his predecessor. Only through the impeachment process, he said, could the House compel release of those papers.[7]

The use of confidential funds by President Lincoln resulted in a Supreme Court decision. Under a contract with the President, made in July 1861, an individual by the name of William A. Lloyd was to proceed South and ascertain the number of troops stationed at different points in the insurrectionary States, procure plans of forts and fortifications, and gain such other information as might be beneficial. Instead of being paid $200 a month, as agreed to in the contract, he was only reimbursed his expenses. When his inheritors tried to recover compensation for the services, the Court of Claims dismissed the petition, partly because it was divided as to the authority of the President to bind the United States by the contract.

The Supreme Court said it had no difficulty as to the President's authority: "He was undoubtedly authorized during the war, as commander-in-chief of the armies of the United States, to employ secret agents to enter the rebel lines and obtain information respecting the strength, resources, and movements of the enemy: and contracts to compensate such agents are so far binding upon the government as to render it lawful for the President to direct payment of the amount stipulated out of the contingent fund under his control." The Court emphasized, however, that such contracts, by their very nature, are forever confidential. Both President and agent "must have understood that the lips of the other were to be for ever sealed respecting the relation of either to the matter." Any disclosure might compromise or embarrass the Government or endanger the life or injure the character of the agent. To allow action in the Court of Claims would expose the very details which were to be kept secret. On that principle the claim was denied.[8]

20TH CENTURY USAGE

In 1916, on the eve of America's entry into World War I, Congress authorized the Secretary of the Navy to make a certificate of expenses for "obtaining information from abroad and at home." Such certificates would be deemed a sufficient voucher for the sum expended. That provision is still part of current law.[9]

On August 25, 1941, just prior to American involvement in World War II, Congress authorized the President to use up to $2.5 million in unvouchered expenditures from his Emergency Fund. Several months later, after the bombing of Pearl Harbor, the President received an Emergency Fund of $100 million, of which $10 million could be spent on a confidential basis. The level of confidential funds rose to $25 million in July 1942 and $50 million in October 1942. It was increased an additional $25 million in July 1943.[10]

At one time confined to diplomatic and wartime expenses, confidential funds became a regular feature of many appropriation accounts. By fiscal 1973, twenty different accounts for executive agencies contained confidential funds. Four were tied directly to the President: Compensation of the President; White House Office, Salaries and Expenses; White House Office, Special Projects; and Executive Residence, Operating Expenses. Six were associated with diplomatic or military matters: Emergencies in the Diplomatic and Consular Service; Contingencies, Defense; and the Operation and Maintenance accounts for Army, Navy, Air Force, and Defense Agencies. Confidential funds for the latter six accounts were several million dollars each.

Three other accounts had national security overtones: Atomic Energy Commission ($100,000 in confidential funds), National Aeronautics and Space Administration, Research and Development Programs ($35,000), and Federal Bureau of Investigation ($70,000). The remaining confidential funds were found in District of Columbia, Chief of Police ($200,000), Bureau of Narcotics and Dangerous Drugs ($70,000), Immigration and Naturalization Service ($50,000), Bureau of Customs ($50,000), U.S. Secret Service ($50,000), Coast Guard ($15,000), and Department of Justice, Salaries and Expenses, General Legal Activities ($30,000). Not included in this list are funds for the U.S. intelligence community (to be discussed later in this chapter) as well as a number of other agencies whose expenditures are not subject to GAO audit.[11]

In addition to confidential funds that are inserted each year in appropriation bills, the executive branch has access to other funds for confidential purposes. The Foreign Assistance Act of 1961, as amended, grants the President a special authority to spend up to $50,000,000 in confidential funds. That is a cumulative amount, not annual. Available to the Agency for International Development are annual amounts of $50,000 for confidential expenses and $2,000 in confidential funds for the Inspector General, Foreign Assistance. The Peace Corps has access to $5,000 a year in confidential funds.[12]

Confidential funds are usually easy to spot in appropriation bills. For example, the "Operation and Maintenance, Defense Agencies" account for fiscal 1973 included $4.3 million to be spent on the approval or authority of the Secretary of Defense, "and payment may be made on his certificate of necessity for confidential military purposes, and his determination shall be final and conclusive upon the accounting officers of the Government." More difficult to find is the $200,000 fund for the D.C. Chief of Police. Language in the appropriation bill merely stated that the "limitation on expenditures of funds by the Chief of Police for prevention and detection of crime during the current fiscal year shall be $200,000." To understand that the funds may be handled by certificates rather than vouchers, one must check back to 1960 legislation. Similarly, language in the appropriation bill for the State Department sets aside $2.1 million for "Emergencies in the Diplomatic and Consular Service." Cross-checking a reference to the U.S. Code is necessary before one discovers that the funds may be accounted for by certificates.[13]

Unvouchered expenditures are often justified as necessary to pay informers. The $70,000 in FBI funds is used for "criminal and security investigations where the name of the informant or the nature of the expenditure must be kept secret so as not to jeopardize the investigative operations. The personal safety of the recipient of the funds is the paramount consideration in situations of this type." The $200,000 for the D.C. Chief of Police is available for expenses involved in investigating such activities as narcotics traffic and gambling. Undercover men use the funds when making purchases of narcotics or during visits to restaurants and bars.[14]

Most of the provisions for confidential funds were vulnerable to a point of order, since they lacked authorizing language.[15] Beginning in 1973, Members took advantage of that situation as the Watergate affair dramatized the need to place curbs on executive actions, as did the shocking revelations of Federal expenditures on President Nixon's homes at San Clemente and Key Biscayne.[16] On June 20, 1973, Bob Eckhardt, Democrat of Texas, offered an amendment to delete the $15,000 confidential Coast Guard fund. To the suggestion that Members of Congress should have faith in the integrity of executive officials, Eckhardt responded:

> I am sort of losing faith in the officers of the Government who are permitted to expend money without the General Accounting Office having any authority over the matter, and I am particularly losing faith in such inves-

209

tigations by officers of the Government unless we know what it is all about.[17]

The Eckhardt amendment was adopted by voice vote and the $15,000 fund was subsequently eliminated from the Transportation appropriation bill that became law.[18]

Eckhardt also attempted to delete the $100,000 confidential fund for the AEC. When advised that Congress should trust the AEC chairman to use those funds with discretion, Eckhardt countered: "I thank the gentleman but I would trust the Comptroller [General] also." Later in the debate the ranking members of the House appropriations subcommittee handling the bill—Joe Evins and John Rhodes—developed some legislative history. They said that the Comptroller General could look behind the certificate of an AEC chairman to make sure that the matter was actually of a confidential nature. With that assurance Eckhardt withdrew his amendment. A subsequent investigation by House Appropriations disclosed that the AEC confidential fund was used on such rare occasions (and probably not at all for a number of years) that there was no need to appropriate $100,000 for that purpose. Consequently, the fund was omitted from the AEC appropriation bill for fiscal 1975.[19]

Confidential funds in the D.C. appropriation bill were subject to a point of order because of a lack of substantive legislation. As a result of a point of order by Rep. H. R. Gross in 1973, followed by Senate action against other D.C. confidential accounts, six confidential funds were struck from the bill. The only remaining fund was $200,000 for the Chief of Police. An authorization bill, enacted October 26, 1973, authorized seven D.C. confidential funds: for the Chief of Police, the D.C. Commissioner, the chairman of the D.C. Council, the Superintendent of Schools, the President of the Federal City College, the President of the Washington Technical Institute, and the President of the D.C. Teachers College.[20]

The largest confidential funds are found in Defense Department accounts. In 1973 and 1974 Eckhardt was successful in raising points of order against the "Contingencies, Defense" account, since it constituted legislation in an appropriation bill. However, each time the funds were restored by the Senate and the conference committee. His efforts did result in the reduction of the account from $5 million to $2.5 million (in the fiscal 1975 act) and led to a softening of the language. Instead of the money being accounted for "solely" on the certificate of the Defense Secretary, payments "may be made on his certificate." The change in language was an invitation to GAO to audit.[21]

A similar development occurred with confidential funds in the Operation and Maintenance (O&M) accounts for the military. Eckhardt made points of order against them in 1973 on the ground that authorization was lacking. He was sustained by the Chair. Although the Senate and conference committee once again restored the funds to the appropriation bill, the prospect for GAO auditing improved. Language in the fiscal 1973 bill, to the effect that Defense Department determinations "shall be final and conclusive upon the accounting officers of the Government," was later changed to provide simply that "payments may be made" on the certificate of the Secretary of the department. Eckhardt withdrew a point of order against confidential funds for Air Force O&M, in the fiscal 1975 bill, after obtaining from Mahon the understanding that such funds could be audited and reviewed by the GAO.[22]

Confidential funding for "White House Office, Special Projects" dates back to a 1955 request by the Budget Bureau. From an initial amount of $1,250,000, the Special Projects account was generally funded at an annual level of $1.5 million. During hearings in 1973, the House Committee on Appropriations asked whether the fund had been used to finance the Special Investigations Unit operating out of the White House (the so-called plumbers group of Watergate fame). The Committee requested OMB to furnish a list of individual vouchers and expenditures for the account. When the Administration declined to supply the information, the Committee deleted the entire budget request.[23]

The Senate Appropriations Committee restored $1 million, inserting a requirement to provide both Appropriations Committees with quarterly reports of a "detailed accounting" of expenditures for the Special Projects account.[24] In floor action, Senator Mondale offered an amendment to strike the $1 million. He placed his amendment in the context of these developments:

> . . . a little thing has happened along the way called Watergate, which opened up for the American public to see the tremendously dangerous tendency that exists when we grant, without specification, without control, without information, substantial funds to the White House which are used by them behind the protection of executive privilege and the separation of powers to do as they please.[25]

Although the Mondale amendment was defeated by a 52-36 vote, House and Senate conferees agreed to delete all funds for the Special Projects account. No funds for that purpose were included in the Treasury-Post Office appropriation bill signed by President Nixon. And as a result of legislative history stimulated by Congressman Dingell, in 1973, confidential funds in other White House accounts were subject to greater scrutiny by the GAO.[26]

Eckhardt offered a more general amendment in 1973 to require that expenditures made solely on the certificate of an executive officer be subject to the scrutiny of the Comptroller General, who would determine whether the expenditure was indeed of a confidential or special nature. Eckhardt himself ran afoul of a point of order. His amendment was rejected because it was legislation in an appropriation bill. He also introduced the same proposal in bill form to allow the Comptroller General to examine confidential expenditures and to report to Congress any apparent irregularities.[27] No action was taken on the bill during the 93d Congress (1973-75).

A number of reasonable arguments can be presented to justify the need for confidential funding, whether for national security, foreign affairs, or domestic investigations. However, some elementary principles should be followed.

First, authorize confidential funds by substantive law (passed by authorization committees) rather than including them in appropriation bills surrounded by waivers to protect against points of order. That would simply adhere to House and Senate rules. Second, the appropriation bill should state the amount, repeat the authorizing language, and cite the authority. To illustrate: "not to exceed (dollar amount) can be used for emergencies and extraordinary expenses, as authorized by (U.S. Code citation), to be expended on the approval or authority of the Secretary, and payments may be made on his certificate of necessity for confidential purposes." At the present time, in many appropriation bills, it is impossible to detect the presence of confidential funds. Third, some form of GAO audit should be carried out to ensure that funds are spent in accordance with legislative authority. Hundreds of agency officials share knowledge about the funds; we can extend the same trust to GAO officials. Fourth, have agencies report annually on the *degree* to which the authority is used. For example: "Of $50,000 in confidential funds authorized, the agency used $37,500."

SECRET FUNDS

Confidential funding is overt to the extent that such funds are cited in appropriation bills. In that sense the appropriation is public while the expenditure and auditing are concealed from Congress and the public. Secret funding, in contrast, is covert at every stage: from appropriation straight through to auditing.

An early case of secret funding involved President Madison. Concerned that certain territory south of Georgia might pass from Spain to another foreign power, he asked Congress for authority to take temporary possession. Voting in secret session, in 1811, Congress provided $100,000 for that purpose. The public did not know of the action until years later, in 1818, when Congress published the secret statute.[28]

Secret funding was employed during World War II to develop and produce an atomic bomb. Administration officials contacted three leaders of the House of Representatives: Speaker Rayburn, Majority Leader McCormack, and Minority Leader Martin. An additional $1.6 billion was needed to manufacture the bomb, an amount the Administration wanted without "a trace of evidence" as to how it would be spent. Clarence Cannon, chairman of House Appropriations, and John Taber, ranking majority member, agreed to make an inscrutable appropriation. Some of the money was tucked away under two accounts: "Engineer Service, Army" and "Expediting Production." Only a handful of Congressmen knew how the money was being used. About $800 million was spent before some members of House Appropriations knew of the project.[29]

CENTRAL INTELLIGENCE AGENCY

The Central Intelligence Act of 1949 contained extraordinary authority over the transfer and application of funds. It provided that sums made available to the CIA "may be expended without regard to the provisions of law and regulations relating to the expenditure of Government funds. . . ." For objects of a confidential nature, expenditures could be accounted for solely on the certificate of the CIA Director, with each certificate deemed a sufficient voucher for the amount certified. In addition, rather than appropriating funds directly to the CIA, Congress authorized the agency to transfer to and receive from other Government agencies "such sums as may be approved by the Bureau of the Budget" for the performance of any functions or activities autho-

214

rized by the National Security Act of 1947. Other agencies were authorized to transfer to or receive from the CIA such sums "without regard to any provisions of law limiting or prohibiting transfers between appropriations."[30]

This transfer authority converts a number of appropriation accounts into a vast mixing bowl. Although explicit sums are voted for departments and agencies, that tidiness is quickly upset by siphoning off agency funds and funneling them to the CIA. The funds for the CIA are initially appropriated to the Defense Department. After the chairmen of the Appropriations Committees inform OMB of the level of the CIA budget, OMB approves the transfer of that amount from the Defense Department to the CIA.[31]

The total budget of the entire U.S. intelligence community has been estimated at $6 billion a year. A study by *Newsweek* in 1971 reported that a dozen agencies employed 200,000 and spent some $6 billion annually. Senator Proxmire released comparable figures in 1973. The CIA portion came to $750 million. The largest amount for the intelligence community was $2.8 billion for the Air Force, followed by the National Security Agency with $1 billion. Other amounts: $775 million each for the Army and Navy intelligence activities, $100 million for the Defense Intelligence Agency, and $8 million for the State Department. Intelligence expenditures of the FBI, the AEC, and the Treasury Department were not estimated.[32]

Current criticism of the CIA results from its evolution as an intelligence-gathering agency, confined to foreign activities, to that of a participant-catalyst of military and political operations. Harry Howe Ransom, the leading scholar on the subject, writes that nothing in the public record "nor in such archives as are accessible (for example, in the Truman Library) suggests that Congress ever intended to create or knew that it was creating an agency for para-military operations and a wide range of foreign political interventions." Senator Stennis, during debate in 1974, said that he came to the Senate soon after the original CIA bill was passed "and there was nothing clearer around here, not anything that sounded louder, than the fact that the CIA act was passed for the purpose of foreign intelligence." He said he was "shocked and disappointed and considerably aroused" when he learned of CIA's involvement in the Watergate affair.[33]

During the last decade the CIA has come under heavy fire for its secret funding of private organizations, Radio Free Europe and Radio Liberty, military operations in Laos, domestic intelligence gathering, and financial support in Chile for opponents of Allende.

With regard to private organizations, in 1967 it was reported in the press that the CIA had been secretly subsidizing religious organizations, student groups, labor unions, universities, and private foundations. President Johnson appointed a three-member committee, headed by Under Secretary of State Katzenbach, to review the relationship between the CIA and private American voluntary organizations. The committee reported that covert CIA assistance had been made available by the last four Administrations, dating back to October 1951. It recommended that "no federal agency shall provide any covert financial assistance or support, direct or indirect, to any of the nation's educational or private voluntary organizations." President Johnson accepted the committee's statement of policy and directed all agencies of the Government to implement it fully.[34]

A footnote in the committee's report explained that its statement of policy did not entirely close the door to covert financing of private voluntary organizations. Exceptions might be necessary: "Where the security of the nation may be at stake, it is impossible for this committee to state categorically now that there will never be a contingency in which overriding national security interests may require an exception—nor would it be credible to enunciate a policy which purported to do so. In no case, however, should any

216

future exception be approved which involved any educational, philanthropic, or cultural organization."[35]

The CIA continued to finance the broadcasting that had been conducted by Radio Free Europe (to Eastern Europe) and by Radio Liberty (to Soviet Russia). In 1971 Senator Case estimated that several hundred million dollars had been expended from CIA budgets over the previous decades to fund the two radios. He introduced legislation to require that, in the future, the two stations be subject to annual appropriations by Congress. Starting with a continuing appropriation act in 1971, funding for the two radios has been overt. A GAO report revealed that between 1949 and mid-1971 the Federal Government had spent $482 million in covert funds to support the two radios.[36]

Senator Case, member of both the Appropriations and the Foreign Relations Committees, had to rely on an article in the *Christian Science Monitor* to learn that the Administration had agreed to finance Thai troops in Laos. Further investigation by Senate staff members disclosed that the CIA was covertly financing Thai troops fighting in northern Laos. The cost of the operation ran to several hundred million dollars a year. An amendment by Senator Symington, to establish a ceiling of $200 million on U.S. expenditures in Laos during fiscal 1972, had to be raised to $350 million. Symington later said that the secret war in Laos was done without knowledge on the part of members of the Senate Armed Services Committee.[37]

CONGRESSIONAL OVERSIGHT

A five-man Senate Armed Services subcommittee, responsible for reviewing CIA activities, met with CIA witnesses twice in 1970, not at all in 1971, and only once in 1972. The other CIA subcommittee in the Senate, located in the Appropriations Committee, did not have a more attractive record. With regard to CIA operations in Laos, Senator Ellender (at that time chairman of the Appropriations

217

Committee) said he "did not know anything about it." He did not ask, in his oversight function, whether CIA funds were being used to carry on the war in Laos: "It never dawned on me to ask about it."[38] This frank exchange then took place between Senators Ellender and Cranston:

> MR. CRANSTON. . . . I am sure I never would have thought to ask such a question. But it appeared in the press that perhaps that was happening. I would like to ask the Senator if, since then, he has inquired and now knows whether that is being done?
> MR. ELLENDER. I have not inquired.
> MR. CRANSTON. You do not know, in fact?
> MR. ELLENDER. No.
> MR. CRANSTON. As you are one of the five men privy to this information, in fact you are the No. 1 man of the five men who would know, then who would know what happened to this money?
> The fact is, not even of the five men, and you are the chief one of the five men, know the facts in the situation.
> MR. ELLENDER. Probably not.[39]

House supervision of the CIA does not appear to be much better. Congressman Norblad, in a floor statement in 1963, said that he had been on the CIA subcommittee of House Armed Services: "We met annually—one time a year, for a period of 2 hours in which we accomplished virtually nothing." Congressman Nedzi, chairman of that subcommittee in later years, suggested in 1971 that only the Budget Bureau and the Kremlin had a full understanding of intelligence activities: "Perhaps they are the only ones. We simply don't have that kind of detailed information. . . . I have to be candid and tell you I don't know whether we are getting our money's worth." A step toward closer review was taken by the Committee Reform Amendments of 1974, which expands the jurisdiction of the House Foreign Affairs Committee to include oversight functions of "intelligence activities relating to foreign policy." Beginning February 21, 1975, the CIA began sharing budget details with the entire defense subcommittee of House Appropriations, rather than a select few from that subcommittee.[40]

With respect to the budgets of the U.S. intelligence community, several proposals have been advanced for greater legislative control. In 1971 Senator Symington proposed a ceiling of $4 billion for expenses of the CIA, the National Security Agency, the Defense Intelligence Agency, and for "intelligence work performed by or on behalf of the Army, Navy, and the Air Force." The motion was rejected by a vote of 56 to 31. Part of the opposition came from those who considered Symington's language too broad, possibly applying even to tactical intelligence. No one could suggest a means of distinguishing between intelligence needed to conduct a battle and intelligence to be covered by the $4 billion.[41] Rather than approach the issue from this abstract conceptual plane, Members of Congress could have proceeded on a more down-to-earth level by simply naming the agencies and bureaus to be made subject to the budget ceiling.

Congress did succeed, in the Foreign Assistance Act of 1971, in placing restrictions on CIA expenditures and transfer authority. The Act imposed a ceiling of $341 million for assistance to Cambodia. The statutory language was broad in its coverage. Notwithstanding any other provision of law, no funds authorized to be appropriated by the Foreign Assistance Act of 1971 or any other law could be obligated in any amount in excess of $341 million for the purpose of carrying out directly or indirectly any economic or military assistance for Cambodia. The effect was to limit CIA's ability to transfer its funds to supplement the Cambodian operation.[42] (For further background on this legislation, see pages 107-10.)

As a means of imposing a more general control on the CIA, Senator McGovern introduced a bill in 1971 to require publication in the budget of "proposed appropriations, estimated expenditures, and other related data" for the CIA. Each of the items would be shown as a single sum. Furthermore, the bill would have prohibited the CIA from spending funds that had been appropriated for other departments or agencies. The standard practice has been to inflate certain military appropriation accounts, allowing the superfluous funds to be transferred to the CIA and other intelligence agencies. "As a result," noted McGovern, "we are led to believe that some programs are better financed than, in fact, they are. We have no way of knowing what these programs and agencies might be."[43]

Similar criticism has been voiced by other Senators. During debate in 1971 on the defense appropriation bill, Senator Fulbright remarked that when "you look at an item in this bill you wonder if it is really the amount of money for the A-14, for example, or if it is for the NSA. One cannot tell what it is."[44] One Senator told me that in one of his economy drives he made an attack on a particular appropriation. Later he received a call from a colleague, who sat on one of the oversight subcommittees, and was advised that the money was actually for the CIA.

To appropriate directly to the CIA would preserve the integrity of other accounts and make for more rational debate and decision by Congress. But how would Congress know that a lump sum amount would be too much or too little unless it knew how the money was to be spent? Congress imposed one restriction in 1974 when it prohibited the CIA from spending funds for operations in foreign countries, "other than activities intended solely for obtaining necessary intelligence. . . ." The restriction can be lifted if the President finds that an operation is important to the national security and reports to Congress on the nature and scope of the operation. In 1975, Senator Proxmire introduced a bill to authorize the GAO to audit and analyze the expenditures of intelligence agencies.[45]

Would publication of the *aggregate* budget figures for the intelligence community jeopardize national interests? CIA Director Colby, as well as his predecessor James Schlesinger, testified that the release of such information would not violate national security. Colby said that the question was basically up to Congress, adding that he had found Congress "at least as responsible on this as our friends elsewhere in government, and we have, as you know, shared with Congress some very sensitive material which has been successfully protected by the Congress." He volunteered the view that the American constitutional structure might require publication of more budget information than might be convenient from a narrow intelligence point of view. However, after he was confirmed as CIA Director, Colby was quoted by Senator Pastore as being opposed to revealing the size of his agency's budget: "Please do not do this. If you want to make my job easier, please do not do this."[46]

Schlesinger was asked about the CIA budget during his nomination hearing as Secretary of Defense. He expressed some misgivings at releasing a "free floating figure, unsupported and unsupportable in public," possibly inviting flat percentage cuts in intelligence activities. But he felt that publishing a gross figure would have only a "minimal" effect on security concerns. While he would be more concerned about the component figures, "for the gross national intelligence program figures I think we could live with that on a security basis, yes."[47]

LITIGATION

Pressure for public funding of the CIA has been building from yet another source: the courts. William B. Richardson, a resident of Greensburg, Pa., sought judgment to declare the Central Intelligence Act in violation of the Statement and Account Clause of the Constitution. He had written to the Government Printing Office in 1967 to request the document which would satisfy that clause. He examined available Treasury documents but could find no listing of CIA expenses. His administrative remedies exhausted, he turned to the courts.

In 1968 a U.S. District Court in Pennsylvania held that Richardson lacked standing to raise a justiciable controversy. A month later, in the church-state case of *Flast* v. *Cohen*, the Supreme Court substantially broadened the grounds on which taxpayers could establish standing, but the district court holding against Richardson was affirmed by the U.S. Court of Appeals for the Third Circuit. The Supreme Court denied certiorari to review the Richardson case; only Justice Douglas supported his motion for review.[48]

Richardson initiated a new suit in 1970, this time asking that a three-judge court be convened to determine the constitutionality of the CIA act. Once again the district court decided he lacked standing. Moreover, the subject matter raised "political questions in a governmental sense and the subject is not open to a United States District Court for adjudication in any manner."[49] Up to that point Richardson had been blocked by three procedural hurdles: standing, jurisdiction, and justiciability.

But this time he was successful when he brought the matter to the court of appeals. On July 20, 1972, by a 6-3 vote, the circuit court vacated the district court ruling and directed that a statutory three-judge court be designated to adjudicate the issue. Judge Max Rosenn, writing the opinion, underscored the importance of the Statement and Account Clause:

A responsible and intelligent taxpayer and citizen, of course, wants to know how his tax money is being spent. Without this information he cannot intelligently follow the actions of the Congress or of the Executive. Nor can he properly fulfill his obligation as a member of the electorate. The Framers of the Constitution deemed fiscal information essential if the electorate was to exercise any control over its representatives and meet their new responsibilities as citizens of the Republic.[50]

The Supreme Court agreed to review the procedural aspects of the case, i.e., whether Richardson had standing to request a three-judge court. A separate writ of certiorari by Richardson, urging the Court to examine the substance and constitutionality of the issue, was rejected.[51]

The Court's decision was handed down June 25, 1974. Chief Justice Burger, writing for a 5-4 majority, held that Richardson lacked standing to maintain his suit. Relief was available, noted Burger, through the electoral process. If citizens felt that Members of Congress were delinquent in performing their duties, they could elect others to produce the publication of CIA expenditures. In a dissenting opinion, Justice Douglas denied that Congress was at liberty to suspend a constitutional provision. To claim that Congress had the power to read the Statement and Account Clause out of the Constitution, he said, was "astounding."[52]

OTHER DARK CORNERS

Beyond the question of confidential and secret funds lie other veiled areas of the Federal budget. Before discussing a few examples directly under the President, brief consideration can be given to a regulatory agency: the Federal Reserve System. Although it spends half a billion dollars a year, its funds are not appropriated by Congress. Nor is there any auditing by GAO. By buying and selling Government securities held in its portfolio, the "Fed" derives income from interest on the bonds. Federal Reserve earnings in calendar 1973 came to $5 billion. After deducting $495 million for its operating expenses, plus additional amounts for dividends to banks, losses on securities, etc., it returned the balance ($4.3 billion) to the Treasury. The House of Representatives passed legislation in 1974 to provide for a measure of GAO auditing, but no action was taken by the Senate.[53]

FREE WORLD FORCES

The financing of the war in Vietnam illustrates how billions can be spent for programs known to a handful of Congressmen. In September 1966, President Johnson expressed his "deep admiration as well as that of the American people for the action recently taken by the Philippines to send a civic action group of 2,000 men to assist the Vietnamese in resisting aggression and rebuilding their country." Other announcements from the White House created the impression that not only the Philippines but also Thailand, South Korea, and other members of the "Free World Forces" had shown a willingness to sacrifice blood and resources in the stand against Communism.[54]

Hearings held by the Symington subcommittee in 1969 and 1970 revealed that the United States had offered sizable subsidies. The Philippines received river patrol craft, engineering equipment, a special overseas allowance for its soldiers, and additional equipment to strengthen Filipino forces at home. It cost the United States $38.8 million to send one Filipino construction battalion to Vietnam. Senator Fulbright remarked that "all we did was go over and hire their soldiers in order to support our then administration's view that so many people were in sympathy with our war in Vietnam." Although the Philippine government denied that U.S. contributions represented a subsidy or a fee in return for sending the construction battalion, a GAO investigation confirmed that *quid pro quo* assistance had indeed been given. Moreover, there was evidence that the Johnson Administration had increased other forms of military and economic aid to the Philippines.[55]

The Symington subcommittee also uncovered an agreement that the Johnson Administration had entered into with the Royal Thai Government in 1967. The United States agreed to cover any additional costs associated with

the sending of Thai soldiers to Vietnam: payment of overseas allowances, modernization of Thai forces, and the deployment of an anti-aircraft Hawk battery in Thailand.
After the Foreign Ministry of Thailand denied that U.S.
payments had been offered to induce Thailand to send
armed forces to Vietnam, the GAO reported that U.S. funds
had been used for such purposes as training Thai troops,
payment of overseas allowances, and payment of separation bonuses to Thai soldiers who had served in Vietnam.
The GAO estimated that the United States had invested
"probably more than $260 million in equipment, allow-
ances, subsistence, construction, military sales concessions,
and other support to the Thais for their contribution under
the Free World Military Assistance program to Vietnam."[56]

Subsidies were also used to support the sending of South
Korean forces to Vietnam. Assistance included equipment
to modernize Korean forces at home, equipment and all
additional costs to cover the deployment of Korean forces
in Vietnam, additional loans from the Agency for International Development, and increased ammunition and communication facilities in Korea. To ensure that the dispatch
of men to Vietnam would not weaken the defensive capa-
bilities of the Republic of Korea, the Johnson Administration agreed to finance the training of forces to replace those
deployed in Vietnam, and to improve South Korea's anti-
infiltration capability. From fiscal 1965 to fiscal 1970,
Korea's military presence in Vietnam cost the United States
an estimated $927.5 million.[57]

The legal basis for assistance to Free World Forces in
Vietnam derived from legislation passed in 1966. Funds
were made available to support Vietnamese "and other
free world forces in Vietnam, and related costs . . . on such
terms and conditions as the Secretary of Defense may determine." Assistance was broadened in 1967 to include local
forces in Laos and Thailand. Reports on such expenditures
were submitted only to the Armed Services and Appropriations Committees of both Houses. The general language of

the statutes did not reveal the types of financial arrangements the Administration might enter into, or with what country. Staff members who had access to the reports told me they did not know the nature and dimension of financing the Free World Forces until hearings were held by the Symington subcommittee.[58]

MILITARY ASSISTANCE

On the basis of a GAO report, Senator Edward Kennedy announced that money appropriated for refugee programs, for public health, agriculture, economic and technical projects, and for the "Food for Peace" program had been diverted to pay for CIA-directed paramilitary operations in Laos. The term "refugee" was a euphemism created by the Agency for International Development to describe the development and support of those operations. Hearings in 1972 confirmed that AID funds had been used to supply Lao military and paramilitary forces with food and medical care and supplies.[59]

Hearings by the Joint Economic Committee in 1971 highlighted the fact that nearly $700 million in Food for Peace funds had been channeled into military assistance programs over the past six years. Since 1954, when the Food for Peace (P.L. 480) program was enacted, $1.6 billion of those funds had been allocated to military assistance. Statutory authority existed, but few Members of Congress were aware that Food for Peace was such a capacious vehicle for military assistance. Nor could they have gained that understanding by reading the budget, which described Food for Peace in these terms: "The United States donates and sells agricultural commodities on favorable terms to friendly nations under the Agricultural Trade Development and Assistance Act (Public Law 480). The program combats hunger and malnutrition, promotes economic growth in developing nations, and develops and expands export markets for U.S. commodities." Senator Proxmire castigated the use of rhetoric by the Administration to conceal the nature of the Food for Peace program. "This seems to me," he said, "to be kind of an Orwellian perversion of the language; food for peace could be called food for war."[60]

The budget itself was deceptive in how much was spent for military assistance. For example, 1971 outlays for military assistance were estimated at $1.175 billion in Defense Department funds, plus an additional $504 million in supporting assistance. The apparent total: $1.679 billion. However, Senator Proxmire obtained from the Pentagon its estimates for military assistance for fiscal 1971: $3.226 billion in the Military Assistance Program, Military Assistance Service Funded, and related programs; $600 million in supporting assistance; $7 million in additional public safety programs; $143 million in Food for Peace funds used for common defense purposes; and $2.339 billion for military export sales. Under that calculation the total rose to $6.317 billion.[61]

Even when Congress appropriates overtly it can act "in the blind" by providing funds for activities that are justified in vague terms by the Administration. In 1972 Congressman Harrington declared that the defense authorization bill contained $830 million that members of the Armed Services Committee "know nothing about. Some of the members of the Armed Services Committee, including the gentleman from New York (Mr. Stratton) and myself, have asked for and been refused information. . . ." Three members of that same committee complained in 1973 that the military assistance program for Vietnam and Laos had been "pro forma justified" to the committee. In the words of one member: "All of the backup figures for the $1.185 billion allegedly justified are *Secret* Classified. I haven't seen the figures and the Committee has no idea what program is justified in this area." The dispute continued in 1974 when Senator Fulbright charged that $490 million in military assistance was hidden in the Pentagon's budget. The money was earmarked for "War Reserve Materials"—stockpiled equipment and munitions destined for Vietnam, Thailand, and Korea.[62]

Although the Statement and Account Clause can be interpreted to allow room for a modest amount of confidential funding, particularly in the diplomatic area, we have reached the point where probably $10 billion to $15 billion in the Federal budget is obscured because of confidential funds, secret funds, or cryptic budget justifications. Members of Congress cannot act intelligently on vast portions of the budget because they are denied basic data. Their constituents cannot hold the Members accountable because the issues and amounts are obfuscated. Elementary accounting practices by the GAO are rendered impossible.

In Federalist 58 James Madison claimed that the power over the purse "may, in fact, be regarded as the most complete and effectual weapon with which any constitution can arm the immediate representatives of the people, for obtaining a redress of every grievance, and for carrying into effect every just and salutary measure." Without public knowledge, without public debate, we have traveled far from that basic underpinning of democratic government.

10

Executive Commitments

Article I, Section 9 of the Constitution states that "No money shall be drawn from the Treasury but in consequence of appropriations made by law." It was axiomatic that Congress, and Congress alone, would have complete authority to decide how to spend the taxpayers' money.

Nonetheless, Presidents and executive officials have found it expedient at times to enter into financial obligations not authorized by Congress. Previous chapters detailed the kinds of commitments entered into by such methods as transfers, reprogramming, and covert financing. This chapter will identify other techniques that permit executive officials to commit the Government prior to congressional action.

EARLY PRECEDENTS

One of the most controversial and widely discussed actions was the decision by President Jefferson to accept France's offer to sell the whole of Louisiana for $11,250,000—plus an additional $3,750,000 to cover private claims against France—even though the offer exceeded instructions set forth by Congress. Jefferson also relied on executive prerogative in 1807 after a British vessel fired on the American ship *Chesapeake*. Without statutory authority he ordered military purchases for the emergency and disclosed his actions to Congress when it came back in session. "To have awaited a previous and special sanction by law," said Jefferson, "would have lost occasions which might not be retrieved."[1]

In 1861, after the firing on Fort Sumter, and while Congress was adjourned, Lincoln directed his Secretary of the Treasury to advance $2 million to three private citizens, the money to be used for "military and naval measures necessary for the defense and support of the Government. . . ." Lincoln acted without statutory authority, but the regular channels in the Treasury Department had become suspect since many of the officials were Southern sympathizers.[2]

Also in the category of unauthorized commitments was the decision by Theodore Roosevelt to send an American fleet around the world as a show of strength, despite congressional threats not to finance the expedition. Roosevelt replied that he had enough money to take the fleet halfway around the world. If Congress did not appropriate enough to get the fleet back, Roosevelt said "it would stay in the Pacific. There was no further difficulty about the money." A less successful effort involved Roosevelt's habit of appointing extralegal, unsalaried commissions to study social and economic issues. To publish the findings of one of his commissions he asked Congress for $25,000. Not only did Congress refuse, it enacted a prohibition against the appointment of commissions without legislative authority. Roosevelt protested that Congress had no right to issue such an order, and that he would ignore it, but he did not get the money. A private organization had to publish the study.[3]

During the Administration of Franklin Roosevelt, Congress discovered that the President had created agencies by Executive Order and was using appropriated funds to finance agency activities without any legislative support. An amendment known as the "Russell Rider" was adopted in 1944 to prohibit the use of any appropriation for an agency unless Congress had specifically authorized the expenditure of funds by the agency.[4]

The Supreme Court occasionally reviewed some of the financial initiatives taken by executive officers. In one case, decided in 1833, the Court addressed itself to the question of whether the head of an executive department could allow payments not authorized by law. A unanimous decision observed that a "practical knowledge of the action of any one of the great departments of the government, must convince every person that the head of a department, in the distribution of its duties and responsibilities, is often compelled to exercise his discretion. He is limited in the exercise of his powers by the law; but it does not follow that he must show a statutory provision for every thing he does. No government could be administered on such principles."[5]

Another Court decision involved an agreement made by John B. Floyd, Buchanan's Secretary of War. A Government contractor, lacking sufficient funds to complete his order, was allowed to draw time-drafts and have them purchased by his suppliers to provide interim financial assistance. The Government subsequently accepted drafts of $5 million, but over a million dollars remained unpaid. Holders of the unpaid drafts contended that Floyd's acceptances were binding on the Government. The Supreme Court, however, dismissed their claims, denying that Floyd possessed either constitutional or statutory authority to enter into his agreements.[6]

Administrative discretion in the handling of funds regularly provoked the ire of Congress. The Gilmer Committee reported in 1842: "Under color of what are termed *regulations*, large amounts of money are often applied to purposes never contemplated by the appropriating power, and numerous offices are sometimes actually created in the same way." Funds generated from such governmental activities as the postal service or customs collection invited executive discretion as to their use. William Barry, Postmaster General from 1828 to 1835, borrowed large sums of money on the credit of the Post Office. His practice was defended on the grounds that the Post Office Department "created its own funds" and that bank loans were therefore simply a claim on future postal revenues. A Senate report in 1834 condemned such practices and justifications. In 1842 the House Committee on Public Expenditures complained that the Secretary of the Treasury was using customs revenue to finance a naval force for the collection of revenue. "He appropriates and pays," the committee said, "without the sanction of Congress, and even without its knowledge."[7]

COERCIVE DEFICIENCIES

Early in the 19th century, Congress authorized agency officials to draw on surpluses as a means of covering deficiencies. The practice of transferring funds allowed agencies to accomplish a similar result. But in 1870 Congress prohibited executive departments from spending in a fiscal year any sum in excess of appropriations for that year; nor could any department involve the government in any contract for the future payment of money in excess of such appropriations.[8]

The thrust of that law was regularly blunted by the incurring of deficiencies. If a department ran out of money before the end of the fiscal year, there was little that Congress could do except pass supplemental appropriations. The fault was not entirely that of the departments. James Garfield, chairman of House Appropriations from 1871 to 1875, made this observation: "One of the vicious party devices too often resorted to for avoiding responsibility for extravagance in appropriations is to cut down the annual bills below the actual amount necessary to carry on the Government, announce to the country that a great reduction has been made in the interest of economy, and, after the elections are over, make up the necessary amount by deficiency bills."[9]

Legislation in 1884 attempted to instill some accountability in the executive branch by requiring all deficiency requests to be transmitted to Congress through the Secretary of the Treasury.[10] Budget discipline was difficult to encourage during that time; the Federal Government enjoyed surpluses year after year, from 1866 to 1893. Deficits began to appear toward the end of the 19th century. After a brief flurry of surpluses, the budget returned to a deficit position in 1904.

ANTIDEFICIENCY ACT

As a technique for compelling agencies to distribute their funds evenly over the course of the year, rather than spending at a disproportionate rate, the Antideficiency Act of 1905 required monthly or other allotments to prevent "undue expenditures in one portion of the year that may require deficiency or additional appropriations to complete the service of the fiscal year. . . ." The Act also provided that any person violating the procedure "shall be summarily removed from office and may also be punished by a fine of not less than one hundred dollars or by imprisonment for not less than one month." The removal power, however, was in the hands of the President (except for impeachment), while the punishment by fine or imprisonment was never invoked. Moreover, the 1905 law allowed departmental heads to waive or modify allotments by written order.[11]

To legislate against deficiencies proved a frustrating assignment. Some deficiencies arose because statutes required compensation, as in the case of paying jurors in the Federal courts. Other deficiencies occurred when there were judgments against the United States, whether rendered by the Court of Claims, treaties, or some other source. In none of those cases did Congress have any option but to appropriate the necessary amount. A third class of deficiency resulted from inaccurate budget estimates by agency officials, sometimes the result of incompetence, sometimes by design. A fourth reason for deficiencies was deliberate underfunding by Congress. Leonidas Livingston reminded his colleagues in the House that it was a well-recognized fact that "if we wanted to make an impression of economy, or if we had a short session and were in a great hurry, we cut appropriations rather than investigated them and said: 'Oh, well; they could go to the Senate or they could come in with a deficiency.' "[12]

Departmental heads used the waiver technique with such frequency, and for such routine purposes, that the Anti-deficiency Act was rewritten in 1906. To emphasize that the apportionment process was not to be waived on a casual basis, Congress changed the language to stipulate that apportionments could be waived or modified only in the event of "some extraordinary emergency or unusual circumstance which could not be anticipated at the time of making such apportionment. . . ."[13]

While such language may have represented a warning against deficiencies, exhortation alone could never eliminate them. In some cases the practice of passing deficiency bills was a convenience for Congress. If deficiencies were totally forbidden, Congress might have to vote larger appropriations to cover all possible contingencies. But with the deficiency system, legislators could cut deeply into any budget request that looked suspicious. The burden would then be on executive officials to show why they could not survive on the reduced amount. Also, Congress might find it impracticable to predict the exact amount an agency needs for certain operations. For example, Congress deliberately underfunds the firefighting program in Interior's Bureau of Land Management. The Bureau enters into whatever obligations are necessary to cover emergency fire suppression costs. For interim financing the Bureau borrows funds from other agencies within Interior. Later the Bureau comes to Congress for a supplemental appropriation.[14]

So intractable were deficiencies that Congress created special subcommittees to handle them each year. During hearings in 1945, the following exchange took place between Congressman Mike Monroney, Vice Chairman of the Joint Committee on the Organization of Congress, and Ben Jensen, Republican member of House Appropriations:

> THE VICE CHAIRMAN. Is it not a fact that there are dozens of items carried each year in the deficiency bill? I mean, the department plans to come before the deficiency committee just as they come before the Interior or Agriculture Appropriations Committees, and ask for this additional money, and it is planned a year ahead that they are going to ask for these deficiencies?
>
> MR. JENSEN. I am afraid that is right, which, of course, should never happen. They should not anticipate letting an item be left out of the regular appropriation and then say that they will go before the deficiency committee and get it. I think that is entirely wrong. I say they should make such requests to their regular subcommittee.[15]

The Antideficiency Act was rewritten in 1950 to encourage agencies to set aside surpluses for unanticipated expenses (see pages 154-57). The Act also sanctioned two types of deficiencies: (1) cases in which Congress enacted legislation after the President submitted his budget, requiring expenditures beyond administrative control, and (2) emergencies involving the "safety of human life, the protection of property, or the immediate welfare of individuals. . . ."[16]

ANTIDEFICIENCY VIOLATIONS

A 1955 study by House Appropriations demonstrated that the Antideficiency Act was far from self-executing. The most serious violations were committed by the Defense Department, partly because it had been slow in issuing directives but also because it displayed an unwillingness to comply with the statute. The study singled out other reasons for violations by the Defense Department and the civilian agencies. An excessive number of allotments were issued in too small amounts, at too low a level in the departments, to permit accountability. Also, there were inadequate records of obligations incurred, a failure to give adequate weight to seasonal variations when making apportionments, and negligence in following established procedures.[17]

The Pentagon's regulations to control deficiencies were issued in 1952 and revised in 1955 and 1958. Still, the Defense Department continued to outdo all other agencies in the frequency and dollar amounts of deficiencies. From 1963 through 1973, executive agencies committed 278 violations of the Antideficiency Act, totaling $188 million. The Pentagon committed 216 of those violations, representing a dollar value of $165 million. In addition to *reported* violations, the General Accounting Office often advises Congress of antideficiency violations that were never reported by the agencies.[18]

The granddaddy of all violations was a $110 million deficiency by the Navy. By letter of April 12, 1972, Defense Secretary Laird informed Congress that the Navy had over-obligated and overspent in the "Military Personnel, Navy" account. An investigation by House Appropriations suggested that certain individuals in the Navy made willful adjustments to accounting records in an effort to conceal the infraction. In order to liquidate the deficiencies, the Administration wanted to use balances available from prior years (so-called "M" account money). But since it had been the adjustment of "M" account balances that kept the violation from becoming immediately apparent, House Appropriations preferred to appropriate new money rather than give any appearance of condoning the Navy's action.[19]

In reporting to Congress on violations of the Antideficiency Act, Pentagon officials frequently explain that they are the result of "misinterpretation or nonobservance of service procedures and controls." Individuals responsible for overobligations will argue that, although members of the Army Comptroller Officer Career Program for a number of years, they have received no training in governmental accounting. By asserting that they did not "willfully or knowingly" intend to violate the law, they can escape the fine and imprisonment penalties of the Antideficiency Act.[20]

Disciplinary action usually takes the form of oral or written reprimand. On rare occasions an individual is relieved of duty. Sometimes the Pentagon has been unable to fix individual responsibility. In other cases, by the time the responsible official has been identified he has retired.[21]

In the mid-1960s, a joint committee on legislative reform made specific recommendations with respect to deficiencies. The final report of the Joint Committee on the Organization of the Congress proposed that the Appropriations Committees include in their reports on supplementals and deficiencies "a comprehensive explanation of why the request is of an emergency nature and could not have been made in the current or the next regular appropriation bills." The joint committee believed that congressional fiscal responsibility was best exercised through the regular appropriation bills. Programs were not to be funded through supplementals or deficiencies unless there was a "compelling necessity" to do so. The report also charged that the Appropriations Committees had engaged in the misleading practice of projecting an image of economy by voting modest sums, with the knowledge that a supplemental would be required at some later point to compensate for their underfunding. The joint committee's recommendations were not included in the eventual legislative product, the Legislative Reorganization Act of 1970.[22]

Two types of deficiency reports are submitted to Congress and referred to the Appropriations Committees. First, an agency may have incurred an actual deficiency, that is, obligated in excess of the amount available to it. Such actions are often referred to as "overobligations." The second type of situation does not involve an actual deficiency or violation. Rather, an appropriation has been apportioned by OMB on a basis that indicates the necessity for a supplemental appropriation.[23]

In earlier years Congress used to act separately on deficiency requests from the agencies, appropriating whatever amounts were necessary in a deficiency bill. But in recent years deficiencies have been mixed in with other requests in a supplemental appropriation bill. No longer is it possible to discover in such legislation which funds are being provided to cover deficiencies. Nor is it possible to tell whether the deficiencies were sanctioned by Congress (as with firefighting funds) or were coercive in nature (the result of unilateral agency commitments). Unless information is displayed in that manner, Congress has no idea of the extent to which the Antideficiency Act is being violated from year to year.

FEED AND FORAGE LAW

Through an obscure funding technique, the Pentagon has been able to skirt the appropriations process and obligate hundreds of millions of dollars. Executive officials make the commitment; at some later point, in perfunctory fashion, Congress pays for it.

The process involves a unique form of contract authority. On most occasions Pentagon officials must come to Congress to justify their budget requests, obtaining authorizations and appropriations with the support of both Houses. Only after that point are executive officials permitted to obligate funds. With the "feed and forage law" the process is reversed. The Pentagon is allowed to enter into obligations first—without any participation by Congress in the decision—and then come to Congress at some later point to obtain funds to liquidate the obligation. By that time the hands of Congress are tied. The obligation is legal and binding. Members of Congress must appropriate whatever is necessary.

The technique of contract authority is not unique. Nor is it new. On any number of occasions Congress has authorized executive officials to enter into contracts in advance of appropriations. The Clean Water Act, discussed in Chapter Eight, is a recent example. Earlier examples can be found as far back as 1789.[24] But such authority was available for a fixed period of time, after which it lapsed. The extraordinary fact about the Pentagon's authority is that it has been available without interruption for more than a century, capable of being invoked at any time. Just as impressive are the amounts of money involved and the statute's inconspicuous quality. The law is a "sleeper," generally unknown to Members of Congress and their staffs.

At present the law is found in title 41 of the U.S. Code, section 11. Sometimes it is referred to as Revised Statute 3732. More familiarly it is known as the "feed and forage law," a name that captures the ancient flavor of this legislation. The law allows the Army, Navy, and Air Force to make contracts and purchases—in advance of appropriations—for clothing, subsistence, forage, fuel, quarters, transportation, or medical and hospital supplies. The authority remains in force year after year, decade after decade, without any action required by Congress other than to appropriate funds to liquidate the obligations.[25]

Besides designating the categories that can be funded, the law contains only one other restriction: obligations incurred "shall not exceed the necessities of the current year." Basically it is open-ended authority, invoked whenever the Department of Defense decides it is time, invoked for whatever amounts the Department thinks necessary.

I have been unable to obtain a full record of how much has been obligated under this authority. However, in the brief period from 1960 to 1972 the Pentagon relied on the feed and forage law to obligate $1.7 billion. Even those statistics, compiled by the Comptroller's Office in the Department of Defense, are quite fragmentary. In the case of the Navy, the Pentagon could not locate data prior to 1966.[26]

Most of what is written and said about the feed and forage law is erroneous and misleading. It is believed to be a Civil War law, since the basic language was adopted in 1861. The Secretary of Defense, a congressional committee, and a number of newspaper accounts have characterized it as a Civil War measure, suggesting that at a time of genuine emergency Congress entrusted to executive officials this extraordinary authority.[27] The argument could then be made that we continue to live under crisis conditions and that therefore this statute, though passed in a different era and under different circumstances, retains its relevance for today.

This account, plausible as it sounds, is mistaken. The feed and forage law is not a Civil War statute. The legislation dates back not to 1861 but to 1799, when Congress authorized the Secretary of War to make purchases and enter into contracts or obligations for "clothing, camp utensils and equipage, medicines and hospital stores" whenever necessary for the troops and armies for the succeeding year.[28] The purpose was to provide American soldiers, particularly those situated in remote outposts, with advance funding authority for essentials.

During the next two decades Members of Congress became concerned about the manner in which executive departments were applying—and misapplying—public funds. Legislation in 1820 represented an important effort to tighten congressional control over the purse. The House Ways and Means Committee reported out a bill to restrict the availability of unexpended balances for the War and Navy Departments. A week later the bill was recommitted to Ways and Means.[29] As rewritten, the bill included additional restrictions on the military departments, such as the practice of transferring funds from one year to the next or from one account to another. The bill also included the following section:

240

SEC. 6. *And be it further enacted*, That no contract shall hereafter be made by the Secretary of State, or of the Treasury, or of the Department of War, or of the Navy, except under a law authorizing the same, or under an appropriation adequate to its fulfilment; and excepting, also, contracts for the subsistence and clothing of the army or navy, and contracts by the Quartermaster Department, which may be made by the Secretaries of those Departments.[30]

During that period it was the responsibility of the Quartermaster's Department to provide all forage, fuel, straw, and stationery for the use of the troops, to provide for their quartering and transportation, and for the transporting of all military stores, camp equipment, and artillery.[31] When the feed and forage law was rewritten in later years, omitting reference to the Quartermaster's Department, it was necessary to add the categories of forage, fuel, quarters, and transportation.

The 1820 bill passed both Houses in substantially the same form as the revised version reported out by Ways and Means. Several Members of the House criticized the executive departments for entering into contracts prior to congressional appropriation. In restricting that practice, Congress decided to allow some flexibility in the case of contracts for the subsistence and clothing of the War and Navy Departments and contracts by the Quartermaster's Department. An element of flexibility seemed particularly appropriate since other forms of executive discretion—access to unexpended balances and transfer authority—were being brought under closer legislative control. A desire to supply the elementary needs of the military was the primary impulse behind enactment of section 6 of the 1820 law. A similar consideration led to the retention of transfer authority in 1852 in the case of Presidential shifts of funds for subsistence of the Army, for forage, medical and hospital departments, and the Quartermaster's Department.[32]

Several years later, in *The Floyd Acceptances* (1868), a dissenting opinion by Justice Nelson expressed this appreciation for the feed-and-forage provision:

> It will thus be seen that contracts for the subsistence and clothing of the army and navy, by the secretaries, are not tied up by any necessity of an appropriation or law authorizing it. The reason of this is obvious. The army and navy must be fed, and clothed, and cared for at all times and places, and especially when in distant service. The army in Mexico or Utah are not to be disbanded and left to take care of themselves, because the appropriation by Congress, for the service, has been exhausted, or no law can be found on the statute book authorizing a contract for supplies.[33]

Part of that flexibility was needed because of inadequate transportation and communication facilities. In 1840, whether by rivers, canals, or turnpikes, it took almost one week to travel from New York to Cleveland and three weeks to go from New York to Chicago.[34] It was not until 1844 that a telegraph message was transmitted over the first experimental line running from Baltimore to Washington. The telephone was not available for distant communication until 1884, marking a conversation held between New York and Boston. While those advances in technology brought the major cities together, they offered little help in relaying messages from Washington to military outposts.

Limited contract authority was also needed whenever Congress failed to pass the regular Army or Navy appropriation bill on time. Although Congress changed the fiscal year in 1842, to begin July 1 instead of January 1, the six months additional time was still insufficient to avoid late appropriations. For example, in August 1856 Congress adjourned without having passed the Army appropriation bill. President Pierce, calling Congress back in special session for that purpose, recognized that he had partial authority to contract for the supply of clothing and subsistence. But he warned the legislators that failure to appropriate funds for the Army would require contracts of enlistment to be broken and the Army disbanded. To discharge large numbers of men in remote places, he said, would be an injustice, particularly where employment opportunities were few. Pierce also raised the specter of Indian attacks. Disbandment of the Army would invite "hoards of predatory savages from the Western plains and the Rocky Mountains to spread devastation along a frontier of more than 4,000 miles in extent and to deliver up the sparse population of a vast tract of country to rapine and murder." Nine days later the Army appropriation bill was enacted into law.[35]

LEGISLATION IN 1860-61

The feed and forage law encountered a curious experience in 1860 and 1861. When the Legislative, Executive, and Judicial Appropriation Bill was reported out of House Ways and Means on March 19, 1860, it contained a prohibition on transfer of funds between fiscal years, a prohibition on transfer of funds between appropriation accounts, and repeal of a section which had given departmental heads authority to cover deficiencies by drawing on surpluses. The restriction on transfers between years was removed during House debate. The Senate deleted the other restrictions, but did adopt an amendment with several features, including a variant of the feed and forage law, a requirement for agencies to advertise their needs before buying supplies, and a restriction on the purchase of patented inventions. All three features were retained in the compromise measure agreed to by the two Houses.[36]

At this point the picture becomes confusing. Early in 1861 Members of both Houses expressed concern about the restriction on patented arms and the requirement to advertise, claiming that they limited the Navy's access to improved forms of weapons and military supplies. By the time

Congress had completed action on the naval appropriation bill, modifying the 1860 language, it inadvertently repealed the feed-and-forage provision.[37] Within a few weeks Congress remedied its error by adding the following provision to the Sundry Civil Expenses Act:

> No contract or purchase shall hereafter be made, unless the same be authorized by law or be under an appropriation adequate to its fulfilment, except in the War and Navy Departments, for clothing, subsistence, forage, fuel, quarters, or transportation, which, however, shall not exceed the necessities of the current year.[38]

CONTEMPORARY FORM

Current authority (41 U.S.C. 11) differs from the 1861 law in three respects. The feed and forage law now applies to the Army, Navy, and Air Force. A second change occurred in 1906 with the addition of the words "medical and hospital supplies" after "transportation." Third, the defense appropriation act of 1966 added a reporting requirement for any exercise of authority granted in 41 U.S.C. 11.[39]

The fact that Congress waited until 1966 to require reports is remarkable testimony to the weakness of legislative oversight. For more than a century executive officials were allowed to contract in advance of appropriations without telling Congress. Just as serious, the reports that have been made since 1966 are of limited utility. They merely state that, pursuant to the feed and forage law, the Pentagon has authorized deficiencies to be incurred in certain appropriation accounts, e.g., "Operation and Maintenance, Navy." No dollar amounts are mentioned. I was advised by staff people that the Pentagon could not give dollar figures until the deficiency was actually incurred (when contracts were entered into). And yet a subsequent discussion with someone in the Pentagon, who actually administered the law, showed that to be false. Dollar figures are known at the time the reports are sent to Congress. A DOD directive requires military services to indicate the amount of the deficiency (overobligation) when they apply to the Comptroller of the Defense Department. If he approves their request, the anticipated dollar figures are used as ceilings on the authority of a military service to incur deficiencies.[40] In short, budget officials in the Pentagon know the dollar amounts but Members of Congress and their staffs do not.

The basic mechanism of the feed and forage law has been amplified. In 1959 Congress passed a law allowing the Secretary of Defense, upon determination by the President that such was necessary, to provide for the cost of an airborne alert by contracting in advance of an appropriation. The cost would be an excepted expense under the feed and forage law. In 1961 Congress provided the same financial authority for increasing the number of military personnel on active duty. Both of those features —for airborne alerts and military personnel—have been repeated each year in defense appropriation bills.[41]

In 1974 Senator Abourezk offered an amendment to repeal the feed and forage law. After Senator Stennis, chairman of the Armed Services Committee, promised to hold hearings at some point during 1974, and on the basis of those hearings make recommendations, Abourezk withdrew his amendment.[42] Hearings were not held that year.

Is the feed and forage law necessary for military operations? It is apparent that the original conditions giving rise to the law have long since disappeared. The financial embarrassments facing departmental heads more than a century ago have no counterpart today. If Congress fails to pass appropriations for the Defense Department by the start of the fiscal year, the Department is covered by a continuing resolution. As a stopgap funding measure, the resolution enables the Pentagon to continue operations uninterrupted while awaiting final action on the regular appropriation bill. At various times in the year the

Defense Department can come to Congress for supplemental assistance to meet unusual and unanticipated expenses.

A century ago the feed and forage law was needed to protect soldiers located in remote frontier outposts, living a precarious existence and forced to disband in the event that Congress failed to appropriate funds on time. No one could make that argument today. Also, Congress is no longer a part-time legislative body. The 19th and 20th centuries differ markedly in the length of congressional sessions. From 1851 to 1861 the long session of a Congress (the first year) averaged 236 days, while the short session (the second year) averaged only 90 days. Today there is virtually no short session. As a practical matter Congress is in session year-round, capable of providing emergency assistance to any agency.

A century ago executive agencies were being stripped of their authority to transfer funds between accounts, to use balances on hand from prior years, and other forms of discretionary spending authority. Today the Defense Department has ample use of multi-year funds, transfers, reprogrammings, contingency funds, stock funds, and other means of adjusting to new and unexpected demands. No longer are the military departments subjected to line-item control, as was the case in the 19th century. Large lump-sum amounts are made available for military personnel and for operation and maintenance; within those accounts the Pentagon is allowed considerable leeway in reprogramming funds.

The feed and forage law is redundant for yet another reason. The Congressional Budget and Impoundment Control Act of 1974 signaled an intention by Congress to regain control over funding totals and budget priorities. The feed and forage law converts Congress into a perfunctory agency instead of a vital instrument for determining national priorities. Its constitutional responsibilities over war are impaired by the availability of the feed and forage law. In 1973, when Defense Secretary Richardson appeared before the Senate Appropriations Committee, he said that the Pentagon could continue to bomb Cambodia even if Congress denied the request for an additional $500 million in transfer authority. Said Richardson: "We will consider that we have the authority to do it anyway. We can find the money to do it anyway. . . . We could invoke section 3732 authority. . . ."[43]

Nothing is more basic in constitutional terms than reserving to Congress the decision of where to commit public funds. Congress should not tolerate the continued existence of a law that allows the Pentagon to circumvent the appropriations process. The feed and forage law served a useful purpose a century ago. It no longer does.

CONTRACT NEGOTIATION

The Armed Services Procurement Act of 1947 established a general rule of competition. It also provided for 17 situations in which the rule could be waived. Instead of relying primarily on free market competition, with the contract awarded to the lowest bidder, administrators have invoked the 17 exceptions and depended heavily on sole-source procurement. Other broad powers are also available to executive officials. They decide claims against the Government and waive penalty provisions in contracts; accept goods with poor performance, late delivery, or reduced service life; make advance and progress payments to contractors; and change specifications, adjust prices, and restructure contracts. Such decisions can lead to billions in additional costs.[44]

The design of a contract often puts Congress in the position of having to appropriate hundreds of millions to cover "cost overruns" and "cost growth." The total-package procurement contract for the C-5A cargo plane was supposed to act as a brake on large cost increases. When the contract was drawn up with Lockheed, it appeared to have a firm price commitment. Nevertheless, a complex repricing formula allowed for built-in increases (what critics called a "get-well clause" or the "golden handshake").

As late as September 1968 the Air Force was telling Congress that costs were in line with earlier estimates. Two months later A. E. Fitzgerald, a cost analyst with the Air Force, revealed to Congress that the original estimate of $3.37 billion for 120 C-5A aircraft had soared to $5.33 billion. At that point Congress was faced with unattractive options: appropriate the extra $2 billion to cover the cost overrun or allow fewer aircraft to be produced at the original total cost. Had Congress known the full cost at the outset, it might have decided not to proceed with the project at all. But the Pentagon permitted Lockheed to "buy in" with an unrealistically low bid and then concealed the cost overrun for as long as possible.[45]

In 1974 Congress passed legislation to create a centralized office to oversee Federal procurement of goods and services. Part of the responsibility of the Office of Federal Procurement Policy, located within OMB, is to establish policies, procedures, and practices which will require the Government to utilize competitive procurement methods to the maximum extent practicable.[46] Reduction in sole-source procurement may be one result. One would hope that the Office could establish principles so that contracts will be designed with fewer opportunities and incentives for buy-ins and cost overruns.

The Office may also want to examine a 1958 statute which authorizes the President to modify any defense contract "whenever he deems that such action would facilitate the national defense." The Defense Department contended that enactment of the law "would cause no apparent increase in the budgetary requirement of the Department of Defense," but no such restriction appeared in the statute. The 1958 statute remains in effect during a national emergency declared by Congress or by the President. The United States is currently in a state of national emergency because of a proclamation issued by President Truman on December 16, 1950, following China's intervention in Korea. A quarter century later that proclamation has yet to be terminated.[47]

From 1959 through 1970, the Pentagon's authority to modify contracts was invoked 3,407 times, amounting to a total of $69,916,000. The average dollar amount for those twelve years was less than $6 million a year, ranging from a low of $2,420,000 to a high of $14,469,000.[48] Considering the magnitudes of defense contracting, such adjustments were modest.

In 1971 the top blew off. The contract with Lockheed Aircraft for the C-5A was modified at a cost of $500 million. In that same year the contract with Lockheed for the AH-56A Cheyenne helicopters was modified at a cost of $123 million. With those two actions, the cost of the contract waiver law soared to $629,004,000 in 1971. Thereafter it settled back to more normal levels: $2,840,000 in 1972 and $5,330,000 in 1973.[49]

The experience with Lockheed led to legislative restrictions in 1973. The defense authorization act contained a provision to limit the contract modification law to $25 million unless the Armed Services Committees are notified in writing prior to the proposed obligation by the Pentagon. During the following 60 days of continuous session either House may adopt a resolution of disapproval. Similar restrictions were placed on loans by the Pentagon and on advance payments to defense contractors.[50]

GENERAL ACCOUNTING OFFICE

It is widely assumed that the General Accounting Office is empowered to decide the legality of a payment of public funds and that such determinations are binding on adminis-

249

trative officials. Several decisions have indeed been issued by the Comptroller General to disapprove expenditures by the executive branch.[51]

However, large areas of executive activity are outside the scope of GAO review. In the case of contract modifications by the Pentagon, pursuant to the 1958 law, GAO has no legal authority to go behind a determination by the Pentagon that the exercise of that authority is necessary. Confidential funds, secret funds, and other parts of the budget are inaccessible to GAO auditing.[52]

Furthermore, it is possible for the executive branch to invoke its own sense of prerogatives and oppose a GAO decision. In a letter directed to the Secretary of State on December 13, 1960, the Comptroller General advised that program funds under the Mutual Security Act would no longer be available because of the Secretary's failure to forward certain documents and records to Congress or to the GAO, as required by the Act. The Attorney General rejected that opinion on the ground that Congress could not infringe on the right of "executive privilege" by forcing the President to release information which he considered to be injurious to the national security or the public interest. Congress rewrote the Act to allow the President to withhold information on the condition that he issue a certification that he has forbidden the release and state his reason for so doing.[53]

Also in 1960, the Defense Department entered into a written agreement with a consortium of five NATO countries formed to produce Hawk surface-to-air missiles in Europe. The Pentagon, lacking sufficient funds to fulfill its part of the agreement, inserted a clause stating that the U.S. commitment was "subject to availability of funds." GAO reached the following conclusions: no express authorization existed in law to allow DOD to enter into the purchase agreement; the commitment did not comply with the intent of the Antideficiency Act; and the Pentagon had firmly committed the United States to buy four missile systems at an unknown cost. Although GAO advised the Pentagon to take certain actions, the Defense Department in December 1970 stated that it did not agree that there had been any violation of law and that it did not consider any corrective action necessary.[54]

The GAO also clashed with the executive branch over the legality of the "Philadelphia Plan." In order to work on Federally assisted projects, contractors had to set specific goals for hiring members of minority groups. In 1969 the Comptroller General held that the Plan conflicted with the 1964 Civil Rights Act, which prohibited any kind of preferential treatment on the basis of race, color, or national origin. The Comptroller General said it did not matter whether one called the hiring commitment a "goal" or a "quota."[55]

The Secretary of Labor promptly announced that the Administration would continue to press ahead with the Philadelphia Plan. He said that the interpretation of the Civil Rights Act had been vested by Congress in the Justice Department, which had approved the plan as consistent with the Act. The U.S. Court of Appeals for the Third Circuit later upheld the legality of the Philadelphia Plan. The court justified this use of Presidential power partly on the Chief Executive's implied power—as it relates to economical procurement policy—to ensure that "the largest possible pool of qualified manpower" be available for the accomplishment of federal projects.[56]

GAO investigations, as in the case of payments to Free World Forces, have been hampered by refusals on the part of executive officials to allow GAO to have access to future planning information, routine evaluative reports, and program evaluation group reports. To offset such constraints, it has been proposed that the Comptroller General have subpoena power to compel agencies to make available books, accounts, and other contractor records required for a GAO investigation. Approximately 40 executive agencies, independent boards, and commissions have subpoena authority now.[57]

MILITARY COMMITMENTS

In a number of other cases the President has presented Congress with a *fait accompli* and in effect compelled it to appropriate the necessary funds. The commitment of troops to Korea by President Truman is one postwar example. Military intervention began prior to the second United Nations resolution of June 27, 1950, and, despite the provisions of the United Nations Participation Act of 1945, no attempt was made to obtain congressional approval for the venture.[58]

The war in Southeast Asia, including the intervention in Cambodia by President Nixon, is another example of Presidential commitment first and a request for congressional support second. In the Paris Agreement of January 27, 1973, the Nixon Administration attempted to commit the Government to heavy reconstruction costs without any participation or involvement by Congress. Article 21 of the Agreement states that the United States "will contribute to healing the wounds of war and to postwar reconstruction of the Democratic Republic of Vietnam and throughout Indochina." The Administration contemplated a $7.5 billion five-year reconstruction program, a third of that earmarked for North Vietnam. Two years later President Ford expressed his own view of the commitment to the South Vietnamese. As he looked back at the Paris Agreement and "the promises that were made, as long as they were willing to fight against aggression and invasion, that we had an obligation to help them with military equipment on a replacement basis."[59]

The subordinate position in which members of the executive branch place Congress is illustrated by President Ford's request, early in 1975, for supplemental military assistance of $300 million to South Vietnam and $222 million to Cambodia. In his words: "We—the Executive and Legislative Branches together—must meet our responsibilities." Note the "We." It was first person singular when the executive branch committed forces to Vietnam, escalated the military activity, and conducted negotiations leading to the Paris Agreement. When it comes time to appropriate funds the plural enters. Vice President Rockefeller, with more than three decades of experience in Federal public policy, demonstrated his own understanding of the Constitution by claiming: "We have a moral obligation that was made by the Secretary of State."[60]

Has executive preeminence in foreign affairs reached the point where multibillion-dollar commitments can be entered into without legislative participation, other than paying the bills? That would be intolerable even if the commitment had been fashioned as a treaty, backed by Senate ratification. The Senate is not at liberty, in conjunction with the President, to consent to treaties that commit the Nation to vast expenditures. Although treaties (and even Presidential agreements) are regarded as binding upon the United States under international law, practical limits exist. Otherwise, the fiscal prerogative of the House of Representatives would be gravely impaired. Dean Acheson, scarcely a champion of legislative power, recognized that fact two decades ago:

> Today it is of new and pressing importance that the House have understanding of foreign affairs. The time has passed when the Senate monopolized the congressional function in this field, since it is the execution of policy, calling for legal authority, funds, and men, which is the ultimate test of success or failure.[61]

Throughout the history of the Federal Government, dating back to the first Administration, the House of Representatives has asserted itself whenever international agreements affected the purse. The House joined with the

Senate in 1792 in authorizing the Postmaster General to make arrangements with foreign postmasters for the reciprocal receipt and delivery of letters and packets.[62] In such matters, directly affecting revenue, the House shared a coequal status with the Senate.

During the dispute over the Jay Treaty, in 1796, Albert Gallatin explained to his colleagues in the House that certain powers delegated to Congress as a whole, such as the authority to regulate trade, might clash with the treaty-making power. Must the House acquiesce in decisions made solely by the President and the Senate? Gallatin disagreed, adding that the general power of Congress to grant appropriations was another restraining force on treaties. On April 7, 1796, the House adopted a resolution stating that whenever a treaty stipulated regulations on any of the subjects submitted by the Constitution to the power of Congress, it was the constitutional right and duty of the House of Representatives to "deliberate on the expediency or inexpediency of carrying such Treaty into effect, and to determine and act thereon, as, in their judgment, may be most conducive to the public good."[63]

On other occasions the House has offered opposition to treaties that required appropriations, two examples being the Gadsden purchase treaty with Mexico in 1853 and the Alaskan purchase treaty with Russia in 1867. The need to have support from the House of Representatives for certain treaties was recognized in a reciprocity treaty with the Hawaiian Islands in 1876. A proviso made the treaty dependent on legislative consent by both Houses.[64]

If the President and the Senate, acting jointly through the treaty process, are restricted in their ability to commit the Nation to financial obligations, surely the President acting unilaterally is under even greater restraint. As Louis Henkin has noted, while Congress "usually feels legally, politically, or morally obligated to appropriate funds to maintain the President's foreign affairs establishment and to implement his treaties and other foreign undertakings, Con-

254

gress can readily refuse to appropriate when it believes the President has exceeded his powers."[65]

Congress has tried in recent years to impose procedural limitations on Presidential initiatives in foreign and military affairs. The National Commitments Resolution, adopted by the Senate in 1969 by a vote of 70 to 16, defined a national commitment as "the use of the armed forces of the United States on foreign territory, or a promise to assist a foreign country, government, or people by the use of the armed forces or financial resources of the United States, either immediately or upon the happening of certain events." The resolution declared it to be the sense of the Senate that a national commitment by the United States results "only from affirmative action taken by the executive and legislative branches of the United States Government by means of a treaty, statute, or concurrent resolution of both Houses of Congress specifically providing for such commitment."[66] As a sense-of-the-Senate resolution it is not legally binding, but was intended to express the view that commitments are not to be made by unilateral executive actions.

In 1972 Congress passed a statute requiring that all international agreements, other than treaties, be transmitted to Congress (both Houses) within 60 days of their execution. Legislation since that time has proposed that executive agreements shall come into force 60 days after being transmitted to Congress, unless both Houses pass a concurrent resolution within that period disapproving the agreement. Such legislation passed the Senate in 1974, toward the end of the 93d Congress, but the House did not act.[67] In order to comprehend the financial implications, Congress should require the executive branch to estimate the long-term costs over a five- or ten-year period for each agreement that exceeds a certain dollar threshold.

The War Powers Resolution of 1973, touted as a restraint on Presidential power, has the potential of widening it. Although the purpose was to insure that the collective judgment of both branches will apply to the introduction of U.S. Armed Forces into hostilities, the procedures established do not guarantee congressional involvement. The President is merely directed "in every possible instance" to consult with Congress before introducing U.S. forces.[68]

In each of these situations, whether it be a financial commitment under an executive agreement, or a military commitment under the War Powers Resolution, much will depend on the attitude of the President and his advisers. Shall they act alone, avoiding what they perceive to be the infirmities of the legislative process? Shall a premium be placed on speed and secrecy, thus denying Congress any significant role? Or shall commitments be entered into after public debate and appropriate legislative action, with executive officials confident that the moral obligation of an international agreement will receive the necessary domestic support? The destructive consequences of the past decade counsel against independent executive action. Will we heed the counsel? Will we, after a few years, even remember it? Keeping that lesson fresh in our minds may provide the most effective guarantee for close consultation and cooperation between the two branches.

Conclusion

In the minds of the Framers, the power of the purse was fixed indelibly as a prerogative of Congress. Alexander Hamilton declared that the Constitution was designed to secure these important ends: "that the *purpose* the *limit* and the *fund* of every expenditure should be ascertained by a previous law." No money could be spent unless a law prescribed an object, defined the extent, and established a fund. More briefly, in the words of James Madison, "the legislative department alone has access to the pockets of the people. . . ."[1]

Events have so transpired that instead of public laws determining how taxpayer funds are spent today, the crucial commitments are often made by administrative officials. The constitutional system has deteriorated in part because of an impractical construction placed upon the separation of power doctrine. With a passion for order and precise jurisdictions, some political observers would restrict Congress to "broad policy" questions while reserving to administrators all of the "day to day" decisions. This pure form of separated powers was advanced by Woodrow Wilson in one of his veto messages:

> The Congress and the Executive should function within their respective spheres. Otherwise, efficient and responsible management will be impossible and progress

impeded by wasteful forces of disorganization and obstruction. The Congress has the power and the right to grant or deny an appropriation, or to enact or refuse to enact a law, but once an appropriation is made or a law is passed the appropriation should be administered or the law executed by the executive branch of the Government.[2]

Public policy is not so easily apportioned into watertight compartments. Policy-making is a dynamic, ongoing phenomenon, beginning with the inception of an idea and carrying through to its enactment and implementation. Although we think of legislation and administration as consecutive steps, they continually interact and fold back into a larger process. If Congress is to play the role of major policy-setter, it must avoid situations where budget execution becomes a controlling factor, locking Congress into commitments and decisions ahead of time.

The record shows that Congress has been active in trying to monitor the expenditure of funds, but generally it is after an abuse has been committed, after the Administration has already involved the Government in substantial outlays. Legislative efforts have been sporadic and *ad hoc* rather than systematic and sustained. Congress succeeds in closing the door but only after the horse has gone.

The weakness of legislative oversight in the spending area is part of a long-standing paradox. Legislators derive credit and satisfaction from the steps needed to enact a bill. To pursue its implementation is regarded as tedious and frustrating, as indeed it is, and of little value in advancing in committee ranks or in being reelected. The public is similarly shortsighted in understanding the constitutional significance of the expenditure phase. A student of English history has noted that numerous revolts have been triggered by high or unauthorized taxation, and yet there is only one known instance of a revolt against "extravagant

258

or unauthorised expenditure—that of Robin of Redesdale in 1469. . . ." The principle of taxation by the consent of the people has always been a clear issue; there is no comparable concern about the spending of the tax proceeds.[3]

A customary congressional control has been to delegate broad discretionary authority, confining that discretion by a combination of statutory guidelines and a trust in the integrity and good-faith efforts of executive officials. That may be a reasonable and practical approach when dealing with career men and women, who adhere to professional standards and must maintain good relationships—year in and year out—with Members of Congress and their staffs. Valuable indeed is the official who cultivates trust on Capitol Hill, who earns a reputation for honesty and dependability, who strives to carry out the intentions of Congress instead of finding ways to circumvent them. No finer tribute exists than the praise bestowed upon William Jump, former budget official with the Department of Agriculture. A Member of the House of Representatives recalled: "Members of Congress through long experience knew that they could trust Mr. Jump. They admired his vast knowledge and understanding of Departmental activities and finances, but over and above and beyond that they respected his integrity in always giving them the full and true picture of Departmental activities."[4]

Delegation has had less happy results when Congress deals with appointees recruited from the outside, brought in with or without professional standards, often with little or no interest in maintaining healthy relationships with Congress. Their main motivation is to accomplish a particular job within a particular span of time. If accomplishing that task happens to antagonize Congress, if trust is broken and discretion abused, that is of less importance. Within a few years the appointees can return to private life, leaving to their replacements and to careerists the job of patching up relations with Congress.[5]

This problem, of increasing seriousness, requires a new attitude on the part of Congress toward the confirmation power. Generally Congress feels an obligation to go along with a Presidential appointment unless the individual is known to have committed a loathsome crime. But Members of Congress should not have the slightest compunction in rejecting outright anyone who displays ineptitude for the task about to be assumed. Mediocrity, incompetence, lack of commitment to congressional programs and policies, rigidity of thought, inadequate background and experience —those are a few of the traits sufficient to disqualify an appointee. Secretaries and assistant secretaries are not mere assistants to a President; they are being called upon to administer the programs enacted by Congress. Rather than have Congress under pressure to consent to a President's choice, the burden should be on the President to select a person with impeccable credentials.[6]

Unless Congress strengthens its control over budget execution, it cannot legislate back to reality its vaunted "power of the purse." In the Steel Seizure Case of 1952 Justice Jackson reminded us of the adage, "The tools belong to the man who can use them." His parting observation then retains its pertinence today: "We may say that power to legislate for emergencies belongs in the hands of Congress, but only Congress itself can prevent power from slipping through its fingers."[7] Lest we neglect our own duties as citizens, I should add that Members of Congress are constantly being educated and re-educated as to their proper responsibilities.

Up to this point I have discussed the role of Congress in "administrative" matters, be it execution of policy or the appointment of officials. In urging a fresh examination of congressional duties in the budget oversight area, I do not mean to parrot the current cry for legislative "reassertion." I do not want to offer expedient interpretations to satisfy momentary passions. The conclusions reached here are grounded upon the historical record, the perspective of the last two centuries, and what I think our constitutional system requires.

Reform advocates can learn something from past efforts. Regardless of good intentions, reforms have mixed and sometimes perverse results. It frequently happens that the adoption of a reform proposal, intended to drive out one evil, simply creates another that proves harder to extirpate. If executive officials have a pressing need for flexibility, the prohibition of one type of discretionary action will be but a prelude to a new form of administrative behavior, which, when discovered, will be the subject of additional legislative controls. Take away the power to make transfers and agency officials pad their budgets. Eliminate discretionary authority altogether and agencies incur deficiencies. Give the President the power to apportion funds—as a means of preventing deficiencies—and he uses that power to impound funds and further his own policies. So, first, let us fully appreciate and understand the historical record.

Second, the impulse to deny discretionary authority altogether should be resisted. There are any number of reasons why obligations and outlays by administrators may have to differ from appropriations by legislators. Appropriations are made many months, and sometimes years, in advance of expenditures. Congress acts with imperfect knowledge in trying to legislate in fields that are highly technical and constantly undergoing change. New circumstances will develop to make obsolete and mistaken the decisions reached by Congress at the appropriation stage. It is not practicable for Congress to adjust to each new development by passing separate supplemental appropriation bills. Were Congress to control expenditures by confining administrators to narrow statutory details, it would perhaps protect its power of the purse but it would not protect the purse itself. The realities and complexities of public policy require executive discretion for the sound management of public funds.

Third, while it is an easy matter to justify the need for executive flexibility, that is an abstract term capable of hiding much mischief. Executive officials regularly complain about the vast amount of "uncontrollables" in the budget that deny them room to maneuver. Nevertheless, when exigencies arise, they manage to come up with a hundred million or so to finance the Cambodian intervention. The Pentagon, crying poverty, repeatedly demonstrates a talent for uncovering a few hundred million here and there to finance new aspirations. It is evident that in a number of areas, including covert financing, impoundment, reprogramming, transfers, and unauthorized commitments, Congress has yet to find an effective means of controlling executive actions. Public policy is then decided by administrators rather than elected officials.

The results are often incongruous. Congress goes through the exercise of authorizing and appropriating funds but the money is never spent. On the other hand, Congress can find itself compelled to pay for administrative commitments it never authorized. The expenditure process, by its very nature, requires substantial discretion for administrators. They need to exercise judgment and take responsibility for their actions, but those actions ought to be directed toward executing congressional, not administrative, policy. Let there be discretion, but channel it and use it to satisfy the programs and priorities established by Congress.[8]

Such a recommendation presupposes that Congress state clearly what it wants. Frequently that is not so. Agencies receive mixed signals from Congress, resulting from different laws sponsored and cleared by different committees, or from loose-ends and ambiguities arising out of awkward compromises in conference committees. The door is then left ajar for the Executive to substitute his interpretation for whatever the legislative compromises were intended to be.

Fourth, as a means of harnessing discretionary actions, much more is needed in the way of visibility. We need to know more about how funds are spent. For a number of years the Joint Committee on the Reduction of Federal Expenditures has prepared a "scorekeeping report" to keep Congress informed of its actions on budget requests. A comparable document could be devised to let Congress know what is happening to the money it appropriates. Much of the material is already available. Hundreds of valuable agency reports are sent to Congress and parcelled out to committees and subcommittees. The only public notice is a seldom read section in the Congressional Record called "Executive Communications," which lists agency reports on transfers, deficiencies, contract modifications, use of contingency funds, etc. GAO reports are summarized in the Record each month. Still other studies are published by the committees, the Congressional Research Service, and private organizations.

What is lacking is a central legislative body (such as the new Congressional Budget Office) to compile this information, analyze it, and present the results to all Members of Congress. Essential aspects should be printed in the Congressional Record. Other evaluations can be made available in the form of House and Senate documents. The structure and content of CBO reports would be sharpened by regular hearings on budget execution by the Budget Committees, the Appropriations Committees, the Government Operations Committees, and other committees devoted to oversight questions. If discretionary actions are soundly based, exposure and analysis cannot hurt. If they are not, all the more reason to make them known.

Fifth, the compilation, analysis, and dissemination of budget execution material must be done with a fine sense of selectivity. Distinctions need to be made between the routine and the significant. If not, agencies will be burdened and distracted by time-consuming paperwork, taxpayer funds wasted on useless reporting, and Congress bewildered and stupefied by a snowstorm of facts and figures. The indiscriminate call for special messages on all impoundments was a major defect of the budget reform act of 1974. Painstaking efforts are needed to select from the thousands of administrative actions the relative few that deserve congressional attention.

This appeal, I know, is partly whistling in the dark. Individual Members of Congress are free to discuss matters as they like. Political needs, pressures of time, and lack of access to information will not always dovetail with standards of objective and accurate reporting. I recall that in 1971 both Houses expressed dismay when OMB reported the impoundment of more than $12 billion. A senior official in OMB subsequently spent hours of his time in distinguishing between funds withheld for routine financial administration ($10.5 billion) and funds withheld for policy reasons ($1.7 billion). Congress ignored his efforts. Members continued to decry the impoundment of "$12 billion." Perhaps statistics developed by CBO and GAO would have a firmer footing in Congress, although there is no assurance of that.

Sixth, we need better techniques of accountability. Congress has little recourse at present when faced with administrative violations and abuses. The party who is officially responsible, at the departmental level, rarely knows what is going on in the bowels of his own organization, where some of the infractions occur. Woodrow Wilson correctly counseled us that there is "no danger in power, if only it be not irresponsible. If it be divided, dealt out in shares to many, it is obscured; and if it be obscured, it is made irresponsible."[9] Statutory penalties against executive violations, in the form of fines and imprisonment, are too heavy-handed to be invoked. To penalize an agency by cutting

264

back its budget is to cripple the very programs that Congress has brought into existence.

Visibility and accountability are harsh standards for members of the legislative and executive branches who prefer doing business in less public ways. "Government in the sunshine" is not in their interest. Yet Congress is moving in that direction: the procedures for reprogramming, reports on transfers and contingency funds, the mechanism contemplated by the budget reform act of 1974, open committee meetings and amendments to the Freedom of Information Act. The force of that direction grows stronger from year to year.

Last, the principle of accountability applies equally to Congress as it does to the agencies. In many instances decisions regarding budget execution are handled by subcommittees and agencies when they should have been brought to the floor for action by the full Congress. Members can use their influence to force agencies to bend the law in order to satisfy constituent needs. Here we have a situation where an agency may prefer less discretion from Congress, may indeed ask for precise statutory directives, to limit the opportunity for that kind of abuse.

To permit agency flexibility, while at the same time providing for congressional control, we need to establish criteria. What should be the *form* of congressional control: provisions in public law, or nonstatutory directives? What should be the *scope* of control; how do we separate out the routine actions, for agency operations, and allow only those actions of policy significance to come to Congress for review? At what *level* should control be exercised? Under what conditions can matters be safely delegated to committees and subcommittees? When must they be resolved by Congress operating as a whole?

Congress has to rely on the expertise of executive agencies and legislative committees without allowing either to become autonomous and independent. As matters now stand, options are sometimes closed by actions taken and decisions made before a bill ever reaches the floor. In each case the desired system is one that preserves for Congress the freedom to work its will.

References

The only unusual shorthand expression in this section is my handling of committee reports and congressional documents. For example, instead of House Report No. 548, 91st Congress, 2d session, page 53 (1970), I abbreviate the reference to H. Rep. 548, 91-2 (1970), 53. Moreover, a number of standard works are cited with such frequency that I have adopted the following abridgments:

Farrand, *Records*   Max Farrand, ed., *The Records of the Federal Convention of 1787* (4 vols., New Haven: Yale University Press, 1937).

Gallatin, *Writings*   *The Writings of Albert Gallatin*, Henry Adams, ed. (3 vols., Philadelphia: J. B. Lippincott, 1879).

Hamilton, *Papers*   *The Papers of Alexander Hamilton*, Harold C. Syrett, ed. (New York: Columbia University Press, 19 vols., in progress, 1961-73).

————, *Works*   *The Works of Alexander Hamilton*, Henry Cabot Lodge, ed. (12 vols., New York: G. P. Putnam's, 1904).

Jefferson, *Papers*   *The Papers of Thomas Jefferson*, Julian Boyd, ed. (Princeton: Princeton University Press, 19 vols., in progress, 1950-74).

Jefferson, *Writings*	*The Writings of Thomas Jefferson,* Paul Leicester Ford, ed. (10 vols., New York: G. P. Putnam's 1892-1899).
Madison, *Writings*	*The Writings of James Madison,* Gaillard Hunt, ed. (9 vols., G. P. Putnam's, 1900-10).
Polk, *Diary*	*The Diary of James K. Polk,* Milo Milton Quaife, ed. (4 vols., Chicago: A. C. McClurg, 1910).
Richardson, *Messages and Papers*	James D. Richardson, ed., *A Compilation of the Messages and Papers of the Presidents* (20 vols., New York: Bureau of National Literature, 1897-1925).
Roosevelt, *Public Papers*	*The Public Papers and Addresses of Franklin D. Roosevelt,* comp. by Samuel I. Rosenman (13 vols., New York, 1938-50).
Wkly Comp. Pres. Doc.	*Weekly Compilation of Presidential Documents,* published each week by the Government Printing Office since 1965.

INTRODUCTION

[1] Woodrow Wilson, "The Study of Administration," originally published in June 1887 in the *Pol. Sci. Q.* and reprinted there in Dec. 1941. The quotation from Wilson is from the latter, 56 *Pol. Sci. Q.* 481, 482 (1941).

[2] *Improving Federal Budgeting and Appropriations,* hearings before the House Committee on Government Operations, 85-1 (1957), 137. The questioner is Clarence J. Brown of Ohio.

CHAPTER ONE

[1] It would be tedious to recount here all of the studies that have created this impression. A sampling, I hope, will do. Former Budget Director Maurice Stans has written that prior to 1921

"the federal government had no President's budget nor any budgetary system worthy of the name in operation. In that relatively uncomplicated period of our national life, each department and agency of the government decided unilaterally how much money it wanted, and then sent a statement of its requirements to the Treasury. There the estimates were bundled up without any editing or review and sent on to Congress." Maurice Stans, "The President's Budget and the Role of the Bureau of the Budget," 9 *Fed'l Accountant* 5 (1959). Another former Budget Director, Percival Brundige, maintained that prior to 1921 the different departments and branches of the Federal Government prepared their financial requests, which were "assembled in the Treasury Department and presented to Congress without comment or revision." *The Bureau of the Budget* (1970), 3.

Another account claims that "until the adoption of the Budget and Accounting Act in 1921, the Treasury Department simply compiled the various departmental budget requirements and passed them on to Congress. There was no executive budget policy and therefore no fiscal function for the President to perform." Gerhard Colm, "The Executive Office and Fiscal and Economic Policy," 21 *Law & Contemp. Prob.* 710 (1956). See also Horace W. Wilkie, "Legal Basis for Increased Activities of the Federal Budget Bureau," 11 *G.W. L. Rev.* 265, 266 (1943).

The early budget leadership of Alexander Hamilton as "finance minister" is treated as an aberration, a short-lived effort to implant English parliamentary practices onto American soil. By 1800, in the words of a leading scholar on the U.S. budget, "centralized Executive authority in budgetary matters was to remain in abeyance for over a century. Executive departments were to deal directly with the Congressional committees. The Secretary of the Treasury was merely to transmit the departmental Book of Estimates, and the President was to have no direct budgetary responsibilities." Arthur Smithies, *The Budgetary Process in the United States* (1955), 53.

That was also the conclusion of Leonard D. White in his 4-volume history of the Federal Administration. He wrote that after the years of war and military defense from 1811 to 1815, estimates were compiled in the Treasury "without any effort by either the Secretary of the Treasury or the President to review departmental requests or the policy contained in them." During the period from the Jeffersonians to the Civil War, the responsibility of the Treasury Department with respect to the estimates was "limited to that of collecting them into a single document and transmitting them to Congress." The latter half of the 19th century appeared to offer no relief from this pattern. According to White, Presidents from Grant to McKinley "had little, if anything, to do with the level of content of the estimates. . . ." For these three observations by Leonard White, see his *The Jeffersonians* (1951), 68-69; *The Jacksonians* (1954), 77-78; and *The Republican Era* (1958), 97.

[2] See Louis Fisher, *President and Congress* (1972), 15-16. Statutes creating the Departments of Foreign Affairs and War: 1 Stat. 28, 49.

[3] *Annals of Congress*, 1st Cong., 384-89 (May 19 and 20, 1789).

[4] *Ibid.* at 592-93.

[5] *Ibid.* at 594.

[6] 1 Stat. 65, sec. 2 (Sept. 2, 1789). See *Annals*, 1st Cong., at 604, 607. Leonard White concludes that Hamilton drafted the bill; *The Federalists* (1948), 118n.

[7] *Annals*, 1st Cong., 231-32 (April 29, 1789). For activities of this committee see *ibid.* at 291 (May 8, 1789), 621 (July 9, 1789), and *American State Papers*, Finance, i, 11-14. Also *Annals*, 1st Cong., 670-71 (July 24, 1789) and 895 (Sept. 17, 1789).

[8] *Annals*, 2d Cong., 1-2 Sess., 703-08 (Nov. 20, 1792).

[9] *Ibid.* at 899-963 (Feb. 28 to March 1, 1793); *Annals*, 3d Cong., 1-2 Sess., 458 (Feb. 19, 1794); *ibid.* at 463-66 (Feb. 24, 1794) and 954 (Dec. 2, 1794). See Broadus Mitchell, *Alexander Hamilton* (1957-62), ii, 245-86. For breadth of activity, see Mitchell, *Alexander Hamilton*, ii, 297-307, 354-57.

[10] *Annals*, 3d Cong., 1st Sess., 532-33 (March 26, 1794); *ibid.*, 4th Cong., 1st Sess., 159 (Dec. 18, 1795). History of committee is covered by Patrick J. Furlong, "The Origins of the House Committee on Ways and Means," 25 *Wm. & Mary Q.* 587, 603 (1968). For Senate Finance, see *Annals*, 14th Cong., 1st Sess., 20 (Dec. 11, 1815); *ibid.*, 14th Cong., 2d Sess. [referred to hereafter as 14-2], 19, 30, 32 (Dec. 5, 10, and 13,

1816); and *History of the Committee on Finance, United States Senate*, S. Doc. 57, 91-2 (1970), 14ff.

[11] *Annals*, 7-1, 412 (Jan. 7, 1802); *ibid.*, 13-2, 1627-28, 1695 (Feb. 24-26, 1814); *ibid.*, 14-1, 1090-91, 1297-99 (Feb. 28 and March 30, 1816). For criticism of the expenditure committees, see Lucius Wilmerding, Jr., *The Spending Power* (1943), 208-23.

[12] 2 Stat. 80 (1800). Regarding Gallatin, see Henry Adams, *History of the United States of America* (1889-91), i, 238-40, and Gallatin, *Writings*, i, 25.

[13] Henry Adams, *Life of Albert Gallatin* (1879), 389. See also Gallatin, *Writings*, i, 117.

[14] Raymond Walters, Jr., *Albert Gallatin* (1957), 148. See Henry Adams, *History of the United States*, i, 241-42, 272.

[15] Henry Adams, *History of the United States*, iv, 156-67, 366-67; vi, 126-27, 157-58; Henry Adams, *Life of Albert Gallatin*, pp. 167-75.

[16] Monroe's complaint: Charles Francis Adams, ed., *Memoirs of John Quincy Adams* (1874-77), iv, 500-01; vi, 439. Confrontation with Crawford: *ibid.*, vii, 81; see also vi, 388, 390, 394. It has been suggested that this story was "greatly exaggerated by the time it got to Adams." Philip Jackson Green, *The Life of William Harris Crawford* (1965), 221. A contemporary admirer of Crawford wrote that his "efforts to apply, as far as practicable, a rigid accountability to every branch of his department, and to induce the nation to adopt, where it was needed, the Jeffersonian system of retrenchment and economy, have brought upon him the appellation of a Radical." Benjamin F. Butler (Pseud. Americanus), *Sketches of the Life and Character of William H. Crawford* (1824), 34.

[17] *Memoirs of John Quincy Adams*, vii, 359. See also vii, 195, 247.

[18] Richardson, *Messages and Papers*, iii, 1288, 1300-01.

[19] Van Buren's attitude: *ibid.*, iv, 1554 (Sept. 4, 1837). First Annual Message: *ibid.*, iv, 1596 (Dec. 5, 1837); last message: *ibid.*, iv, 1826 (Dec. 5, 1840).

[20] *Ibid.*, iv, 1867-68 (March 4, 1841).

[21] *Ibid.*, iv, 1890-91 (April 9, 1841); see also *ibid.*, iv, 1939-40 (Dec. 7, 1841).

22 *Ibid.*, v, 2056 (Dec. 6, 1842), 2079 (Feb. 13, 1843), and 2122 (Dec. 1843).

23 Polk, *Diary*, i, 48.

24 *Ibid.*, iii, 125-42.

25 *Ibid.*, iii, 213-21; iv, 165-81.

26 Richardson, *Messages and Papers*, vii, 3055 (Dec. 6, 1858). Similar expressions of Administration scrutiny regarding estimates appear in Buchanan's Third Annual Message, *ibid.*, vii, 3104, 3106-07 (Dec. 19, 1859).

27 *Ibid.*, vii, 3279-80 (May 26, 1862), and 3303 (Feb. 14, 1862).

28 1 Stat. 346 (1794); 1 Stat. 621 (1799); 3 Stat. 783 (1823); 4 Stat. 137 (1826); 4 Stat. 175 (1826); 4 Stat. 704 (1834); 5 Stat. 158 (1837); 5 Stat. 668 (1844); 11 Stat. 102 (1856).

29 *Cong. Globe*, 40-1, 10 (March 6, 1867). The membership and powers of the Appropriations Committee were decided the following day, *ibid.* at 12. John Sherman, chairman of the Finance Committee, later explained: "it was agreed that the duties of the [Finance] committee should be divided by referring all appropriations to a committee on appropriations, and I was to choose between the two committees. The House of Representatives had already divided the labors of the committee of ways and means, a corresponding committee to that on finance, among several committees, and the experiment had proved a success." John Sherman, *Recollections* (1895), 335.

30 *Cong. Globe*, 38-2, 1312 (March 2, 1865). For a history of House Appropriations, concentrating mainly on the committee chairmen between 1865 and 1941, see *A History of the Committee on Appropriations: House of Representatives*, by Edward T. Taylor, H. Doc. 299, 77-1 (1941).

31 Grant: Richardson, *Messages and Papers*, ix, 3993 (Dec. 6, 1869). House resolution: 2 Cong. Rec. 211-14 (1873).

32 James A. Garfield, "National Appropriations and Misappropriations," *No. Am. Rev.*, No. 271 (June 1879), 586; also reprinted in James A. Garfield, *Works* (1882), ii, 740-52.

33 Commerce: 7 Cong. Rec. 18-26 (1877); 10 Cong. Rec. 200, 663, 1261 (1880). Agriculture and Forestry: 10 Cong. Rec. 683-86 (1880).

34 17 Cong. Rec. 168-76 (1885). Randall-Morrison dispute: De Alva Stanwood Alexander, *History and Procedure of the*

House of Representatives (1916), 239-50; also recounted by Joseph Cannon, H. Doc. 264, 66-1 (1919), 12-15.

[35] 17 Cong. Rec. 286 (1885).

[36] Thomas B. Reed, "Spending Public Money: Appropriations for the Nation," *No. Am. Rev.*, No. 424 (March 1892), 319, 321.

[37] S. *Journal*, 44-2, 120 (Jan. 17, 1877). 28 Cong. Rec. 42, 132-34 (1895). Comment on "monopolistic dominance": 28 Cong. Rec. 1288 (1896). Dismantling at 32 Cong. Rec. 1212 (1899). For further details see *Committee on Appropriations, United States Senate*, S. Doc. 21, 90-1 (1967), 7-8; David Rothman, *Politics and Power* (1966), 65-67; and Francis S. Hewitt, "Senate Appropriations Process," 16 *Fed'l Accountant* 129, 136-38 (1966-67).

[38] Reed: Henry Jones Ford, "Budget Making and the Work of Government," *The Annals*, Vol. 62 (Nov. 1915), 12. Rollo Ogden, "The Rationale of Congressional Extravagance," 6 *Yale Rev.* 37, 46-47 (May 1897).

[39] As related on May 26, 1915, by Rep. John J. Fitzgerald, chairman of the House Committee on Appropriations, to the New York Constitutional Convention Committee on Finances; "Budget Systems," *Municipal Research*, No. 62 (June 1915), 326.

[40] Veto message: Richardson, *Messages and Papers*, x, 4708 (Aug. 1, 1882). Nast cartoon: *Harper's Weekly*, Aug. 12, 1882, p. 497. Bill enacted into law: 22 Stat. 191 (1882). For resistance by Polk to rivers and harbors bills, see Richardson, *Messages and Papers*, v, 2314 (Aug. 3, 1846); *ibid.*, vi, 2460-63 (Dec. 15, 1847); and Polk, *Diary*, iv, 190. The latter reference is to his discovery that rivers and harbors projects had been smuggled into the Treasury estimates; he directed that they be struck out.

[41] *History of the Committee on Finance: United States Senate*, S. Doc. 91-57, 91-2 (1970), 78. Statistics for pension outlays are from William H. Glasson, *Federal Military Pensions in the United States* (1918), 123. For references to earlier pension frauds, see Leonard D. White, *The Jacksonians*, 413. See also 17 Cong. Rec. 7764-65 (1886), regarding the inability of Congress to consider intelligently the thousands of private pension bills introduced each year, and Talcott Powell, *Tattered Banners* (1933), 130, a caustic treatment of pension agents. The num-

ber of deserters during the Civil War was officially estimated at over a half million, prompting Charles Francis Adams to call the soldiers "far more battle-scared than battle-scarred." He marveled at the amount of "cant and fustian—nauseating twaddle, perhaps, would not be too strong a term," that had been used by Members of Congress in praise of veterans. Henry F. Pringle, *The Life and Times of William Howard Taft* (1929), II, 641.

[42] *Presidential Vetoes, 1789-1968*, compiled by the Senate Library (1969), 31-56.

[43] Richardson, *Messages and Papers*, x, 5001-02 (May 8, 1886).

[44] Claimant with measles: *ibid.* at 5028 (June 23, 1886); deserter: *ibid.* at 5033-34 (June 23, 1886).

[45] *Harper's Weekly*, July 3, 1886, p. 421. For the 43 pension vetoes, see Richardson, *Messages and Papers*, x, 5020-37, and xi, 5038-40 (June 21-23, 1886). The Cleveland pension vetoes are also evaluated by Edward Campbell Mason, *The Veto Power* (1890), 87-93.

[46] Richardson, *Messages and Papers*, xii, 5978 (Dec. 3, 1894); xiii, 6169 (Dec. 7, 1896); and xiii, 6186 (Feb. 22, 1897). For more on the 1888 election, see William H. Glasson, *Federal Military Pensions in the United States* (1918), 226, 278. Tanner's performance in office created such opposition that he had to submit his resignation, which President Harrison immediately accepted. See Harry J. Sievers, *Benjamin Harrison: Hoosier President* (1968), 117-28. Still another target of Cleveland's economy program was the free distribution of seeds by congressmen to their constituents, a program that had grown from $1,000 in 1839 for the distribution of rare and improved varieties of seeds, to a level of $135,000 by 1893 for the distribution of ordinary seeds, bulbs, and cuttings. Cleveland eliminated $100,000 from the estimates, suggesting that the remaining funds be used for the purchase of new and improved seed varieties. Richardson, *Messages and Papers*, xii, 5888-89 (Dec. 4, 1893). Congress ignored his suggestion and appropriated $135,400; 27 Stat. 738-39.

[47] Oscar Kraines, "The Cockrell Committee, 1887-1889: First Comprehensive Congressional Investigation into Administration," 4 *West. Pol. Q.* 583 (1951). For Cockrell-Dockery Commission in 1893-95, see Lloyd Milton Short, *The Development*

of National Administrative Organization in the United States (1923), 278-80; Gustavus A. Weber, *Organized Efforts for the Improvement of Methods of Administration in the United States* (1919), 67-70; and Fred W. Powell, comp., *Control of Federal Expenditures: A Documentary History, 1775-1894* (1939), 706-915.

[48] See *Letters of Theodore Roosevelt* (Morison ed., 1951-54), IV, 1201-02, and *Works of Theodore Roosevelt* (Executive Edition, 1914), IV, 694-98. See also Richardson, *Messages and Papers*, XIV, 6988-90 (Dec. 5, 1905) and 7105 (Dec. 3, 1907); Harold T. Pinkett, "The Keep Commission, 1905-1909: A Rooseveltian Effort for Administrative Reform," 52 *J. Am. Hist.* 297 (1965); and Oscar Kraines, "The President Versus Congress: The Keep Commission, 1905-1909: First Comprehensive Presidential Inquiry into Administration," 23 *West. Pol. Q.* 5 (1970). Budget surpluses and deficits are obtained from U.S. Bureau of the Census, *Historical Statistics of the United States of America, Colonial Times to 1957* (1960), p. 711; yearly shifts in revenue and expenditure are taken from the *Annual Reports of the Secretary of the Treasury on the State of the Finances.*

[49] 33 Stat. 1257, sec. 4 (1905); 34 Stat. 49 (1906). See debate at 40 Cong. Rec. 1272-90 (1906).

[50] *Annual Report of the Secretary of the Treasury, 1908/09*, at 25.

[51] 35 Stat. 1027, sec. 7 (1909). This act was anticipated by George B. Cortelyou, Secretary of the Treasury from 1907 to 1909, in his article "Regulation of the National Budget," *No. Am. Rev.*, Vol. 189, No. 4 (1909), 500. For background of the Act see Henry Jones Ford, *The Cost of the Our National Government* (1910). An early appeal for budget reform is by Allen Johnson, "American Budget Making," 18 *Yale Rev.* 363 (1910). Taft's direction to departmental heads: Richardson, *Messages and Papers*, XV, 7423 (Dec. 7, 1909). Scrutiny of budget estimates: *Annual Report of the Secretary of the Treasury, 1908/09*, at 5; *1909/10*, at 1.

[52] Taft's advice to Congress: Richardson, *Messages and Papers*, XV, 7423-24 (Dec. 7, 1909). The text of the Executive Order is reprinted in Henry Jones Ford, *The Cost of Our National Government* (1910), 115-16. Taft's chagrin: "Budget

Systems," *Municipal Research*, No. 62 (1915), 349: remarks by Taft before the New York Constitutional Convention Committee, June 10, 1915.

[53] 36 Stat. 703 (1910). Congress subsequently granted the Commission $75,000 (36 Stat. 1364), $10,000 (37 Stat. 643), and $75,000 (37 Stat. 417). For progress reports and comments on the Commission by Taft, see Richardson, *Messages and Papers*, xv, 7698-7719, 7736-45; and xvi, 7829-35.

[54] *The Need for a National Budget*, H. Doc. 854, 62-2 (1912), 138. Emphasis in original.

[55] Taft's review of departmental estimates: his Second Annual Message, Dec. 6, 1910, reprinted in Richardson, *Messages and Papers*, xv, 7505. Influence of income tax on budget reform is discussed by James W. Good, 58 Cong. Rec. 7083 (1919), and by James A. Tawney, "Federal Appropriations: Their Rapid Increase," *Review of Reviews*, Vol. 42, No. 3 (1910), 343. At the time of their remarks, both men served as chairman of House Appropriations.

[56] 37 Stat. 415.

[57] William Howard Taft, *Our Chief Magistrate and His Powers* (1916), 64-65. For model budget, see 49 Cong. Rec. 3985 (1913). Rep. Swager Sherley, soon to be chairman of House Appropriations, was the only legislator to express support; *ibid.* at 4349ff. Frederick A. Cleveland, "The Federal Budget," *Proceedings of the Academy of Political Science*, Vol. 3, pp. 167-68 (1912-13) provides more background on the dispute.

[58] Wilson's interest: Ray Stannard Baker, ed., *Woodrow Wilson: Life and Letters* (1927-29), vii, 291-92 (Wilson to Rep. Fitzgerald). See also iv, 212 (Jan. 30, 1913). Fitzgerald's proposals: "Budget Systems," *Municipal Research*, No. 62 (June 1915), 312, 322, 327, 340. See also William Franklin Willoughby, *The Problem of a National Budget* (1918), 146-49.

[59] Willoughby, *Problem of a National Budget*, 29. For 1916 party positions, see Edward Stanwood, *A History of the Presidency* (1898-1916), ii, 344-45, 349, 358. See also Charles Wallace Collins, "The Coming of the Budget System," 15 *So. Atl. Q.* 308 (1916).

[60] December 1917 message: Richardson, *Messages and Papers*, xvii, 8405. Cabinet review of estimates: 58 Cong. Rec. 7143

(1919). Remarks are by Rep. Gilbert N. Haugen, chairman of the House Agriculture Committee.

[61] H. Doc. 1006, 65-2 (1918).

[62] Joseph G. Cannon, *The National Budget*, H. Doc. 264, 66-1 (1919), 28-29, and Edward Fitzpatrick, *Budget Making in a Democracy* (1918), viii-ix, 117.

[63] Cable to Sherley: *New York Times*, Feb. 12, 1919, 7:3. Dependence on treaty: David Houston, *Eight Years With Wilson's Cabinet* (1926), ii, 7-8.

[64] H. Rep. 362, 66-1 (1919), 4.

[65] *Ibid.* at 5.

[66] See *ibid.* at 7. For an example of an "executive budget" concept, which would have reduced the power of Congress in committee and on the floor, see Charles Wallace Collins, "Constitutional Aspects of a National Budget System," 25 *Yale L. J.* 376 (1916).

[67] Wilson's support: Richardson, *Messages and Papers*, xvii, 8810 (Dec. 2, 1919). S. Rep. 524, 66-2 (1920), 2.

[68] Conference report: H. Rep. 1044, 66-2 (1920), 3. Veto: H. Doc. 805, 66-2 (1920), 2. House override attempt: 59 Cong. Rec. 8614 (1920). Modified bill: *ibid.* at 8627 and 8647-58.

[69] 42 Stat. 20 (1921).

CHAPTER TWO

[1] H. Rep. 373, 66-1 (1919), 10. See also 59 Cong. Rec. 8102-21 (1920).

[2] 58 Cong. Rec. 7126 (1919).

[3] 62 Cong. Rec. 3419-20 (1922). See entire debate at 3418-32. Current system is described in Senate Rule xvi, Clause 6(a).

[4] See Richard F. Fenno, Jr., *The Power of the Purse* (1966), 162-63.

[5] U.S. Bureau of the Budget, *Circulars*, "First Budget Regulations," Circular No. 4 (July 1, 1921). Emphasis in original.

[6] Circular No. 51 (Dec. 21, 1921). Circular No. 55 (March 3, 1922). For the development of the Budget Bureau in these early years, see Fritz Morstein Marx, "The Bureau of the Budget: Its Evolution and Present Role" (2 Parts), 39 *Am. Pol. Sci. Rev.* 657, 869 (Aug. and Oct. 1945), and Robert E. Mer-

riam, "The Bureau of the Budget As Part of the President's Staff," *The Annals*, Vol. 307 (1956), 15-23.

[7] Cited in Henry P. Seidemann, "The Preparation of the National Budget," *The Annals*, Vol. 113 (May 1924), 43.

[8] Horace W. Wilkie, "Legal Basis for Increased Activities of the Federal Budget Bureau," 11 *G.W. L. Rev.* 265, 271 (1943).

[9] Circular No. 49 (Dec. 19, 1921). Richard E. Neustadt, "Presidency and Legislation: The Growth of Central Clearance," 48 *Am. Pol. Sci. Rev.* 641, 643-44 (1954).

[10] Early studies on central clearance include Carl R. Sapp, "Executive Assistance in the Clearance Process," 6 *Pub. Adm. Rev.* 10 (1946), and John H. Reese, "The Role of the Bureau of the Budget in the Legislative Process," 15 *J. Pub. L.* 63 (1966). For a critical study of the manner in which the Budget Bureau discharged its review function, see Arthur Maass, "In Accord With the Program of the President?," 4 *Public Policy* 77 (1953).

Recent studies of central clearance include Robert S. Gilmour, "Central Legislative Clearance: A Revised Perspective," 31 *Pub. Adm. Rev.* 150 (1971), and Allen Schick, "The Budget Bureau That Was: Thoughts on the Rise, Decline, and Future of a Presidential Agency," 35 *Law & Contemp. Prob.* 519, 525-28 (1970). For additional views on contacts and relationships between Budget Bureau personnel and executive agencies, see James W. Davis and Randall B. Ripley, "The Bureau of the Budget and Executive Agencies: Notes on Their Interaction," 29 *J. Pol.* 749 (1967), and L. L. Wade, "The U.S. Bureau of the Budget: As Agency Evaluator; Orientations to Action," 27 *Am. J. Eco. & Soc.* 55 (1967). With regard to clearance of Executive Orders and Proclamations, see Office of Management and Budget Manual, Section 200-3, reprinted at S. Rep. 7, 93-1 (1973), 9. See Executive Order 11030 of June 19, 1962 (27 Fed. Reg. 5847), as amended by Executive Order 11354 of June 1, 1967 (32 Fed. Reg. 7695).

[11] Hoover's request for authority: 75 Cong. Rec. 4109, 9640 (1932). Authority: 47 Stat. 382, Part II, Titles I and IV (1932). His Executive Orders: 76 Cong. Rec. 233 (1932). House disapproval: 76 Cong. Rec. 2103-06. Last two economy measures: 47 Stat. 1517, sec. 16 (1933) and 47 Stat. 1602, Title II, sec. 4 (1933).

278

[12] Economy Act: 48 Stat. 8 (1933). Executive Order 6166: 77 Cong. Rec. 5708 (1933); 5 U.S.C. 132 (1934 ed.). For Presidential message to the Congress transmitting Executive Order 6166, see Roosevelt, *Public Papers*, II, 222-25.

[13] Executive Order 7126 (Aug. 5, 1935), as amended by Executive Order 7150 (Aug. 19, 1935) and Executive Order 7174 (Sept. 5, 1935). Executive Orders were not published in the *Federal Register* until the next year. These three Orders are cited in *Investigation of Executive Agencies of the Government*, a report by the Brookings Institution for the Senate Select Committee to Investigate the Executive Agencies of the Government [Byrd Committee], S. Rep. 1275, 75-1 (1937), 100.

[14] The President's Committee on Administrative Management, *Report of the Committee*, submitted to the President and the Congress in accordance with Public Law No. 739, 74-2 (1937), 21.

[15] *Ibid.* at 22.

[16] A. E. Buck, "Financial Control and Accountability," a study for the President's Committee on Administrative Management (1937), 1, 5, 26.

[17] Harvey C. Mansfield, "The General Accounting Office," a study for the President's Committee on Administrative Management (1937), 33, 37.

[18] *Investigation, supra* note 13, at 126, 113. See Richard Polenberg, *Reorganizing Roosevelt's Government* (1966), 39, 45.

[19] Roosevelt, *Public Papers*, v, 668; vi, 498.

[20] Woodrum's recommendation: 83 Cong. Rec. 355 (1938). Opposition: *ibid.* at 387 and 4630. See A. J. Wann, *The President as Chief Administrator* (1968), 72-98.

[21] Reorganization Act and impoundment authority: 53 Stat. 561. For the transition from Roosevelt's explanation in 1937 (that reorganization was not an instrument for major savings) to the provisions of the 1939 Act (listing spending reduction as the first purpose), see Polenberg, *supra* note 18, 7-8, 19, 33-35, 132-33, 186-87. Transfer of BOB to EXOP: 53 Stat. 1423. Executive Order 8248: 4 Fed. Reg. 3864. For specific studies on the Budget Bureau during the FDR period, see A. J. Wann, "Franklin D. Roosevelt and the Bureau of the Budget," 9 *Bus. & Govt. Rev.* 32 (1968); Harold D. Smith, "The Bureau of the

Budget," 1 *Pub. Adm. Rev.* 106 (1941); and Norman M. Pearson, "The Budget Bureau: From Routine Business to General Staff," 3 *Pub. Adm. Rev.* 126 (1943).

[22] Charles G. Dawes, *The First Year of the Budget of the United States* (1923), xi.

[23] Percival F. Brundage, *The Bureau of the Budget* (1970), 29-30, and Edward H. Hobbs, *Behind the President* (1954), 36-37.

[24] Lewis H. Kimmel, *Federal Budget and Fiscal Policy* (1959), 192-204. For Division of Fiscal Analysis, see Gerhard Colm, "Fiscal Policy and the Federal Budget," in *Income Stabilization for a Developing Democracy*, Max F. Millikan, ed. (1953), 229.

[25] Stephen Kemp Bailey, *Congress Makes a Law* (1950), 243-48, secs. 3(c) and 6. For an early study encouraging the use of the Federal budget as a stabilization tool, see J. Weldon Jones, "The Execution of the Federal Budget," 17 *Accounting Rev.* 88 (1942). See also Louis Fisher, *President and Congress* (1972), 157-73, and Gerhard Colm, "The Executive Office and Fiscal and Economic Policy," 21 *Law & Contemp. Prob.* 710 (1956).

[26] 42 U.S.C. 4201-44 (1970) and 33 Fed. Reg. 16487 (1968).

[27] For a detailed contemporary description of the functions of the Office of Management and Budget, see its budget justifications reprinted at *Treasury, Postal Service, and General Government Appropriations for Fiscal Year 1975* (Part 3), hearings before the House Committee on Appropriations, 83-2 (1974), 665-703.

[28] *Public Papers of the Presidents, 1970*, 260-61.

[29] Brownlow Committee: The President's Committee on Administrative Management, *Report of the Committee* (1937), 16. Budget and Accounting Procedures Act of 1950: 64 Stat. 834, sec. 104. Hoover Commission: Commission on Organization of the Executive Branch of the Government, *Budget and Accounting* (June 1955), 5.

[30] *Public Papers of the Presidents, 1970*, 258-59. Emphasis in original. For studies on the policy-administration distinction, see Woodrow Wilson, "The Study of Administration," 2 *Pol. Sci. Q.* 481 (1887); Frank J. Goodnow, *Politics and Administration* (1900); and Dwight Waldo, *The Administrative State* (1948),

104-29. A contemporary critique of the policy-administration distinction between the Domestic Council and the Office of Management and Budget is by John E. Moore, "Policy Implications of the Office of Management and Budget," paper presented at the 1971 Annual Meeting of the American Political Science Association, Chicago, Illinois, at 4-5. Also, a good discussion of the frustration encountered in trying to separate foreign policy into "policy" and "operations" appears in I. M. Destler, *Presidents, Bureaucrats, and Foreign Policy* (1972), 18-22.

[31] Hugh Heclo, "OMB and the Presidency—the problem of 'neutral competence,'" *Public Interest*, No. 38 (Winter 1975), 89.

[32] *Reorganization Plan No. 2 of 1970 (Office of Management and Budget; Domestic Council)*, hearings before a subcommittee of the House Committee on Government Operations, 91-2 (1970), 126. John F. Griner, National President.

[33] *Ibid.* at 139-41.

[34] H. Rep. 1066, 91-2 (1970), 10. Nixon's intention to delegate: *Public Papers of the Presidents, 1970*, 260.

[35] Blatnik and Holifield legislation: H.R. 17376, 91-2 (1970). Response to Cambodia: see Dom Bonafede, "Lobbying Brings Last-Minute Victory for Nixon's Reorganization Plan," *National Journal*, May 16, 1970, pp. 1018-20.

[36] H. Rep. 1066, 91-2 (1970), 4-6, 11.

[37] *Ibid.* at 21.

[38] *Reorganization Plan No. 2 of 1970*, hearing by a subcommittee of the Senate Committee on Government Operations, 91-2 (1970), 20. Ribicoff's three earlier statements in this paragraph are at pages 22, 28, and 46. The responsiveness theme was also elaborated by five Republicans who dissented from the report issued by House Government Operations: John N. Erlenborn, Guy Vander Jagt, Paul Findley, John H. Buchanan, Jr., and Sam Steiger. They remarked: "An almost universal outcry is circulating today to the effect that government is not responsive to the needs of the public. Students protest against foreign involvement; Blacks against poverty; women against inequality; the taxpayers against inefficiency and ineconomy; the victims against the rising incidence of lawlessness and crime; and, of course, every one against economic malfunctioning." H. Rep. 1066, 91-2 (1970), 22.

REFERENCES TO PAGES 51-56

[39] The letters are reprinted at 116 Cong. Rec. H4336-37 (daily ed. May 13, 1970). House upholding President: *ibid.* at H4346. Executive Order 11541: 35 Fed. Reg. 10737.

[40] Dec. 20, 1972 article in the *Washington Post*, reprinted at 119 Cong. Rec. S1107 (daily ed. Jan. 23, 1973).

[41] S. Rep. 7, 93-1 (1973), 3.

[42] 119 Cong. Rec. S1975-79 (daily ed. Feb. 2, 1973); S2088 (Feb. 5).

[43] *Ibid.* at S1973 (Feb. 2).

[44] *Confirmation of the Director and Deputy Director of the Office of Management and Budget,* hearings before the House Committee on Government Operations, 93-1 (1973), 16-22.

[45] Rhodes: *ibid.* at 31. Administration's position: *ibid.* at 163-66.

[46] H. Rep. 109, 93-1 (1973), 3-4.

[47] House action: 119 Cong. Rec. H3228 (daily ed. May 1, 1973); for Steelman amendment, see H3221-27. Senate action: *ibid.* at S8232 (May 3).

[48] Veto: S. Doc. 16, 93-1 (May 21, 1973). Senate and House override attempts: 119 Cong. Rec. S9601-06 (daily ed. May 22, 1973) and *ibid.* at H3911-20 (May 23).

[49] S. Rep. 237, 93-1 (1973). The Senate voted 72-12 in favor of the bill, amending it to require reconfirmation of the OMB Director and Deputy Director with the beginning of a new Presidential term. 119 Cong. Rec. S11894-98, S11920-21 (daily ed. June 25, 1973). House Government Operations: H. Rep. 697, 93-1 (1973). House action is at 119 Cong. Rec. H11544-46 (daily ed. Dec. 17, 1973).

[50] P.L. 93-250, 88 Stat. 11.

[51] *Watergate: Its Implications for Responsible Government,* A report prepared by a Panel of the National Academy of Public Administration at the request of the Senate Select Committee on Presidential Campaign Activities, March 1974, p. 43. The President's Committee on Administrative Management, *Report of the Committee* (1937), 17-18. The exception was Paul O'Neill, Human and Community Affairs. He was politically appointed but from career status. For background of other political appointees, see *National Journal,* Jan. 23, 1971, at 161, and *National Journal Reports,* Oct. 27, 1973, at 1590-91.

282

[52] *Supra* note 27, at 636.

[53] 121 Cong. Rec. S1393 (daily ed. Feb. 3, 1975).

CHAPTER THREE

[1] Madison, *Writings*, ii, 38-39. Emphasis in original.

[2] 1 Stat. 95 (1789); 1 Stat. 104 (1790); and 1 Stat. 190 (1791).

[3] 1 Stat. 226 (1791), and 1 Stat. 327 (1793).

[4] Gallatin, *Writings*, i, 73; Richardson, *Messages and Papers*, i, 317 (Dec. 8, 1801); and Hamilton, *Works*, vii, 256-57.

[5] Gallatin, *Writings*, iii, 117 (Nov. 12, 1796).

[6] *Writings of Thomas Jefferson* (Washington ed.), iv, 529-30, 533. For Gallatin report, see *American State Papers*, Finance, i, 757.

[7] 12 Stat. 344.

[8] *Uncle Joe Cannon*, as told to L. White Busbey (1927), 186-91. See also 31 Cong. Rec. 2602-21 (1898), and 30 Stat. 274 (1898).

[9] 48 Stat. 351.

[10] 79 Cong. Rec. 2014 (1935). I first came upon the Vandenberg statement in Charles S. Hyneman, *Bureaucracy in a Democracy* (1950), 79.

[11] Arthur W. Macmahon, John D. Millett, and Gladys Ogden, *The Administration of Federal Work Relief* (1941), 53-65. See 49 Stat. 115 (1935), and John Morton Blum, *Roosevelt and Morgenthau* (1970), 108-47.

[12] *Congressional Digest*, xvi, 172 (June-July 1937). See Gerhard Colm, "Comment on Extraordinary Budgets," 5 *Social Research* 168 (1938). Congress appropriating directly to agencies: Elias Huzar, "Legislative Control Over Administration: Congress and the W.P.A.," 36 *Am. Pol. Sci. Rev.* 51, 52, 57 (1942). Arthur W. Macmahon *et al.*, *The Administration of Federal Work Relief* (1941), 387.

[13] H. Doc. 854, 62-2 (1912), 210.

[14] Frank J. Goodnow, "The Limits of Budgetary Control," *Proceedings of the American Political Science Association*, 9th annual meeting, Dec. 28-31, 1912 (1913), 75; W. F. Wil-

loughby, "Allotment of Funds by Executive Officials: An Essential Feature of Any Correct Budgetary System," *ibid.*, 80.

[15] 58 Cong. Rec. 7101 (1919).

[16] *Ibid.*

[17] Roosevelt, *Public Papers*, iv, 40. A. E. Buck, "Financial Control and Accountability," President's Committee on Administrative Management (1937), 6.

[18] Harold D. Smith, "The Budget as an Instrument of Legislative Control and Executive Management," 4 *Pub. Adm. Rev.* 181, 185 (1944).

[19] Commission on Organization of the Executive Branch of the Government, *Budgeting and Accounting* (Feb. 1949), 12.

[20] Recommendation in 1949: *ibid.* at 13. Estimate of appropriation items eliminated: *Financial Management in the Federal Government*, S. Doc. 50, 92-1 (1971), i, 133. Volume i is also S. Doc. 11, 87-1 (1961). Commission on Organization of the Executive Branch of the Government, *Budget and Accounting* (June 1955), 12-13.

[21] 40 Cong. Rec. 1283 (1906).

[22] 107 Cong. Rec. 21477 (1961).

[23] H. Rep. 712, 86-1 (1959), 8; H. Rep. 1798, 86-2 (1960), 13; 74 Stat. 779. See also S. Rep. 1849, 86-2 (1960), 10, and William L. Morrow, *Congressional Committees* (1969), 165-67. A more general treatment is contained in William L. Morrow, "Legislative Control of Administrative Discretion: The Case of Congress and Foreign Aid," 30 *J. Pol.* 985 (Nov. 1968).

[24] Peace Corps: Executive Order 10924, 26 Fed. Reg. 1789 (1961). Funds included in 75 Stat. 721. For President's financing, see H. Rep. 1115, 87-1 (1961), 66. Commission on Civil Disorders: S. Rep. 1576, 90-2 (1968), 28.

[25] 106 Cong. Rec. 9037 (1960). For specific dollar examples on the use of the contingency fund to restore congressional cuts, see remarks by Senator Long at *ibid.*, 9040-41.

[26] H. Rep. 1798, 86-2 (1960), 15; S. Rep. 1849, 86-2 (1960) 10; 74 Stat. 777.

[27] S. Rep. 620, 93-1 (1973), 71. The interest of Rep. Daniel J. Flood (D-Pa.) in the Bahamas project is described in the *Washington Post*, Feb. 9, 1975, A1:3.

[28] H. Rep. 742, 93-1 (1973), 7. For funding, see 87 Stat. 1050.

[29] Most of the information on the helicopter deal was obtained from officials in AID and OMB. But see 120 Cong. Rec. S20540 (daily ed. Dec. 4, 1974); *Fiscal Year 1975 Foreign Assistance Request*, hearings before the House Committee on Foreign Affairs, 93-2 (1974), 329; and General Accounting Office, "Funding of Presidential Gifts and Grants to Middle East Countries," B-181244 (Oct. 31, 1974). The statutory restriction appears at P.L. 93-559, 88 Stat. 1803, sec. 28(c). This restriction, which had its origin in the House Foreign Affairs Committee, was directed specifically at the helicopter gift. See H. Rep. 93-1471, 93-2 (1974), 41. For appropriated amount of $1.8 million, to cover the helicopter, see 121 Cong. Rec. S4306 (daily ed. March 19, 1975) and P.L. 94-11, 89 Stat. 18.

[30] S. Rep. 625, 89-1 (1965), 53; H. Rep. 439, 88-1 (1963), 63. For original expectations regarding the use of this fund, see H. Rep. 574, 87-1 (1961), 65.

[31] H. Rep. 1389, 92-2 (1972), 233.

[32] 42 Stat. 1289-90 (1923).

[33] 42 Stat. 1488 (1923).

[34] 43 Stat. 432 (1924).

[35] 66 Cong. Rec. 155-60 (1924).

[36] For early discussion of this, see Arthur W. Macmahon, "Congressional Oversight of Administration: The Power of the Purse" (Part II), 58 *Pol. Sci. Q.* 380 (1943). A more contemporary account is by Michael W. Kirst, *Government Without Passing Laws* (1969).

[37] HUD Act: P.L. 93-414, 88 Stat. 1100-01 (Sept. 6, 1974); DOD Act: P.L. 93-437, 88 Stat. 1220 (Oct. 8, 1974).

[38] P.L. 93-393, 88 Stat. 783; H. Rep. 1274, 93-2 (1974), 7-24.

[39] 65 Stat. 342. See William E. Rhode, *Committee Clearance of Administrative Decisions* (1959), 35.

[40] Ford's observation: Edith T. Carper, "The Defense Appropriations Rider," Inter-University Case Program 359 (1960), 21. Eisenhower's opposition to the committee veto: *Public Papers of the Presidents, 1955*, 688; Johnson's opposition: *ibid.*,

1965, ii, 861, and 111 Cong. Rec. 12639 (1965); Nixon's opposition: *Public Papers of the Presidents, 1972*, 627-28, 686-88. The growth of the legislative and committee veto is covered by Joseph P. Harris, *Congressional Control of Administration* (1964), ch. 8.

CHAPTER FOUR

[1] W. F. Willoughby, "Allotment of Funds by Executive Officials, An Essential Feature of Any Correct Budgetary System," *Proceedings of the American Political Science Association*, 9th Annual Meeting, Dec. 28-31, 1912 (1913), 78-87.

[2] Arthur W. Macmahon, "Congressional Oversight of Administration: The Power of the Purse" (Part ii), 58 *Pol. Sci. Q.* 380, 404 (1943). Elias Huzar, *The Purse and the Sword* (1950), 354-59.

[3] For specific annual figures, see Louis Fisher, "Reprogramming of Funds by the Defense Department," 36 *J. Pol.* 77, 80 (1974).

[4] H. Rep. 2181, 84-2 (1956), 19.

[5] H. Rep. 1049, 85-1 (1957), 11.

[6] H. Rep. 1864, 85-2 (1958), 3.

[7] S. Rep. 871, 91-2 (1970), 3; S. Rep. 1335, 91-2 (1970), 5-6.

[8] S. Rep. 564, 91-1 (1969), 9; S. Rep. 937, 91-2 (1970), 6; H. Rep. 684, 92-1 (1971), 19; S. Rep. 550, 92-1 (1971), 25.

[9] General Accounting Office, "Appropriations Committees Not Advised on Reprograming of Funds by the Internal Revenue Service," B-133373 (May 1, 1973); H. Rep. 1209, 93-2 (1974), 12-13.

[10] John Taber (R-N.Y.) stated in 1955 that foreign aid administrators would have "at least a billion dollars available to them in deobligations and returns from the reserves and that they will have all that money available to them to operate on." 101 Cong. Rec. 10211. Passman: 106 Cong. Rec. 13127 (1960). See also H. Rep. 1798, 86-2 (1960), 7-8; S. Rep. 1849, 86-2 (1960), 5-6; and P.L. 86-704, 74 Stat. 776 (1960). The latter act provided that for technical cooperation "no part of this appropriation shall be used to initiate any project or activity

which has not been justified to the House of Representatives and the Senate." General Accounting Office, "Reappropriation of Receipts, Recoveries, and Unobligated Balances of Prior Year Funds Appropriated for Foreign Assistance," reprinted at *Foreign Assistance and Related Programs Appropriations, Fiscal Year 1974* (Part 2), hearings before the Senate Committee on Appropriations, 93-1 (1973), 1503, 1524.

[11] *Department of Defense Appropriations for 1951* (Part 2), hearings before the House Committee on Appropriations, 81-2 (1950), 1000.

[12] S. Rep. 1582, 83-2 (1954), 1-2.

[13] H. Rep. 1917, 83-2 (1954), 8.

[14] *Department of Defense Appropriations for 1956*, hearings before the House Committee on Appropriations, 84-1 (1955), 562-63.

[15] H. Rep. 493, 84-1 (1955), 8.

[16] Reprinted at *Budgeting and Accounting*, hearings before the Senate Committee on Government Operations, 84-2 (1956), 113-19. For dissatisfaction expressed by House Appropriations in 1956, regarding a defense reprogramming action, see H. Rep. 2104, 84-2 (1956), 13.

[17] H. Rep. 408, 86-1 (1959), 20. Department of Defense Instruction, "Reprogramming of Appropriated Funds—Report on," No. 7250.5 (Oct. 23, 1959). The House Appropriations Committee expressed its satisfaction with this revised procedure; H. Rep. 1561, 86-2 (1960), 26-27.

[18] *Department of Defense Appropriations for 1962* (Part 1), hearings before the House Committee on Appropriations, 87-1 (1961), 105-06.

[19] *Ibid.* at 109.

[20] *Ibid.* (Part 3), at 578.

[21] *Ibid.* at 579-80. Section 412(b) of the Military Construction Act of 1959 provided: "No funds may be appropriated after December 31, 1960, to or for the use of any armed force of the United States for the procurement of aircraft, missiles, or naval vessels unless the appropriated of such funds has been authorized by legislation enacted after such date." 73 Stat. 322.

[22] Mahon letter to McNamara, April 26, 1961. See Harold W. Stoneberger, Colonel, U.S. Air Force, "An Appraisal of Re-

programming Actions," Student Research Report No. 159, Resident School Class of 1968 (Washington, D.C.: Industrial College of the Armed Forces), 48-50. In 1962 House Appropriations noted "with some concern" that DOD instructions had not been revised since 1959, although "significant changes based on mutual instructions" had been agreed upon since that time. The committee asked that the instructions be revised immediately. H. Rep. 1607, 87-2 (1962), 21. The revised DOD directive was issued the following year; Department of Defense Directive, "Reprogramming of Appropriated Funds." No. 7250.5 (March 4, 1963).

[23] Department of Defense Directive, "Reprogramming of Appropriated Funds," No. 7250.5, Sec. II.B, II.C (May 21, 1970). For specific details, see Louis Fisher, "Reprogramming of Funds by the Defense Department," 36 *J. Pol.* 77, 85-86 (1974).

[24] Letter from Secretary Laird to Senator Ellender, May 8, 1972, together with memorandum dated May 9, 1972, amending DOD Instruction No. 7250.10.

[25] Department of Defense Directive, "Reprogramming of Appropriated Funds," No. 7250.5 (May 21, 1970), Sec. II.C.4.

[26] Department of Defense Instruction, "Implementation of Reprogramming of Appropriated Funds," No. 7250.10 (April 1, 1971), sec. V.A.2.

[27] *Supra* note 25, sec. II.D.2.

[28] See Table 2 in Louis Fisher, "Reprogramming of Funds by the Defense Department," 36 *J. Pol.* 77, 88 (1974). A DOD table dated July 22, 1974 shows reprogramming requests of $1.453 billion for fiscal 1973 and $219 million for fiscal 1974.

[29] Statistics on internal reprogramming appear in Table 3 of my article on reprogramming, 36 *J. Pol.* 77, 89.

[30] The average of 100 reprogramming actions a year is detailed at *ibid.*, Table 4, p. 90. The figures for fiscal 1973 and fiscal 1974 appear in a DOD table dated Aug. 9, 1974. For Stoneberger study, see *supra* note 22, at 53-54. The actions and line items for fiscal 1973 and fiscal 1974 come from the same DOD table dated Aug. 9, 1974. See also John T. Parker, "An Inquiry Into Defense Budgetary Reprogramming," *Perspectives in Defense Management* (Winter 1973-74).

[31] For statistics from July 1, 1967 to Feb. 19, 1968, see *Department of Defense Appropriations for 1969* (Part 1), hear-

ings before the House Committee on Appropriations, 90-2 (1968), 351, 355. A DOD table, undated, shows the following reprogramming requests for fiscal 1973: prior approvals, $984,-197,000; notifications, $468,831,000. Of the prior approvals, $788,818,000 represented *transfers* that were subject to the reprogramming procedure. For this development see Chapter Five, pages 112-14.

[32] *Department of Defense Appropriations for 1951* (Part 3), hearings before the House Committee on Appropriations, 81-2 (1950), 1512. H. Rep. 1316, 89-2 (1966), 18.

[33] S. Rep. 962, 92-2 (1972), 107-10.

[34] *Department of Defense Reprograming of Appropriated Funds: A Case Study*, Subcommittee for Special Investigations of the House Committee on Armed Services, 89-1 (1965), 16.

[35] *Department of Defense Appropriations for 1972* (Part 2), hearings before the House Committee on Appropriations, 92-1 (1971), 331. See also 330-42. After the DIA director signed the reprogramming request, almost three months elapsed before the agency came before House Appropriations, making it even more difficult to hold DIA to the original congressional reduction. DIA argued that full compliance with the congressional cut was difficult because almost half the fiscal year was over by the time House Appropriations acted, but committee staff maintained that the cut had taken into account the late appropriation.

[36] H. Rep. 662, 93-1 (1973), 16.   P.L. 93-238, 87 Stat. 1046, sec. 745 (1974).

[37] *Supra* note 35, at 610.

[38] H. Rep. 666, 92-1 (1971), 118-19. S. Rep. 498, 92-1 (1971), 197; and H. Rep. 754, 92-1 (1971), 14.

[39] H. Rep. 662, 93-1 (1973), 17.

[40] *Investigation into Electronic Battlefield Program*, hearings before the Senate Committee on Armed Services, 91-2 (1970), 15, 36. This reference does not explicitly support my statement, but conversations with several officials in DOD's Comptroller Office have confirmed that reprogramming was the initial means of financing the electronic battlefield. Moreover, a private study by McGraw-Hill's DMS Market Intelligence Report stated that the "original FY67 funding of the program was $3.5 million. After creation of the DCPG, the three services quickly upped funding to several hundred times that by reprogramming and

use of emergency funds." 116 Cong. Rec. 23827 (July 13, 1970). I wrote to Defense Secretary Laird on June 22, 1972, attempting to pin down more precisely the relationship between reprogramming and the electronic battlefield. The letter was not acknowledged. A follow-up letter of March 10, 1973, to Defense Secretary Richardson, was not answered either. On September 24, 1974 I tried again, this time to Defense Secretary Schlesinger.

On March 7, 1975 I received a reply from the Comptroller's Office of the Pentagon. I was advised that after the deactivation of DCPG, files were destroyed and/or retired, and personnel had been reassigned and/or retired. Some information, however, was available. The DCPG was initiated through reprogramming in fiscal 1967. A total of $4,875,000 was reprogrammed to the DCPG from the following sources: RDT&E/Army (fiscal 1967 program), $1,939,000; RDT&E/Army (fiscal 1966 program), $2,039,000; RDT&E/Army (fiscal 1965 program), $247,000; and Emergency Fund, Defense, $650,000. An additional $18,090,000 was reprogrammed to the DCPG in fiscal 1968 from the following accounts: RDT&E/Army (fiscal 1968 program), $15,760,000, and Emergency Fund, Defense, $3,-300,000. That amount was in addition to the $10 million originally included in the fiscal 1968 RDT&E/Army program for DCPG.

Two other programs which the Department of the Army identified as related to the DCPG were ADSID (Air Defense Seismic Intrusion Detector) and Dye Marker Communications and Electronic Equipment. The ADSID program was initiated in fiscal 1967 through reprogramming $5,100,000 from the fiscal 1967 Procurement of Equipment and Missiles, Army program. The Dye Marker program was increased from a base of $5,000,-000 in fiscal 1968 through reprogramming of $29,800,000 from the fiscal 1968 Procurement of Equipment and Missiles, Army program.

The comment from Senator Symington appears at 116 Cong. Rec. 23834 (1970).

[41] H. Rep. 698, 91-1 (1969), 75. The conference committee rejected the amount of $8.5 million which had been proposed by the Senate for advance procurement. H. Rep. 766, 91-1

(1969), 6. Navy request in 1970: *Department of Defense Appropriations for 1971* (Part 5), hearings before the House Committee on Appropriations, 91-2 (1970), 1114. See 1100-24 for discussion.

[42] H. Rep. 698, 91-1 (1969), 72.

[43] H. Rep. 666, 92-1 (1971), 89, and S. Rep. 498, 92-1 (1971), 135. Senate Appropriations also wanted to eliminate $56.5 million for the oil tanker, a ship of such "low priority that it can be deferred without endangering the operational capability of the fleet. . . ." S. Rep. 498, 92-1 (1971), 131. The Senate Committee on Armed Services had denied authorization of the oiler because of its admittedly low-priority nature. S. Rep. 359, 92-1 (1971), 68. The oil tanker was eventually funded.

[44] 84 Stat. 2037, sec. 842 (1970). H. Rep. 916 (Part ii), 93-2 (1974), 29. The rescission authority was adopted by the House on Oct. 8, 1974, when it passed H. Res. 988.

[45] *Department of Defense Appropriations for 1972* (Part 2), hearings before the House Committee on Appropriations, 92-1 (1971), 336-37.

[46] *Fiscal Year 1972 Authorization for Military Procurement, Research and Development, Construction and Real Estate Acquisition for the Safeguard ABM and Reserve Strengths* (Part 1), hearings before the Senate Committee on Armed Services, 92-1 (1971), 232-33.

[47] *Department of Defense Reprograming, 1965*, hearings before the Senate Committee on Appropriations, 89-1 (1964), 1-4, 9.

[48] Laird's plan: *supra* note 46, at 97. Ellender: *Department of Defense Appropriations for Fiscal Year 1972*, hearings before the Senate Committee on Appropriations, 92-1 (1971), 1344-45. Stennis: *New York Times*, April 18, 1971, 40.

[49] H. Rep. 666, 92-1 (1971), 105. S. Rep. 498, 92-1 (1971), 18, and H. Rep. 754, 92-1 (1971), 13.

[50] S. 1333, 92-1. A similar bill, H.R. 10429, was introduced that year by Congressman Dante B. Fascell (D-Fla.). Neither bill was acted upon. For an earlier proposal to involve the full Congress in major reprogramming actions, see Stephen Horn, *Unused Power* (1970), 230-31.

Chapter Five

[1] Hamilton, *Works*, VII, 258-59.

[2] *Annals of Congress*, 2d Cong., pp. 890, 899-902.

[3] Jefferson, *Writings*, VI, 168. Jefferson's biographer, Dumas Malone, doubts that Jefferson did the entire draft for Giles. Although Malone agrees that Jefferson sympathized with the move and "probably contributed to it," he suggests that the primary force was Giles, assisted by Jefferson and Madison. Dumas Malone, *Jefferson and the Ordeal of Liberty* (1962), 15, 31-33. For Hamilton's role in the rebuttal by Smith, see Broadus Mitchell, *Alexander Hamilton* (1962), II, 260-63.

[4] 3 *Annals* 890. The speaker is not identified.

[5] Congressional authority: 1 Stat. 264 (1792). Gallatin, *Writings*, III, 117-18. Appropriation: 1 Stat. 404 (1794); see 1 Stat. 403 for act authorizing the expedition after it had taken place.

[6] *Annals*, 7th Cong., 1st Sess., p. 320 (1801).

[7] 2 Stat. 535-36 (1809).

[8] *Annals*, 14th Cong. 2d Sess., pp. 420-21.

[9] 3 Stat. 568, sec. 5 (1820).

[10] John Rogers, Navy Commissioner's Office, Nov. 23, 1829, to John Branch, Secretary of the Navy, *American State Papers*, Class VI, Naval Affairs, III, 401.

[11] *Ibid.* at 378-79 (Amos Kendall, Treasury Department, Fourth Auditor's Office, Nov. 30, 1829, to John Branch, Secretary of the Navy). See also Kendall's report on transfers, dated Dec. 14, 1830, *ibid.* at 823-33. Transfer authority: 4 Stat. 558 (1832).

[12] *American State Papers*, Class VI, Naval Affairs, II, 101.

[13] *Ibid.*, IV, 357-58.

[14] 4 Stat. 742 (1834). Subsequent authority: 5 Stat. 78, sec. 2 (1836); 5 Stat. 223 (1838); and 5 Stat. 533, sec. 23 (1842).

[15] King: *Cong. Globe*, 27th Cong., 2d Sess., p. 970 (Aug. 30, 1842). 5 Stat. 581, sec. 11 (1842). For discussion on transfer authorities, including the restrictions in the 1842 act, see 4 Ops. Att'y Gen. 266-68 (Oct. 23, 1843). In *Gratiot* v. *United States*, 45 U.S. 80, 114 (1846), the U.S. Supreme Court made reference to the principle that a "specific appropriation could not be diverted from its object. . . ."

[16] 9 Stat. 101, sec. 5 (1846).

[17] 9 Stat. 171 (1847); 9 Stat. 271, sec. 9 (1848); 10 Stat. 104, sec. 2 (1852); 10 Stat. 107, sec. 3 (1852); 12 Stat. 103, sec. 2 (1860); and 15 Stat. 36, sec. 2 (1868).

[18] 31 U.S.C. 628 (1970).

[19] Lucius Wilmerding, Jr., *The Spending Power* (1943), 17-18; 68 Cong. Rec. 1151 (1927) and Israel, *State of the Union Messages*, III, 2696.

[20] 47 Stat. 411, sec. 317 (1932); see Wilmerding, *The Spending Power*, 180-84.

[21] 55 Stat. 54, sec. 1(c) (1941); 57 Stat. 367, sec. 3 (1943).

[22] Committee's proposal: S. Rep. 1011, 79-2 (1945), 22-23. As reported by Senate: S. Rep. 1400, 79-2 (1946), 5. Act: 60 Stat. 812 (1946).

[23] 119 Cong. Rec. H3548-49 (daily ed. May 10, 1973).

[24] *Ibid.* at H3549.

[25] H. Rep. 916 (Part II), 93-2 (1974), 29. See *Committee Reform Amendments of 1974* (Part 2), open business meeting of the House Select Committee on Committees, 93-2 (1974), 423, 425-26.

[26] 22 U.S.C. 2360, 2364, 2318 (1970).

[27] *Supplemental Foreign Assistance Authorizations, 1970*, hearings before the Senate Committee on Foreign Relations, 91-2 (1970), 2, 78, 87-88.

[28] *Ibid.* at 2-3.

[29] H. Rep. 1678, 91-2 (1970), 18.

[30] Rogers: *supra* note 27, at 27. Cambodian foreign minister: interview with Henry Bradsher, *Washington Sunday Star*, May 23, 1971, A5:1.

[31] 84 Stat. 1943, sec. 7(a). House conferees: H. Rep. 1791, 91-2 (1970), 5.

[32] 84 Stat. 1943, sec. 7(b).

[33] 84 Stat. 1943, sec. 8 (1971). Related to sections 506(a), 610(a), and 614(a) of the Foreign Assistance Act of 1961, as amended. Broadening of prior-notice requirement: 86 Stat. 28, sec. 304 (1972).

[34] 117 Cong. Rec. S16390 (daily ed. Oct. 19, 1971).

[35] *Ibid.* at S17169-75 (daily ed. Oct. 29, 1971).

[36] Conferees: S. Rep. 590, 92-1 (1971), 28. P.L. 92-226, 86 Stat. 29, sec. 655.

[37] *Public Papers of the Presidents, 1970,* 478.

[38] *Department of State Bulletin,* Vol. LXVIII, No. 1769 (May 21, 1973), at 655. Statement of April 30, 1973.

[39] *Mitchell* v. *Laird,* 476 F.2d 533, 538 (D.C. Cir. 1973). For earlier conclusions by Federal courts that appropriations constituted a sanction of the war policy, see *Orlando* v. *Laird,* 317 F.Supp. 1013, 1018-19 (E.D. N.Y. 1970); *Orlando* v. *Laird,* 443 F.2d 1039, 1042 (2d Cir. 1971); *Berk* v. *Laird,* 317 F.Supp. 715, 724, 728, 730 (E.D. N.Y. 1970); *Berk* v. *Laird,* 429 F.2d 302, 305 (2d Cir. 1970); and *DaCosta* v. *Laird,* 448 F.2d 1368, 1369 (2d Cir. 1971). In *Atlee* v. *Laird,* 347 F.Supp. 689, 708 (E.D. Pa. 1972), *aff'd* on appeal, *Atlee* v. *Richardson,* 411 U.S. 911 (1973), Circuit Judge Adams argued that it would be impossible to decide whether Congress, through its appropriations, meant to authorize the military activities in Vietnam: "to explore these issues would require the interrogation of members of Congress regarding what they intended by their votes, and the synthesization of the various answers. To do otherwise would call for gross speculation in a delicate matter pertaining to foreign relations." Efforts were unsuccessful in 1970 to have the Cambodian intervention declared an unconstitutional war; *Mottola* v. *Nixon,* 318 F.Supp. 538 (N.D. Cal. 1970).

[40] At the time of the first large-scale authority to the Defense Department to transfer funds, for fiscal 1971, House and Senate conferees agreed that all transfers "shall be considered to be matters of special interest to the Committees on Appropriations under the reprograming procedures." H. Rep. 1799, 91-2 (1970), 15. For sample hearings on these transfer requests, see *Department of Defense Appropriations for 1973* (Part 8), hearings before the House Committee on Appropriations, 92-2 (1972), 69-106.

[41] P.L. 92-570, 86 Stat. 1198, sec. 713(d) (1972). Late notification: Letter from Deputy Defense Secretary W. P. Clements, Jr., to George H. Mahon, chairman of House Appropriations. Deficiency-rate spending: In a letter to Rep. Les Aspin, May 18, 1973, Acting Assistant Secretary of Defense (Comptroller) Don R. Brazier explained that the Pentagon had "obligated funds for certain purposes above planned amounts ('above budgeted amounts'). What this means is that under

existing authority appropriations have been used at a faster rate than contemplated at the time the appropriations were made. However, the Department has not exceeded the amount of any appropriation and no deficiency has in fact been created."

[42] *Second Supplemental Appropriation Bill, 1973* (Part 3), hearings before the House Committee on Appropriations, 93-1 (1973), 592.

[43] *Ibid.* at 594.

[44] *Ibid.* at 595.

[45] H. Doc. 66, 93-1 (1973).

[46] *Second Supplemental Appropriations for Fiscal Year 1973* (Part 2), hearings before the Senate Committee on Appropriations, 93-1 (1973), 1984.

[47] *Ibid.* at 1987.

[48] H. Rep. 164, 93-1 (1973), 22-23, 122. The eight members were Joseph P. Addabbo, Joseph J. Flynt, Robert N. Giaimo, Clarence D. Long, David R. Obey, J. Edward Roush, Robert O. Tiernan, and Sidney R. Yates. Another separate statement, signed by two of the eight in conjunction with two other committee members, also dissented from the recommended $430 million transfer authority. *Ibid.* at 127 (Giaimo and Yates along with Edward P. Boland and Frank E. Evans).

[49] Addabbo: 119 Cong. Rec. H3566, H3592-93 (daily ed. May 10, 1973). Long: *ibid.* at H3593, H3598.

[50] S. Rep. 160, 93-1 (1973), 21. Endorsed by the full Senate by voice vote; 119 Cong. Rec. S10128 (daily ed. May 31, 1973).

[51] S. Rep. 160, 93-1 (1973), 133 (sec. 305). Senate action: 119 Cong. Rec. S9843 (daily ed. May 29, 1973); *ibid.* at S10128 (May 31).

[52] Agreement on $75 million: H. Rep. 295, 93-1 (1973), 6. House debate: 119 Cong. Rec. H5266-67 (daily ed. June 25, 1973).

[53] Giaimo: *ibid.* at H5268. Mahon: *ibid.* at H5274.

[54] *Wkly Comp. Pres. Doc.*, IX, 861-62. House override attempt: 119 Cong. Rec. H5487-88 (daily ed. June 27, 1973).

[55] *Ibid.* at H5676 (June 29).

[56] See H. Rep. 350, 93-1 (1973), 3, and P.L. 93-50, 87 Stat. 129, sec. 307. The August 15 deadline was also incorporated in a continuing appropriation enacted on July 1,

1973. Section 108 of that law stated that "notwithstanding any other provision of law, on or after August 15, 1973, no funds herein or heretofore appropriated may be obligated or expended to finance directly or indirectly combat activities by United States military forces in or over or from off the shores of North Vietnam, South Vietnam, Laos or Cambodia." P.L. 93-52, 87 Stat. 134. Cong. Addabbo on bogus issue: 119 Cong. Rec. H5667 (daily ed. June 29, 1973).

⁵⁷ *Drinan* v. *Nixon*, 364 F.Supp. 854, 860, 861 (D. Mass. 1973).

⁵⁸ *Holtzman* v. *Schlesinger*, 361 F.Supp. 553, 565 (E.D. N.Y. 1973); for procedural issues on this case, see 361 F.Supp. 544 (E.D. N.Y. 1973).

⁵⁹ *Holtzman* v. *Schlesinger*, 414 U.S. 1304, 1310 (1973). Footnote omitted. See 119 Cong. Rec. H7194-96 (daily ed. Aug. 1, 1973). On August 4 Justice Douglas vacated the stay, *Holtzman* v. *Schlesinger*, 414 U.S. 1316, but later that same day Justice Marshall reinstated the stay and announced that other members of the Court were unanimous in overruling the Douglas order, *Schlesinger* v. *Holtzman*, 414 U.S. 1321.

⁶⁰ *Holtzman* v. *Schlesinger*, 484 F.2d 1307, 1313-14 (2d Cir. 1973). Also treating military expenditures in Southeast Asia as a political question was *Harrington* v. *Schlesinger*, 373 F.Supp. 1138 (E.D. N.C. 1974).

⁶¹ 120 Cong. Rec. S4491-94 (daily ed. March 27, 1974), statement by Senator Hughes summarizing the findings of the Senate Armed Services Committee. President Nixon approved the bombing on March 17, but the bombing did not begin until the next day. Statement by the Department of Defense to Senator Stennis, chairman of the Armed Services Committee, reprinted at *Bombing in Cambodia*, hearings before the Senate Committee on Armed Services, 93-1 (1973), 170.

⁶² *Bombing in Cambodia, supra* note 61, at 483.

⁶³ *Impeachment of Richard M. Nixon, President of the United States*, H. Rep. 1305, 93-2 (1974), 217.

⁶⁴ *Ibid.* at 219. For a 599-page document entitled "Bombing in Cambodia," which is a collection of evidentiary material, see Book xi of the Statement of Information prepared by the House Committee on the Judiciary (May-June 1974).

⁶⁵ H. Rep. 662, 93-1 (1973), 16. P.L. 93-238, 87 Stat. 1044,

sec. 735. The same restriction was applied the next year, in the defense appropriation act for fiscal 1975. P.L. 93-437, 88 Stat. 1231, sec. 834.

CHAPTER SIX

[1] Hamilton, *Papers*, xviii, 91, 114 (report of Jan. 16, 1795).

[2] 1 Stat. 437, sec. 16.

[3] *Annals*, 16th Cong., 1st Sess., 807-9. See Wilmerding, *The Spending Power* (1943), 83-94. As a result of legislation in 1792 and 1798, the Treasurer acted as agent for the War and Navy Departments; 1 Stat. 280, sec. 2, and 1 Stat. 610, sec. 2. Those provisions were repealed in 1822; 3 Stat. 689.

[4] 3 Stat. 567, sec. 1 (1820). 2 Ops. Att'y Gen. 442, 446 (1831).

[5] 10 Stat. 98, sec. 10 (1852).

[6] 7 Ops. Att'y Gen. 1, 14 (1854). For an additional opinion on the 1852 law, see 13 Ops. Att'y Gen. 181 (1870).

[7] *Cong. Globe*, 41st Cong., 2d Sess., p. 3328 (1870). See also 3327-31.

[8] 16 Stat. 251 (1870). Legislation a few months earlier had already covered into the Treasury certain unexpended balances for the Navy; 16 Stat. 68. For 1870 legislation, see Wilmerding, *The Spending Power*, 122-28.

[9] 13 Ops. Att'y Gen. 290 (1870). Impact of act: James A. Garfield, "National Appropriations and Misappropriations," *No. Am. Rev.*, No. 271 (June 1879), p. 583.

[10] 18 Stat. 110, sec. 5 (1874). See 15 Ops. Att'y Gen. 357 (1877) and Wilmerding, *The Spending Power*, 131-35.

[11] 25 Ops. Att'y Gen. 105 (1904); see also 40 Ops. Att'y Gen. 55 (1948). Farrand, *Records*, ii, 143, 158, 168, 182.

[12] Farrand, *Records*, ii, 323, 329-30.

[13] 83 Stat. 475-79, titles iv & v (1969). H. Rep. 698, 91-1 (1969), 7. S. Rep. 607, 91-1 (1969), 136-37; 83 Stat. 487, sec. 642 (1969).

[14] H. Rep. 1570, 91-2 (1970), 7-8.

[15] *The Department of Defense Appropriations for Fiscal Year 1971* (Part 5), hearings before the House Committee on Appropriations, 91-2 (1970), 95-97.

[16] 84 Stat. 2037, sec. 842 (1970). Multi-year funding was

continued in subsequent appropriation acts for procurement and RDT&E. S. Rep. 962, 92-2 (1972), 115.

[17] 4 Cong. Rec. 4439 (1876).

[18] See *Hinds' Precedents*, IV, 3591-94; *Cannon's Precedents*, VII, 1153-60; *Senate Procedure: Precedents and Practices*, S. Doc. 21, 93-1 (1973), 148 (item 60). *Organization of Congress* (Part 4), hearings before the Joint Committee on the Organization of Congress, 79-1 (1945), 893-94. See also Part 3, at 536, and Part 4, at 782.

[19] Joint committee recommendation: S. Rep. 1011, 79-2 (1946), 22-23. 1946 Act: 60 Stat. 833, sec. 139(c); House Rule XXI, Clause 5; *Senate Procedures: Precedents and Practices*, S. Doc. 21, 93-1 (1973), 121, 152; Senate Manual, S. Doc. 1, 92-1 (1971), sec. 346.3.

[20] H. Rep. 1175, 92-2 (1972), 4. The agriculture appropriation act (86 Stat. 603, 606) provided $150 million for FmHA water and sewer grants, "of which $58,000,000 shall be derived from the unexpended balances," and $500 million for HUD water and sewer grants, "which shall be derived from the unexpended balance. . . ." In neither case would the funds have lapsed. The only genuine reappropriation in the act was $2 million for a special fund under the Agriculture Research Service, which was funded by one-year money; 86 Stat. 593.

[21] 86 Stat. 1190. The change from defense no-years to multi-years was followed by reappropriations each year to prevent money from lapsing.

[22] Authorization for unexpended balances: 22 U.S.C. 2404 (1970). Example of appropriation language: 86 Stat. 50 (paragraph beginning "Unobligated balances . . ."). Passman: 101 Cong. Rec. 10232 (1955). Gross: 106 Cong. Rec. 13138 (1960). Authority for reappropriation in the mutual security act: 69 Stat. 289, sec. 548 (1955).

[23] 107 Cong. Rec. 18133 (1961). For legislation authorizing the reappropriation of foreign assistance funds, see 75 Stat. 462, sec. 645 (1961).

[24] The GAO and CRS Studies are reprinted in *Foreign Assistance and Related Programs Appropriations, Fiscal Year 1974* (Part 2), hearings before the Senate Committee on Appropriations, 93-1 (1973), 1479-1529. Senate Appropriation's

direction in 1973: S. Rep. 620, 93-1 (1973), 33. Legislation in 1974: P.L. 93-559, 88 Stat. 1796, sec. 6.

[25] The Commission on Organization of the Executive Branch of the Government, *Budgeting and Accounting*, A Report to the Congress (Feb. 1949), 14. GAO studies: *Financial Management in the Federal Government*, S. Doc. 50, 92-1 (1971), I, 39, 85. Harry F. Byrd, "The Unexpended Balances of Appropriations," *Commercial and Financial Chronicle*, Vol. 177, No. 5186 (Jan. 15, 1953), 14.

[26] 100 Cong. Rec. 11476 (1954).

[27] 68 Stat. 830-32, sec. 1311 (1954). Clarence Cannon, former chairman of House Appropriations, recalled the genesis of this statutory definition of obligation; see *Congressional Control Over the Budget of the United States*, hearing before a Special Subcommittee of the House Government Operations Committee, 84-1 (1955), 28. Defense reserves: 68 Stat. 1224, sec. 110 (1954).

[28] 60-day restriction: 68 Stat. 1224, sec. 108 (1954). Passman: 101 Cong. Rec. 10208-09 (1955).

[29] H. Rep. 1086, 84-1 (1955), 4; 101 Cong. Rec. 10209.

[30] H. Rep. 1086, 84-1 (1955), 1-2.

[31] 69 Stat. 438, sec. 106 (1955). "Glossary of Key Words Applicable to the AID/MAP Programs," AID photo copy, at 2, undated. Regarding "commitments," see *Department of Defense Appropriations for 1970* (Part 3), hearings before the House Committee on Appropriations, 91-1 (1969), 24-26.

[32] *Legislative Reorganization Act of 1946*, hearings before the Senate Committee on Expenditures in the Executive Departments, 80-2 (1948), 137. For another proposal during that period to abolish carryovers and synchronize appropriations with expenditures, see Herman C. Loeffler, "Alice in Budget-Land," 4 *Nat'l Tax J.* 54 (1951). A rebuttal by Michael S. March and a rejoinder by Loeffler appear at 5 *Nat'l Tax J.* 155, 174 (1952).

[33] Commission on Organization of the Executive Branch of the Government, *Budget and Accounting*, A Report to the Congress, June 1955, at 18-21.

[34] *Ibid.* at 22-25. For a critique of the Hoover Commission's advocacy of contract authority, see George Y. Harvey, "Con-

tract Authorization in Federal Budget Procedure," 18 *Pub. Adm. Rev.* 117 (1957).

[35] J. Harold Stewart, "The Hoover Commission Recommendations on Budgeting and Accounting," 7 *Fed'l Accountant* 8-9 (1958). Stewart was chairman of the task force on budgeting and accounting.

[36] *Improving Federal Budget and Appropriations*, hearings before the House Committee on Government Operations, 85-1 (1957), 133, 135.

[37] H. Rep. 216, 85-1 (1957), 5. For earlier criticism by House Appropriations on contract authority, see H. Rep. 2085, 79-2 (1946), 7-8, and H. Rep. 1797, 81-2 (1950), 4.

[38] 70 Stat. 782 (1956). 72 Stat. 852 (1958). For details on the development of this legislation in 1956 and 1958, see *Financial Management in the Federal Government*, S. Doc. 50, 92-1 (1971), i, 92-108. Eisenhower's experience: H. Rep. 227, 86-1 (1969), 10-12.

[39] See Report of the President's Commission on Budget Concepts (Oct. 1967), 7 [recommendation 5], 36-46; Carl W. Tiller, "Accrual Accounting and Budgeting for the Government," 19 *Fed'l Accountant* 73 (1970); and Ernest Enke, "The Accrual Concept in Federal Accounting," 22 *Fed'l Accountant* 4 (1973). *The Budget of the United States Government, Fiscal Year 1976*, 23, 329.

[40] Wilfred Lewis, Jr., *Federal Fiscal Policy in the Postwar Recessions* (1962), 65, 221-27.

[41] *Ibid.* at 250-72. See also *Public Papers of the Presidents, 1961*, at 41, and *Economic Report of the President, 1962*, at 97-98.

[42] Moot: *Washington Evening Star*, March 31, 1972, A7:1; H. Rep. 349, 90-1 (1967), 35-36; and H. Rep. 1111, 93-2 (1974), 17; S. Rep. 1048, 93-2 (1974), 14; H. Rep. 1270, 93-2 (1974), 5 [amendment 12]; 88 Stat. 768.

[43] U.S. Bureau of the Budget, Circular No. 28 (Sept. 1, 1921); see Aaron Wildavsky, *The Politics of the Budgetary Process* (1964), 31.

[44] H. Rep. 698, 91-1 (1969), 48; *Fiscal Year 1973 Authorization for Military Procurement, Research and Development, Construction Authorization for the Safeguard ABM, and Active Duty and Selected Reserve Strengths* (Part 6), hearings before the

Senate Committee on Armed Services, 92-2 (1972), 3852-53. See also statement by Rep. Les Aspin, "Last Minute Navy Claims Payment," 118 Cong. Rec. H7362 (daily ed. Aug. 8, 1972).

[45] See testimony by Wilfred J. McNeil, former Pentagon Comptroller, at *Improving Federal Budgeting and Appropriations*, hearings before the House Committee on Government Operations, 85-1 (1957), 278. For a representative statute, see 87 Stat. 1041, sec. 719 (1974).

[46] H. Rep. 1607, 87-2 (1962), 48-49, 51.

[47] *Ibid.* at 37. See also S. Rep. 1578, 87-2 (1962), 46.

[48] *Foreign Assistance and Related Programs Appropriations, Fiscal Year 1974* (Part 2), hearings before the Senate Committee on Appropriations, 93-1 (1973), 1524.

[49] *Department of Labor and Health, Education, and Welfare Appropriations for 1975* (Part 5), hearings before the House Committee on Appropriations, 93-2 (1974), 72. For committee investigation and OE response, see 54-83. Dollar breakdown for individual programs appears at 119 Cong. Rec. E4583 (daily ed. July 9, 1973).

[50] H. Rep. 164, 93-1 (1973), 124.

[51] *Ibid.* at 48; S. Rep. 160, 93-1 (1973), 49, 53; H. Rep. 295, 93-1 (1973), 10; P.L. 93-50, 87 Stat. 106 (1973).

[52] See 118 Cong. Rec. S10816-20 (daily ed. June 29, 1972).

[53] Withdrawal of amendment and Weinberger pledge: *ibid.* at S10912, S10915. OMB Bulletin is reprinted *ibid.* at S11201 (July 19, 1972). See Weinberger's testimony at *Foreign Assistance and Related Programs Appropriations for Fiscal Year 1973*, hearings before the Senate Committee on Appropriations, 92-2 (1972), 1089-1116.

[54] P.L. 93-52, 87 Stat. 132, sec. 101(b) (1973). For warning the next year, see H. Rep. 1158, 93-2 (1974), 3.

[55] P.L. 93-324, 88 Stat. 282, sec. 101(b) (1974).

CHAPTER SEVEN

[1] 95 Cong. Rec. 14922 (1949).

[2] 21 Ops. Att'y Gen. 415 (1896); similar statements appear *ibid.* at 392, 422.

[3] *First Supplemental National Defense Appropriation Bill for*

1944, hearings before the Senate Committee on Appropriations, 78-1 (1943), 739. Letter from President Roosevelt to Senator Richard Russell, Aug. 18, 1942.

[4] H. Rep. 1797, 81-2 (1950), 9.

[5] *Ibid.* at 311.

[6] 89 Cong. Rec. 10362 (1943).

[7] Jefferson on contingency funds: Richardson, *Messages and Papers*, I, 325, 354, 366, 382-83, 405, 421, 447. Romney: *Department of Housing and Urban Development; Space, Science, Veterans, and Certain Other Independent Agencies Appropriations, Fiscal Year 1973*, hearings before the Senate Committee on Appropriations, 92-2 (1972), 565; Weinberger: *Caspar W. Weinberger To Be Secretary of Health, Education, and Welfare* (Part 1), hearings before the Senate Committee on Labor and Public Welfare, 93-1 (1973), 29.

[8] Richardson, *Messages and Papers*, I, 348, 360. For a discussion of the historical background on this, see the study by Prof. Joseph Cooper, *Impoundment of Appropriated Funds by the President*, joint hearings before the Senate Committee on Government Operations and the Senate Committee on the Judiciary, 93-1 (1973), 676-77 [hereafter cited as *1973 Ervin Hearings*].

[9] *Decatur* v. *Paulding*, 39 U.S. (14 Pet.) 497 (1840). See also *Reeside* v. *Walker*, 52 U.S. (11 How.) 272, 290, (1850); *Brashear* v. *Mason*, 47 U.S. (6 How.) 92, 102 (1848); *United States ex rel. Tucker* v. *Seaman*, 58 U.S. (17 How.) 225, 230 (1854); and *United States ex rel. Goodrich* v. *Guthrie*, 58 U.S. (17 How.) 284, 304 (1854).

In a decision of March 20, 1973, Judge Lord of the U.S. District Court for the District of Minnesota distinguished between two types of actions by the Secretary of Agriculture: executive (requiring judgment and discretion) and ministerial (actions mandated by statutory laws or agency regulations). The decision of the Secretary to designate an area an "emergency loan area" was his alone. But once a designation had been made, it was the duty of the Secretary to accept loan applications and consider them. *Berends* v. *Butz*, 357 F.Supp. 143, 150 (1973). In *Harrington* v. *Schlesinger*, 373 F.Supp. 1138, 1141 (E. D. N. C. 1974), a U.S. district court maintained that the execution and administration of an appropriation act concerning military expenditures for Southeast Asia "is not merely a ministerial function, but is a function in which the Executive is vested with discretion."

[10] *Executive Impoundment of Appropriated Funds*, hearings before the Senate Committee on the Judiciary, 92-1 (1971), 85 [hereafter cited as *1971 Ervin Hearings*].

[11] *Washington Post*, Jan. 15, 1971, A2:1. New Jersey action: *New York Times*, Apr. 23, 1971, 36:2.

[12] *Washington Post*, June 26, 1971, B1:6; *ibid.*, May 31, 1972, A1:3.

[13] 64 Stat. 768, sec. 1214 (1950); H. Doc. 182, 82-1 (1951). For further details see Louis Fisher, "The Politics of Impounded Funds," 15 *Adm. Sci. Q.* 361, 370 (1970).

[14] 81 Stat. 662. See *Public Papers of the Presidents, 1967*, II, 1173-74.

[15] 82 Stat. 271, sec. 202 (1968); 83 Stat. 82, sec. 401 (1969); and 84 Stat. 406, sec. 501 (1970). See also Louis Fisher, *President and Congress* (1972), 106-10. Evins: *Public Works for Water and Power Development and Atomic Energy Commission Appropriations* (Part 6), hearings before the House Committee on Appropriations, 92-1 (1971), 13. Spending ceiling in 1972: Louis Fisher, "Congress, the Executive and the Budget," *The Annals*, Vol. 411 (Jan. 1974), 102-13.

[16] Rep. Mahon explained the stretchout policy of the Eisenhower Administration at 103 Cong. Rec. A7337 (1957). Budget Director Stans said that the funds were released after the debt ceiling was raised; *The Budget for 1960*, hearings before the House Committee on Appropriations, 86-1 (1959), 40. For reliance by Nixon Administration, see *1971 Ervin Hearings*, at 96, and *1973 Ervin Hearings*, at 270, 366-67.

[17] 31 U.S.C. 13(a) (1970).

[18] *Caspar Weinberger To Be Secretary of Health, Education, and Welfare* (Part 1), hearings before the Senate Committee on Labor and Public Welfare, 93-1 (1973), 30.

[19] Stephen Kemp Bailey, *Congress Makes a Law* (1950), 248 [sec. 6].

[20] *1973 Ervin Hearings*, at 286. See 64 Stat. 765, sec. 1211, codified at 31 U.S.C. 665(c)(2) (1970).

[21] *Second Deficiency Appropriation Bill for 1947*, hearings

before the Senate Committee on Appropriations, 80-1 (1947), 116-17, 125.

[22] *Ibid.* at 137; S. Rep. 175, 80-1 (1947), 1.

[23] "Report and Recommendations by the Director of the Bureau of the Budget and the Comptroller General of the United States with respect to the Antideficiency Act and Related Legislation and Procedures," a 35-page report with appendices submitted to Senator Styles Bridges, chairman of the Committee on Appropriations, June 5, 1947, at 7, 15; draft bill is attached to BOB-GAO report, sec. (c) (2).

[24] BOB-GAO report, at 21. Commission on Organization of the Executive Branch of the Government, *Budgeting and Accounting*, Feb. 1949, at 17. H. Rep. 1797, 81-2 (1950), 311. Examiners Handbook: J. D. Williams, "The Impounding of Funds by the Bureau of the Budget," ICP Case Series No. 28 (University of Alabama Press, 1955), reprinted in *1973 Ervin Hearings*, at 859.

[25] 88 Stat. 332, sec. 1002 (1974). See S. Rep. 688, 93-2 (1974), 72-75.

[26] 84 Stat. 48, sec. 410 (1970); see discussion at 116 Cong. Rec. 5926-27 (1970). 87 Stat. 746 (1973).

[27] 84 Stat. 10, sec. 119. See 22 U.S.C. 2370(s) (1970). Hickenlooper: 22 U.S.C. 2370(e) (1970). Applied against Ceylon: *Foreign Assistance and Related Agencies Appropriations for 1973* (Part 2), hearings before the House Committee on Appropriations, 92-2 (1972), 142.

[28] Civil Rights: 42 U.S.C. 2000(d)(1) (1970); billboards: *Washington Evening Star*, Feb. 27, 1971, A2:6, and *Washington Post*, Feb. 12, 1972, A4:1; welfare payments: 42 U.S.C. 602(a) (23) (1970). Regarding latter, see also *National Journal*, Feb. 20, 1971, at 401-09; *New York Times,* Apr. 1, 1971, 24:3; *ibid.* March 29, 1971, 19:1; *ibid.* Jan. 20, 1971, 15:1; *Washington Post,* Jan. 28, 1971, A18:1; *ibid.* Jan. 9, 1971, A2:1; *ibid.* Jan. 8, 1971, A5:6. Reliance by Nixon Administration on stabilization act: *1973 Ervin Hearings*, at 366. OMB, in its impoundment reports, also relied on the Economic Stabilization Act; see 38 Fed. Reg. 3475 (1973) [check programs covered by Code 6c]. Eagleton amendment: 119 Cong. Rec. S2682 (daily ed. Feb. 19, 1973); S. Rep. 63, 93-1 (1973), 6-7; and 87 Stat.

26 (1973). For authority to withhold highway funds from States that fail to control billboards, see 23 U.S.C. 131 (1970).

[29] Nixon: *Wkly Comp. Pres. Doc.*, IX, 110. For the take-care clause, see *Budget of the United States, Fiscal Year 1973*, hearings before the Senate Committee on Appropriations, 92-2 (1972), 126 (statement by OMB). Repeated by OMB Director Ash at the *1973 Ervin Hearings*, 272. Regarding executive power, see *1971 Ervin Hearings*, 95, and *1973 Ervin Hearings*, 270. Also, Deputy Attorney Sneed doubted whether Congress could legislate against impoundment even in the domestic area: "To admit the existence of such power deprives the President of a substantial portion of the 'executive power' vested in him by the Constitution . . ."; *1973 Ervin Hearings*, 369.

[30] On "Chief Clerk" concept, see remarks by Deputy Attorney General Sneed at *1973 Ervin Hearings*, 369. Brandeis: *Myers v. United States*, 272 U.S. 52, 293 (1926). On 1774-1787 period, see Louis Fisher, *President and Congress* (1972), 1-27, 241-70; Louis Fisher, "The Efficiency Side of Separated Powers," 5 *J. Am. Studies* 113 (1971); and Louis Fisher, "Presidential Tax Discretion and Eighteenth Century Theory," 23 *West. Pol. Q.* 151 (1970).

[31] 37 U.S. (12 Pet.) 524.

[32] *Kendall: ibid.* at 613, 610. *Reeside*: 52 U.S. (11 How.) 272. For further analysis, see Louis Fisher, "Funds Impounded by the President: The Constitutional Issue," 38 *G.W. L. Rev.* 124, 126-27 (1969); *United States* v. *Price*, 116 U.S. 42 (1885); and *United States* v. *Louisville*, 169 U.S. 249 (1898).

[33] *1973 Ervin Hearings*, 368.

[34] 86 Stat. 32, sec. 658. *Foreign Assistance and Related Agencies Appropriations for 1972*, hearings before the House Committee on Appropriations, 92-1 (1971), 275-77 (Part 1) and 70, 181-91, 251-55 (Part 2). See S. Rep. 432, 92-1 (1971), 15. GAO subsequently reported that the domestic funds in question had been released; 118 Cong. Rec. H4098 (daily ed. May 3, 1972).

In 1950 Congress directed the President to make a loan of $62,500,000 to Spain. Truman said he would have to regard the statutory provision as an authorization, not as a directive, "which would be unconstitutional. . . ." However, the loan to

Spain was eventually granted, in part because of domestic pressures generated by the 1950 elections. 64 Stat. 758 (Sept. 6, 1960); *Public Papers of the Presidents, 1950*, at 616; H. Bradford Westerfield, *Foreign Policy and Party Politics* (1955), 73.

[35] *Youngstown* v. *Sawyer*, 343 U.S. 579, 641 (1952).

[36] H. Rep. 1830, 85-2 (1958), 35-36; 72 Stat. 715 (1958). See also 73 Stat. 367 (1959) and 74 Stat. 340 (1960). For contemporary floors in the Armed Services authorization bill for fiscal 1975, see 88 Stat. 402, sec. 401 (1974).

[37] *Public Papers of the Presidents, 1945*, at 259, 320, 343, and 579. See also 58 Stat. 623, sec. 303 (1944); 59 Stat. 304, sec. 607 (1945); 59 Stat. 407 (1945); 59 Stat. 617, sec. 3, 10 (1945); 60 Stat. 6, 221, 600 (1946); and 61 Stat. 572 (1947).

Impoundment was used before, during, and after World War II, sparking numerous objections from Members of Congress but never reaching a major crisis. With war imminent in January 1941, President Roosevelt told Congress that it seemed appropriate to defer construction projects when they competed for manpower and materials needed for defense purposes. On that basis the Roosevelt Administration was generally able to withhold funds from domestic projects in order to promote the war effort. Roosevelt, *Public Papers*, IX, 656. See 58 Stat. 891, sec. 10 (1944), 59 Stat. 11, sec. 2 (1945); J. D. Williams, "The Impounding of Funds by the Bureau of the Budget," ICP Case Series, No. 28 (University of Alabama Press, 1955); and Louis Fisher, "The Politics of Impounded Funds," 15 *Adm. Sci. Q.* 361, 364-65 (1970).

[38] *Military Situation in the Far East* (Part 4), hearings before the Senate Committees on Armed Services and Foreign Relations, 82-1 (1951), 2607.

[39] Soviet Russia intentions: Warner R. Schilling *et al.*, *Strategy, Politics, and Defense Budgets* (1962), 103-07; Hoover Commission: *New York Times*, Dec. 17, 1948, 18:3; *ibid.* April 12, 1949, 1:5; Schneider: Schilling *et al.*, at 110.

[40] Truman vetoes: 93 Cong. Rec. 7073-74, 9303; override: 94 Cong. Rec. 4018-19, 4026, 4051-53. See A. E. Holmans, *United States Fiscal Policy: 1945-1959* (1961), 56-84.

[41] 95 Cong. Rec. 14355, 14591-92. See also exchange between Senators Ferguson and Saltonstall, *ibid.* at 14855. For pointed critiques of the manner in which Congress failed to analyze the defense budget, particularly the justification for an expanded Air Force, see Edward A. Kolodziej, *The Uncommon Defense and Congress* (1966), 87-107, and Schilling *et al.*, *Strategy, Politics, and Defense Budgets* (1962), 71-87.

[42] *Public Papers of the Presidents, 1949*, at 538-39; *Department of Defense Appropriations for 1951: Additional Supplemental Hearing* before the House Committee on Appropriations, 81-2 (1950), 27. See also letter from President Truman to Defense Secretary Johnson, Nov. 8, 1949, *1971 Ervin Hearings*, at 525. For McKellar and Cannon; *New York Times*, Oct. 30, 1949, 3:3, 40:5. See also *Public Papers of the Presidents, 1950*, at 661, and Elias Huzar, *The Purse and the Sword* (1950), 177-92.

[43] *Public Papers of the Presidents, 1960-61*, at 52, 951.

[44] McNamara: *New York Times*, Oct. 28, 1961, 1:5; House Armed Services: H. Rep. 1406, 87-2 (1962), 1, 9.

[45] 108 Cong. Rec. 4694 (1962). Kennedy's reasons for holding up the RS-70 were given at a news conference on March 7, 1972; *Public Papers of the Presidents, 1962*, at 202.

[46] Joint Chiefs and Mahon: *Business Week*, March 17, 1962, at 34. See also remarks by Mahon at 108 Cong. Rec. 4720 (1962). Ford: 108 Cong. Rec. 4714 (1962); Halleck, McCormack, and Albert: Edward A. Kolodziej, *The Uncommon Defense and Congress* (1966), 415-17.

[47] Announcement of new study: 108 Cong. Rec. 4694 (1962). Vinson: *ibid.* at 4694. Representative Leslie Arends called it a "paper victory." He said he would "await the translation of the assurances we now have into affirmative action." *Ibid.* at 4699. Representative Frank Becker claimed that McNamara's offer was "an old legislative trick—that when you want to get rid of something, agree to a study. This is the surest way to brush something under the rug that you want to get rid of." *Ibid.* at 4707. Representative H. R. Gross regretted that the fight had ever been started, "for it is apparent now that it has been lost. This is not a compromise; it is a defeat for the entire House of Representatives." *Ibid.*

at 4714. For studies on the RS-70 and other impoundments of weapons systems, see Gerald Davis, "Congressional Power to Require Defense Expenditures," 33 *Fordham L. Rev.* 39 (1964); John H. Stassen, "Separation of Powers and the Uncommon Defense: The Case Against Impounding of Weapons System Appropriations," 57 *Geo. L. J.* 1159 (1969); Louis Fisher, "The Politics of Impounded Funds," 15 *Adm. Sci. Q.* 361, 366-69 (1970); J. Malcomb Moore, "To . . . Provide for the Common Defense," in *Public Administration*, 2d ed., R. Golembiewski *et al.*, eds., (1972), 371-400.

⁴⁸ Douglas: *Cong. Globe*, 36th Cong., 2d Sess., p. 1177 (1861). Grant: Richardson, *Messages and Papers*, ix, 4331.

⁴⁹ 28 Cong. Rec. 6031 (1896).

⁵⁰ *New York Times*, Feb. 8, 1923, 4:6; *ibid.* Jan. 23, 1923, 20:3. See also 64 Cong. Rec. 3507 (1923).

⁵¹ *Public Papers of the Presidents, 1946*, at 229-30; H. Doc. 136, 80-1 (1947); Arthur Maass, *Muddy Waters* (1951), 215, 237.

⁵² *Public Papers of the Presidents, 1965*, ii, 1083; Department of Agriculture Release No. 1015-69 (1969); see 115 Cong. Rec. 5923 (1969).

⁵³ Aquarium: *1971 Ervin Hearings*, at 139-42, 211-17. The aquarium, to be located in the District of Columbia, had the strong personal backing of Mike Kirwin, then chairman of the House Public Works Committee. Career budget staff in BOB and OMB recommended to both Presidents Johnson and Nixon that construction funds for this "nonessential recreation" project could be safely impounded, especially for a city without representation in Congress. All but the planning and design money was impounded. Kirwin's death on July 27, 1970 left the Administration without a major proponent for the project.

For Barge Canal, see *Public Papers of the Presidents, 1971*, at 43-44. See statements by Representative Bennett at 117 Cong. Rec. E2196 (daily ed. March 25, 1971) and by Representative Sikes at 118 Cong. Rec. H4668 (daily ed. May 17, 1972). Litigation: *Canal Authority of the State of Florida v. Callaway*, 71-92-Civ-J (D. Fla. 1974). Four other civil actions were consolidated with this case.

Public Papers of the Presidents, 1966, ii, at 980-81.

[55] Ibid. at 987-88 and 1406-10. Public Papers of the Presidents, 1967, 219, 357.

[56] Public Papers of the Presidents, 1970, 822-23, 824-25.

[57] Public Works for Water and Power Development and Atomic Energy Commission Appropriations (Part 6), hearings before the House Committee on Appropriations, 92-1 (1971), 22.

[58] Ibid. at 19.

[59] Ibid. at 17. Still another explanation for impounding all of the new congressional projects was that it seemed more "impartial" to do it that way. It was argued by an OMB official that a more selective list, impounding projects in some congressional districts while allowing other add-ons to go forward, might have invited charges of discrimination and political favoritism. Ibid. at 10-11.

[60] New York Times, Jan. 9, 1970, 1:8; ibid. Oct. 2, 1969, 28:1; ibid. Sept. 16, 1969, 16:1; ibid. Sept. 13, 1969, 1:4; ibid. Sept. 11, 1969, 1:1.

[61] 1971 Ervin Hearings, at 310 (Caspar Weinberger). See 1973 Ervin Hearings, at 877-79, and 1971 Ervin Hearings, at 164-65.

[62] Budget of the United States, Fiscal Year, 1973, hearings before the Senate Committee on Appropriations, 92-2 (1972), 129-30.

[63] In his budget message for fiscal 1974, President Nixon quoted the Tenth Amendment and said that the "philosophy of the Founding Fathers embodied in this amendment is also my philosophy" (p. 11). For comments on the Tenth Amendment, see Louis Fisher, President and Congress (1972), 37-39.

[64] Impoundment Reporting and Review (Part 1), hearings before the House Committee on Rules, 93-1 (1973), 229.

[65] 38 Fed. Reg. 3474 (1973).

[66] Definition of contract authority appears in The Budget of the United States Government, Fiscal Year 1974, at 315. OMB Director Weinberger explained that "the authority to obligate the United States comes into existence on the date the allotments to the states are made and the amount of the total obligational authority thus provided is determined by the total amount

allotted." *Nominations of Caspar W. Weinberger, of California, to be Secretary of Health, Education, and Welfare, and Frank C. Carlucci, of Pennsylvania, to be Under Secretary of Health, Education, and Welfare,* hearings before the Senate Committee on Finance, 93-1 (1973), 48. Activity by the Federal courts, regarding clean-water funds, is covered in Chapter Eight.

⁶⁷ For more detail on the Labor-HEW impoundment, see Louis Fisher, "Impoundment of Funds: Uses and Abuses," 23 *Buff. L. Rev.* 141, 195 (1973). The Federal courts consistently upheld the higher level authorized by Congress in the continuing resolution. For example, see *Oklahoma* v. *Weinberger*, Civ-73-425-C (W.D. Okla. 1973), which involved three programs under the Library Services and Construction Act; *Massachusetts* v. *Weinberger*, Civ. Action No. 1308-73 (D.D.C. 1973), concerning impounding of school construction funds: *Pennsylvania* v. *Weinberger*, Civil Action No. 1606-73 (D.D.C. 1973), affecting Title V funds under the Elementary and Secondary Education Act; *American Assn. of Colleges of Podiatric Medicine* v. *Ash*, Civ. Action No. 1139-73 (D.D.C. 1973) and *American Assn. of Colleges of Pharmacy* v. *Ash*, Civ. Action No. 1244-73 (D.D.C. 1973), regarding health grants; and *National Council of Community Mental Health Centers* v. *Weinberger*, Civ. Action No. 1223-73 (D.D.C. 1973).

After numerous defeats in the courts, on December 19, 1973, Deputy Press Secretary Gerald L. Warren announced that President Nixon had directed HEW Secretary Weinberger to proceed with the obligation of funds that had been contested in the courts. *Wkly Comp. Pres. Doc.*, IX, 1473-74.

⁶⁸ Details on these three categories appear in Louis Fisher, "Impoundment of Funds: Uses and Abuses," 23 *Buff. L. Rev.* 141, 193-95 (1973). The proposed rescissions were treated as impoundment by the courts. See *National Assn. of Collegiate Veterans* v. *Ottina*, Civ. Action No. 349-73 (D.D.C. 1973); *Minnesota Chippewa Tribe* v. *Carlucci*, Civ. Action No. 628-73 (D.D.C. 1973); and *National Assn. of State Universities and Land Grant Colleges* v. *Weinberger*, Civ. Action No. 1014-73 (D.D.C. 1973).

⁶⁹ Additional details on impoundment statistics are available in Louis Fisher, "Impoundment of Funds: Uses and Abuses," 23 *Buff. L. Rev.* 141, 191-200 (1973).

CHAPTER EIGHT

[1] *Public Papers of the Presidents, 1972,* 742, 964. Ehrlichman: *Wall Street Journal,* July 27, 1972, 3.

[2] Richard D. Fenno, Jr., "If, as Ralph Nader Says, Congress is 'The Broken Branch,' How Come We Love Our Congressmen So Much?" (paper presented to the Harvard Club, Boston, Mass., Dec. 12, 1972, as part of the Time, Inc. editorial projection on "The Role of Congress"). Reprinted at 119 Cong. Rec. H1582 (daily ed. March 8, 1973). For background and analysis of the 1972 dispute over the spending ceiling, see Louis Fisher, "Congress, the Executive and the Budget," *The Annals,* Vol. 411 (Jan. 1974), 102-13.

[3] *Washington Post,* March 7, 1973, A4.

[4] See statement "The Federal Budget and the Cities" prepared by the National League of Cities and the U.S. Conference on Mayors, reprinted at 119. Cong. Rec. S2066 (daily ed. Feb. 5, 1973).

[5] For this position on REAP and Water Bank, see memorandum from Edward M. Shulman, General Counsel, to Kenneth E. Frick, Administrator of the Agricultural Stabilization and Conservation Service, reprinted in H. Rep. 6, 93-1 (1973), 2-4. For the same position on FmHA emergency loans, subsidized loan and grant programs for rural housing, FmHA water and waste disposal grants, and the REA loan program, see memorandum from John A. Knebel (Shulman's successor), General Counsel, Department of Agriculture, in *REA Loan Program,* hearings before the House Committee on Agriculture, 93-1 (1973), 59-64.

[6] *Comptroller General's Opinion of the Legality of Executive Impoundment of Appropriated Funds,* prepared for the Subcommittee on Separation of Powers of the Senate Committee on the Judiciary, 93d Cong., 2d Sess. (committee print, 1974), 21.

[7] *Impoundment of Funds for Farm and Rural Programs,* hearings before the Senate Committee on Agriculture and Forestry, 93-1 (1973), 491-92.

[8] Memorandum from Edward M. Shulman, General Counsel, to Kenneth E. Frick, Administrator of the Agricultural Stabilization and Conservation Service, reprinted at H. Rep. 6, 93-1

(1973), 3-5. See also *Rural Environmental Assistance Program*, hearings before the House Committee on Agriculture, 93-1 (1973), 123ff for statement by J. Phil Campbell, Under Secretary for the Department of Agriculture.

[9] H. Rep. 6, 93-1 (1973), 8, 11.

[10] Senate action: S. Rep. 49, 93-1 (1973), 35; 119 Cong. Rec. S3811-12 (daily ed. March 1, 1973). House-Senate differences: See conference report, H. Rep. 101, 93-1 (1973). Modified program: P.L. 93-86, 87 Stat. 241. For litigation on REAP, see *Guadamuz* v. *Ash*, Civil Action No. 155-73 (D.D.C. 1973).

[11] Initial announcement, reprinted at H. Rep. 15, 93-1 (1973), 2. Subsequent justifications: *Restore FHA Emergency Loan Program*, hearings before the House Committee on Agriculture, 93-1 (1973), 607. Critics: *ibid.* at 66.

[12] *Berends* v. *Butz*, 357 F.Supp. 143, 148 (D. Minn. 1973).

[13] Two types of secretarial actions and unauthorized actions by Butz: *ibid.* at 151, 157. Butz violating departmental regulations: *ibid.* at 154, 155. For a similar situation in which the Nixon Administration, trying to close down the Office of Economic Opportunity, acted in violation of OEO procedures, see *Local 2677, Am. Fed'n of Gov't Employees* v. *Phillips*, 358 F.Supp. 60 (D.D.C. 1973).

[14] P.L. 93-24, 87 Stat. 24. See S. Rep. 85, 93-1 (1973), 4, and H. Rep. 15, 93-1 (1973), 10.

[15] *REA Loan Program*, hearings before the House Committee on Agriculture, 93-1 (1973), 67-68.

[16] *Wkly Comp. Pres. Doc.*, ix, 107 (1973). News conference of January 31, 1973.

[17] *Impoundment of Funds for Farm and Rural Program*, hearings before the Senate Committee on Agriculture and Forestry, 93-1 (1973), 22.

[18] S. Rep. 20, 93-1 (1973), 7-8.

[19] *Ibid.* at 25-26; H. Rep. 91, 93-1 (1973), 12-13, 19-20, 38.

[20] Butz pledge and conference action: H. Rep. 169, 93-1 (1973), 5, 10. See P.L. 93-32, 87 Stat. 65. Also James T. Easterling, "The Amended Rural Electrification Act: Congressional Response to Administration Impoundment," 11 *Harv. J. Leg.*

205 (1974). Ash assurance: H. Rep. 520, 93-1 (1973), 15-16. *Sioux Valley Empire Electric Association* v. *Butz*, 367 F.Supp. 686 (D. S.D. 1973).

[21] Justification for impoundment: *Restore Rural Water and Waste Disposal Grant Programs*, hearings before the House Committee on Agriculture, 93-1 (1973), 28, 47. Challenge to arguments: *ibid.* at 2-3, 19-20, 44, *passim*.

[22] H. Rep. 21, 93-1 (1973), 3; House passage: 119 Cong. Rec. H1284-85 (daily ed. March 1, 1973); Senate passage: *ibid.* at S5598 (March 22, 1973); failure to override: *ibid.* at H2551-52 (April 10, 1973). For veto message, see *ibid.* at H2454 (April 5, 1973).

[23] Veto overridden: 118 Cong. Rec. H10266-73 (daily ed. Oct. 18, 1972); *ibid.* at S18546-54 (Oct. 17, 1972). See P.L. 92-500. 87 Stat. 816. Letter to William Ruckelshaus, EPA Administrator, from President Nixon, Nov. 22, 1972, reprinted in *Federal Budget for 1974*, hearings before the House Committee on Appropriations, 93-1 (1973), 194-95.

[24] H. Rep. 1465, 92-2 (1972), 113, 115.

[25] 118 Cong. Rec. S16871 (daily ed. Oct. 4, 1972).

[26] *Ibid.*

[27] Harsha: *ibid.* at H9122 (Oct. 4, 1972). Harsha, Jones, and Ford: *ibid.* at H9123.

[28] Veto statement: *Public Papers of the Presidents, 1972*, 992. Muskie: 118 Cong. Rec. S18546, S18549, S18551 (daily ed. Oct. 17, 1972); Harsha: *ibid.* at H10268 (Oct. 18, 1972).

[29] 86 Stat. 816, sec. 101; *ibid.* at 845, sec. 301(b)(1).

[30] Muskie: 118 Cong. Rec. S16870, S16871 (daily ed. Oct. 4, 1972). Jones: *ibid.* at H9117; Blatnik: *ibid.* at H9121; Harsha: *ibid.* at H9122.

[31] *Ibid.* at H10267.

[32] *Ibid.* at H10268.

[33] *Ibid.* at S18547-48.

[34] *Washington Post*, Feb. 5, 1973, A4:5.

[35] Ruckelshaus after veto: *1973 Ervin Hearings*, at 417. Prior to the veto he wrote to the Office of Management and Budget, Oct. 11, 1972; letter reprinted in *A Legislative History of the Water Pollution Control Act Amendments of 1972*, a committee print of the Senate Committee on Public Works, 93-1 (1973), I, 155.

36 Ruckelshaus: *ibid.* at 152, 155. Muskie: 118 Cong. Rec. S18548 (daily ed. Oct. 17, 1972).

37 *City of New York* v. *Ruckelshaus,* 358 F.Supp. 669 (D.D.C. 1973). *City of New York* v. *Train,* 494 F.2d 1033, 1042 (D.C. Cir. 1974).

38 *Minnesota* v. *Fri,* No. 4-73 Civ. 133 (D. Minn. 1973), memorandum form, at 13.

39 *Florida* v. *Train,* Civ. No. 73-156 (N.D. Fla. 1974) and *Texas* v. *Ruckelshaus,* C.A. No. A-73-CA-38 (W.D. Tex. 1973). *Martin-Trigona* v. *Ruckelshaus,* No. 72-C-3044 (N.D. Ill. 1973); *Ohio* v. *Environmental Protection Agency,* Nos. C73-1061 and C74-104 (N.D. Ohio, 1974); and *Maine* v. *Train,* No. 14-51 (D. Maine, 1974). *Brown* v. *Ruckelshaus,* 364 F.Supp. 258, 266 (D. Cal. 1973).

40 *Campaign Clean Water* v. *Ruckelshaus,* 361 F.Supp. 689, 700 (D. Va. 1973). *Campaign Clean Water* v. *Train,* No. 73-1745 (4th Cir. 1973).

41 *Train* v. *City of New York,* at 9-10 (slip opinion, Feb. 18, 1975).

42 *Withholding of Funds for Housing and Urban Development Programs, Fiscal Year 1971,* hearings before the Senate Committee on Banking, Housing and Urban Affairs, 92-1 (1971), 159, 163, 165.

43 Ervin and Ash: *1973 Ervin Hearings,* at 277-78; Romney: speech of Jan. 8, 1973, to the National Association of Home Builders, Houston, Texas, at 5; Romney's position was underscored a week later by Kenneth Cole, Director of the Domestic Council, in a letter of Jan. 15, 1973 to Senator Sparkman, reprinted at 119 Cong. Rec. S1723 (daily ed. Jan. 31, 1973).

44 119 Cong. Rec. E680 (daily ed. Feb. 6, 1973).

45 Legislative efforts: H. Rep. 296, 93-1 (1973), 6. Statement by Rep. Tiernan, *ibid.* at 31. Tiernan's effort on the House floor to mandate spending for community development programs: 119 Cong. Rec. H5217-19 (daily ed. June 22, 1973). Senator Cranston successfully proposed an amendment to prohibit the Secretary of HUD from using any funds for administrative expenses unless the full amount appropriated for community development assistance programs was released during fiscal 1974, as well as funds impounded from prior appropriations; 119 Cong. Rec. S12624 (daily ed. June 30, 1973). A Senate bill specified

that all funds "shall be made available for expenditure except as specifically provided by law . . .", *ibid.* at S12616, and S. Rep. 272, 93-1 (1973), 4. Those amendments to the HUD bill were rejected in conference: 119 Cong. Rec. H6814-15 (daily ed. July 28, 1973) [Amendments 1, 9, and 36]. *Rooney* v. *Lynn,* Civil Action No. 2010-73 (D.D.C. 1974).

⁴⁶ P.L. 93-383, 88 Stat. 633 (1974).

⁴⁷ Speech by Secretary Romney, National Association of Home Builders, Houston, Texas, Jan. 8, 1973, at 7; letter from Mr. Cole to Senator Sparkman, Jan. 15, 1973, reprinted at 119 Cong. Rec. S1723 (daily ed. Jan. 31, 1973).

⁴⁸ Proxmire: *Oversight on Housing and Urban Development Programs: Washington, D.C.* (Part 1), hearings before the Senate Committee on Banking, Housing and Urban Affairs, 93-1 (1973), 256. Lilley: *Washington Post,* Dec. 3, 1973, A1:5.

⁴⁹ *New York Times,* Jan. 9, 1973, 21:4.

⁵⁰ Anthony Downs, "Federal Housing Subsidies: Their Nature and Effectiveness, and What We should Do About Them" (Real Estate Research Corporation, Oct. 1972), 17.

⁵¹ *Ibid.* at 19, 21.

⁵² *Housing Subsidies and Housing Policy,* a committee print of the Subcommittee on Priorities and Economy of the Joint Economic Committee, 93-1 (1973), 6.

⁵³ See exchange between Congressman Moorhead (D-Pa.), HUD Secretary Lynn, and HUD Under Secretary Hyde at *Suspension of Subsidized Housing Programs,* hearing before the House Committee on Banking and Currency, 93-1 (1973), 16-17.

⁵⁴ Richey: *Pennsylvania* v. *Lynn,* 362 F.Supp. 1363 (D.D.C. 1973). On July 31, 1973, in another case, Judge Richey ruled that the Administration's refusal to further process, approve and implement applications for Farmers Home Administration interest credit loans was unlawful; *Pealo* v. *Farmers Home Adm'n,* Civ. No. 1028-73 (D.D.C. 1973). Court of Appeals: *Pennsylvania* v. *Lynn,* No. 73-1835 (D.C. Cir. 1974).

For earlier district court decisions on housing impoundments, see *San Francisco Redev. Agency* v. *Nixon,* 329 F.Supp. 672 (N.D. Cal. 1971), where Chief Judge Carter ruled that there was no precedent to suggest that a U.S. district court may compel the President "to take any action whatsoever," and *Housing*

Authority v. *United States Dep't of Housing and Urban Dev.*, 340 F.Supp. 654, 656 (N.D. Cal. 1972), in which Carter held that Congress had been responsible in its legislation for creating much of the President's discretion to withhold funds.

⁵⁵ 119 Cong. Rec. H6626 (daily ed. June 25, 1973). For Mr. Mahon's previous support of impoundment, see his letter to Senator Ervin of Feb. 25, 1969, reprinted at *1971 Ervin Hearings*, at 501-02. The Mahon bill was H.R. 5193, 93-1 (1973), later changed in the Committee on Rules to H.R. 8480, 93-1 (1973). See *Impoundment Reporting and Review* (2 Parts), hearings before the House Committee on Rules, 93-1 (1973).

⁵⁶ S. 373, 93-1 (1973), which passed the Senate three times: as an amendment to the Par Value Modification Bill (119 Cong. Rec. S6696, April 4, 1973), as an amendment to the Debt Limit Bill (*ibid.* at S12169, June 27, 1973), and as a bill by itself (*ibid.* at S8871, May 10, 1973).

⁵⁷ P.L. 93-344, 88 Stat. 297.

⁵⁸ Public works projects: 121 Cong. Rec. H1602 (daily ed. March 12, 1975); Labor-HEW: H. Rep. 26, 94-1 (1975), 11-12; defense: remarks by Cong. Mahon at 121 Cong. Rec. H1067 (daily ed. Feb. 25, 1975). Mahon said "it is not appropriate, in my view, for the Executive to transmit a rescission proposal that only contains funds which have been enacted into law as a result of the initiative of the Congress. I do not subscribe to the theory that everything the Executive does is correct and right and defensible, and that everything the Congress does by way of providing additional sums or modifying sums is all wrong." 121 Cong. Rec. H1054 (daily ed. Feb. 25, 1975).

⁵⁹ 120 Cong. Rec. S11238 (daily ed. June 21, 1974).

CHAPTER NINE

¹ Statement and Account Clause: Article I, Section 9, Clause 7. 1950 Act: 64 Stat. 834, sec. 111, codified at 31 U.S.C. 65 (1970). Direction to Secretary of the Treasury: 31 U.S.C. 66b(a) (1970).

² Farrand, *Records*, II, 618.

³ *Ibid.*

⁴ *Ibid.* at 618-19.

⁵ *Ibid.*, III, 326.

[6] 1 Stat. 128-29 (1790); 1 Stat. 300 (1793), but see also 2 Stat. 609, sec. 3 (1810); 31 U.S.C. 107 (1970).

[7] Richardson, *Messages and Papers*, v, 2281-86. See *Hinds' Precedents*, II, §1561. Background on this dispute appears in Henry Merritt Wriston, *Executive Agents in American Foreign Relations* (1929), 260-67.

[8] *Totten, Administrator* v. *United States*, 92 U.S. (2 Otto.) 105 (1875).

[9] 39 Stat. 557 (1916); 31 U.S.C. 108 (1970). See also 10 U.S.C. 7202, which authorizes unvouchered expenditures by the Secretary of the Navy for emergency and extraordinary expenses.

[10] 55 Stat. 682 (Aug. 25, 1941); 55 Stat. 818 (Dec. 17, 1941); 56 Stat. 705 (July 25, 1942) and 56 Stat. 996 (Oct. 26, 1942); 57 Stat. 432 (July 12, 1943).

[11] An Administration request in 1973 for confidential funds for the new Bureau of Alcohol, Tobacco and Firearms was rejected by House Appropriations. As a substitute, the Committee provided a lump sum of $100,000 in confidential funds to be disbursed by the Secretary of the Treasury to the bureaus and services under his command. H. Rep. 399, 93-1 (1973), 8. That eliminated the two previous sums of $50,000 each for the Bureau of Customs and the Secret Service. See P.L. 93-143, 87 Stat. 511. Beginning in fiscal 1974 the Drug Enforcement Administration (successor to the Bureau of Narcotics and Dangerous Drugs) received a confidential fund of $70,000. P.L. 93-62, 87 Stat. 644. For restrictions on GAO audit authority, see U.S. General Accounting Office, *Legislation Relating to the Functions and Jurisdiction of the General Accounting Office* (Jan. 1971), Chapter C, and the supplement dated Jan. 1973.

[12] For those four authorities, see Title 22 of the U.S. Code, sections 2364(c), 2396(a)(8), 2384(d)(7), and 2514(d)(7).

[13] Operation and Maintenance account: 86 Stat. 1188. D.C. funds; 87 Stat. 310, sec. 10; 74 Stat. 20. State Department funds: 86 Stat. 1110; 31 U.S.C. 107. The State Department account appears to be used largely to pay for Presidential gifts to foreign countries. See General Accounting Office, "Funding of Presidential Gifts and Grants to Middle East Countries," B-181244 (Oct. 31, 1974), at 11-12, 15-16.

[14] FBI: 119 Cong. Rec. H5701 (daily ed. June 29, 1973),

statement by Rep. Slack. Authority for FBI confidential fund appears at 28 U.S.C. 537 (1970). D.C.: *District of Columbia Appropriations for Fiscal Year 1974* (Part 1), hearings before the Senate Committee on Appropriations, 93-1 (1973), 668.

[15] Exceptions include 3 U.S.C. 102 (Presidential compensation), 3 U.S.C. 103 (Presidential travel), 8 U.S.C. 1555 (immigration), 10 U.S.C. 7202 (Navy), 28 U.S.C. 537 (FBI), 31 U.S.C. 107 (foreign affairs), 31 U.S.C. 108 (Navy), 31 U.S.C. 529d (U.S. Customs Service), 42 U.S.C. 2017 (AEC). See also citations in note 12 above.

[16] See Dan Cordtz, "The Imperial Life Style of the U.S. President," *Fortune*, Oct. 1973, at 142-47, 220-24, and *Federal Expenditures at San Clemente and Key Biscayne*, hearings before the House Committee on Appropriations, 93-1 (1973).

[17] 119 Cong. Rec. H5018 (daily ed. June 20, 1973).

[18] *Ibid.* at H5019; P.L. 93-98, 87 Stat. 330.

[19] Eckhardt, Evins, and Rhodes: 119 Cong. Rec. H5612-13 (daily ed. June 28, 1973). Use of AEC fund: information obtained from staff members of House Appropriations, AEC, and GAO. Several sources in the executive branch told me the fund had not been used since 1959. For fiscal 1975 AEC appropriation bill, see P.L. 93-393, 88 Stat. 782. A reorganization act on Oct. 11, 1974 (P.L. 93-438) broke AEC into two parts, one assigned to the new Energy Research and Development Administration (ERDA) and the other parceled out to the new Nuclear Regulatory Commission (NRC). The authority for the confidential fund remains available to ERDA and probably also to NRC.

[20] Gross: 119 Cong. Rec. H4869 (daily ed. June 18, 1973). Senate action: 119 Cong. Rec. S14082 (daily ed. July 19, 1973); concurred in by conferees: H. Rep. 416, 93-1 (1973), 6. D.C. authorization bill in 1973: P.L. 93-140, 87 Stat. 505, sec. 9, and 87 Stat. 509, sec. 26.

[21] Eckhardt on Contingencies, Defense: 119 Cong. Rec. H10409 (daily ed. Nov. 30, 1973), and 120 Cong. Rec. H7740 (daily ed. Aug. 6, 1974). Compare 86 Stat. 1190, 87 Stat. 1032, and 88 Stat. 1218.

[22] Eckhardt on O&M accounts: 119 Cong. Rec. H10405-06 (daily ed. Nov. 30, 1973). Compare 86 Stat. 1186-88, 87 Stat. 1028-30, and 88 Stat. 1215-16. Eckhardt and Mahon: 120 Cong. Rec. H7760 (daily ed. Aug. 6, 1974).

[23] *General Government Matters Appropriations, 1956,* hear-

ings before the Senate Committee on Appropriations, 84-1 (1955), 1-4. *Treasury, Postal Service, and General Government Appropriations for Fiscal Year 1974* (Part 3), hearings before the House Committee on Appropriations, 93-1 (1973), 601; H. Rep. 399, 93-1 (1973), 25-26.

[24] S. Rep. 378, 93-1 (1973), 21.

[25] 119 Cong. Rec. S15944 (daily ed. Sept. 5, 1973).

[26] Mondale amendment: *ibid.* at S15946; H. Rep. 570, 93-1 (1973), 5; P.L. 93-143, 87 Stat. 510. Dingell: 119 Cong. Rec. H7146-47 (daily ed. Aug. 1, 1973).

[27] Eckhardt amendment: 119 Cong. Rec. H5703 (daily ed. June 29, 1973). His bill: H.R. 10250, 93-1 (1973). See also his remarks at 119 Cong. Rec. E5790-91 (daily ed. Sept. 13, 1973).

[28] 3 Stat. 471-72. See David Hunter Miller, *Secret Statutes of the United States* (1918).

[29] Joe Martin, *My First Fifty Years in Politics* (1960), 100-01. Funding under two accounts: Leslie R. Groves, *Now It Can Be Told* (1962), 360-61. $800 million: Elias Huzar, *The Purse and the Sword* (1950), 338. See also James A. Robinson, *Congress and Foreign Policy-Making* (1967), 36-38.

[30] 50 U.S.C. 403 (1970).

[31] For OMB operation, see letter from OMB Director Ash to Senator Proxmire, April 29, 1974, reprinted at 120 Cong. Rec. S9603-04 (daily ed. June 4, 1974). Senator McClellan stated that only one bill—the defense appropriation bill—contained funds for the CIA; 120 Cong. Rec. S14334 (daily ed. Aug. 5, 1974). The following day, when asked if money to fund the CIA was in the defense appropriation bill, Appropriations Chairman Mahon answered, "That is correct," 120 Cong. Rec. H7709 (daily ed. Aug. 6, 1974).

[32] *Newsweek*, Nov. 22, 1971, at 29. See also at 32 for an organizational chart of the U.S. intelligence community, including details on budgets and functions. The CIA budget was estimated at $750 million. Proxmire: 119 Cong. Rec. S6868 (daily ed. April 10, 1973). Victor Marchetti and John D. Marks, *The CIA and the Cult of Intelligence* (1974), at 58-64, put the CIA budget at $750 million, but noted that the Pentagon also contributes additional amounts in the hundreds of millions of dollars to fund espionage programs and clandestine activities. A story on a $1.5 billion secret program called the National Re-

connaissance Office, funded by Air Force appropriations, appears in the *Washington Post*, Dec. 12, 1973, at A1:1.

[33] Harry Howe Ransom, "Secret Intelligence Agencies and Congress," *Society* (March/April 1975), at 34. Also of the opinion that Congress did not create the CIA to engage in subversion of foreign governments is Jerrold L. Walden, "The C.I.A.: A Study in the Arrogation of Administrative Powers," 39 *G.W. L. Rev.* 66, 82-84 (1970). Stennis: 120 Cong. Rec. S9505 (daily ed. June 3, 1974).

[34] *Public Papers of the Presidents, 1967*, I, 403. For details on CIA subsidies to supposedly private organizations, see Jerrold L. Walden, "Proselytes for Espionage—The CIA and Domestic Fronts," 19 *J. Pub. Law* 179 (1970).

[35] *Wkly Comp. Pres. Doc.*, III, 556.

[36] Case estimate and bill: 117 Cong. Rec. S130 (daily ed. Jan. 25, 1971), and S. 18, 92-1 (1971). Continuing appropriation: 85 Stat. 90 (July 1, 1971). GAO study: *Washington Post*, June 6, 1972, F9:3. See also *Public Financing of Radio Free Europe and Radio Liberty*, hearing before the Senate Committee on Foreign Relations, 92-1 (1971).

[37] Case: 117 Cong. Rec. S7503 (daily ed. May 20, 1971). Senate staff study: *Washington Post*, May 22, 1971, A17:1, and *Laos: April 1971*, staff report for the Senate Foreign Relations Committee (committee print 1971). Symington ceiling: 117 Cong. Rec. S15762-82 (daily ed. Oct. 4, 1971); 85 Stat. 428, sec. 505. Symington also at 119 Cong. Rec. S15364 (daily ed. Aug. 1, 1973).

[38] For record of Senate Armed Services Committee, see remarks of Senator Proxmire, 120 Cong. Rec. S5929 (daily ed. April 11, 1974). Ellender: 117 Cong. Rec. S19527 (Nov. 23, 1971). See Symington at 117 Cong. Rec. S17996 (daily ed. Nov. 10, 1971).

[39] 117 Cong. Rec. S19529 (daily ed. Nov. 23, 1971).

[40] Norblad: 109 Cong. Rec. 15086 (Aug. 15, 1963). Nedzi: *Washington Post*, Dec. 21, 1971, A28:1. For Committee Reform Amendments of 1974, see H. Res. 988, sec. 101, passed by the House on Oct. 8, 1974. CIA relationship with entire defense subcommittee: *Washington Post*, Feb. 22, 1975, A2:1. Congress' record of controlling the CIA is discussed by Marchetti and

Marks, *The CIA and the Cult of Intelligence* (1974), 341-49. For a conclusion (which I do not accept) that the Constitution by itself requires a specific appropriation to the CIA and an accounting to the public about its expenditures, see Note, "The CIA's Secret Funding and the Constitution," 84 *Yale L. J.* 608 (1975). I favor a direct appropriation to the CIA, removal of the authority to transfer funds back and forth between agencies, and GAO auditing, but I would argue on grounds of good public policy rather than constitutional requirements.

[41] 117 Cong. Rec. S19521-30 (daily ed. Nov. 23, 1971).

[42] P.L. 92-226, 86 Stat. 29 (Feb. 7, 1972).

[43] 117 Cong. Rec. S10527 (July 7, 1971); S. 2231, 92-1 (1971).

[44] *Ibid.* at S19526 (Nov. 23, 1971). The practice of padding the defense budget to conceal CIA money brought forth the comment from Senator Cranston that "we have no idea what the figures really are, whether for the C-5A, the B-1 bomber, the Trident, or for military housing. We do not know whether those figures are accurate or inaccurate." 119 Cong. Rec. S15363 (daily ed. Aug. 1, 1973).

[45] Restriction on operations: P.L. 93-559, 88 Stat. 1804, sec. 32 (1974). Proxmire: S. 653, 94-1 (1975). See his remarks at 121 Cong. Rec. S1771-75 (daily ed. Feb. 11, 1975), which include an important study by GAO on auditing of the intelligence agencies. For an evaluation of the McGovern bill, see Stanley N. Futterman, "Toward Legislative Control of the C.I.A.," 4 *N.Y.U. J. Int'l Law & Pol.* 431, 441 (1971). A thorough review of congressional control over the CIA is by Robin Berman Schwartzman, "Fiscal Oversight of the Central Intelligence Agency: Can Accountability and Confidentiality Coexist?" 7 *N.Y.U. J. Int'l Law & Pol.* 493 (1974).

[46] *Nomination of William E. Colby*, hearings before the Senate Committee on Armed Services, 93-1 (1973), 17, 181. Pastore: 120 Cong. Rec. S9605 (daily ed. June 4, 1974).

[47] *Nomination of James R. Schlesinger, To Be Secretary of Defense*, hearing before the Senate Committee on Armed Services, 93-1 (1973), 67-68.

[48] *Richardson v. Sokol*, 285 F.Supp. 866 (W.D. Pa. 1968). *Flast v. Cohen*, 392 U.S. 83 (1968). *Richardson v. Sokol*, 409

F.2d 3 (3d Cir. 1969); the court of appeals did not decide the standing question because it believed the district court lacked jurisdiction. *Richardson* v. *Sokol,* 396 U.S. 949 (1969).

[49] *Richardson* v. *United States,* C.A. No. 7023 (W.D. Pa. 1970); not reported, but reprinted at *United States* v. *Richardson,* "Petition for a Writ of Certiorari to the United States Court of Appeals for the Third Circuit," U.S. Supreme Court Docket No. 72-885, at 55a-58a.

[50] *Richardson* v. *United States,* 465 F.2d 844, 853 (3d Cir. 1972), footnote omitted.

[51] *United States* v. *Richardson,* 410 U.S. 953 (No. 72-885), 955 (No. 72-894).

[52] *United States* v. *Richardson,* 418 U.S. 166, 200-01 (1974). Burger's reference to political remedies, *ibid.* at 179.

[53] See *To Provide For an Audit of the Federal Reserve System by the General Accounting Office,* hearings before the House Committee on Banking and Currency, 93-1 (1973); H. Rep. 585, 93-1 (1973); and 120 Cong. Rec. H4554-87 (daily ed. May 30, 1974). See also 118 Cong. Rec. H973-76 (daily ed. Feb. 9, 1972); *ibid.* at H4818 (May 22, 1972); 119 Cong. Rec. H10366 (daily ed. Nov. 29, 1973); *ibid.* at H11134-36 (Dec. 11, 1973). Calendar 1973 figures obtained from the budget office of the Federal Reserve.

[54] *Public Papers of the Presidents, 1966,* II, 1029.

[55] *United States Security Agreements and Commitments Abroad: The Republic of the Philippines* (Part 1), hearings before the Senate Committee on Foreign Relations, 91-1 (1969), 261, 358. Denial: *New York Times,* Nov. 20, 1969, 13:1. GAO: 116 Cong. Rec. S4453 (daily ed. March 25, 1970).

[56] *United States Security Agreements and Commitments Abroad: Kingdom of Thailand* (Part 3), hearings before the Senate Committee on Foreign Relations, 91-1 (1969), 625-57. Denial: *New York Times,* Dec. 16, 1969, 10:1. GAO: 116 Cong. Rec. S19743 (daily ed. Dec. 9, 1970).

[57] *United States Security Agreements and Commitments Abroad: Republic of Korea* (Part 6), hearings before the Senate Committee on Foreign Relations, 91-2 (1970), 1529-47.

[58] 80 Stat. 37, sec. 401 (1966); 80 Stat. 82, sec. 102 (1966); 81 Stat. 53, sec. 301 (1967); 81 Stat. 248, sec. 639 (1967). For additional details on Free World Forces, see Louis Fisher,

"Presidential Spending Discretion and Congressional Controls," 37 *Law & Contemp. Prob.* 135, 141-42 (1972).

[59] *Problems of War Victims in Indochina* (Part II: Cambodia and Laos), hearings before the Senate Committee on the Judiciary, 92-2 (1972), 38-39. See *Washington Post*, Feb. 7, 1971, A2:8, and *Washington Evening Star*, Feb. 7, 1971, A1:1.

[60] *Economic Issues in Military Assistance*, hearings before the Joint Economic Committee, 92-1 (1971), 2, 293. Hereafter cited as *Economic Issues*. Statutory authority: 7 U.S.C. 1704(c) (1970). *The Budget of the United States Government, Fiscal Year 1972*, at 101. Proxmire: *Economic Issues*, at 61.

[61] *The Budget of the United States Government Fiscal Year 1972*, at 86, 96. *Economic Issues*, at 203.

[62] Harrington: 118 Cong. Rec. H6141 (daily ed. June 27, 1972). Members of the Armed Services Committee: H. Rep. 383, 93-1 (1973), 120. Emphasis in original. The three members are Robert Leggett, Patricia Schroeder, and Ronald Dellums. Fulbright: 120 Cong. Rec. S7062 (daily ed. May 6, 1974). See *ibid.* at E2906-07 (May 9, 1974) and S9972-75 (June 6, 1974).

CHAPTER TEN

[1] Louisiana Purchase: Richardson, *Messages and Papers*, I, 346. Congress initially appropriated $2 million to be applied toward the purchase of New Orleans and the Floridas. 12 *Annals of Congress* 270-71 (1803) and 2 Stat. 202, sec. 1 (1803). Supplemental appropriations: 2 Stat. 245, 247 (1803). See Henry Adams, *History of the United States of America*, II, ch. II. *Chesapeake* incident: Richardson, *Messages and Papers*, I, 416.

[2] Richardson, *Messages and Papers*, VII, 3279. Lincoln's use of secret agents during the war was upheld by the Supreme Court in *Totten, Administrator v. United States*, 92 U.S. (2 Otto.) 105, 106 (1875).

[3] *The Works of Theodore Roosevelt*, XX, 552-53, 416-17.

[4] 58 Stat. 387, sec. 213 (1944), codified at 31 U.S.C. 696 (1970). See 90 Cong. Rec. 6021-39 (1944).

[5] *United States v. Macdaniel*, 32 U.S. (7 Pet.) 1, 14 (1833).

[6] *The Floyd Acceptances*, 74 U.S. (7 Wall.) 666 (1868).

7 Gilmer Committee: H. Rep. 741, 27-2 (1842), 17-18. Emphasis in original. For Barry's practices, see Leonard D. White, *The Jacksonians* (1954), 265-66, and S. Rep. 422, 23-1 (1834). House Committee on Public Expenditures: H. Rep. 756, 27-2 (1842), 6. Other examples where Presidents and executive officials have committed the Nation to expenditures without legislative authority: Wilmerding, *The Spending Power* (1943), 3-19. For a discussion of how the Secretary of the Navy founded the Naval Academy at Annapolis in 1845, without legislative authority, see Lt. Col. Bennet N. Hollander, "The President and Congress—Operational Control of the Armed Forces," 27 *Mil. L. Rev.* 49, 60-61 (1965).

8 See 5 Stat. 533, sec. 23 (1842) and my discussion at pages 125-26. 16 Stat. 251, sec. 7 (1870).

9 James A. Garfield, "National Appropriations and Misappropriations," *No. Am. Rev.*, No. 271 (June 1879), 573, 584.

10 23 Stat. 254 (1884).

11 33 Stat. 1257-58, sec. 4 (1905). See H. Rep. 4861, 58-3 (1905), 5-6, and 39 Cong. Rec. 3687 (1905).

12 See entire debate at 40 Cong. Rec. 1272-90 (1906). Some of the main reasons for deficiencies are discussed *ibid.* at 1273 and 1289. Livingston remarks are at 1281.

13 34 Stat. 48-49, sec. 3 (1906).

14 *Second Supplemental Appropriations for Fiscal Year 1973* (Part 2), hearings before the Senate Committee on Appropriations, 93-1 (1973), 997-1005. See Arthur Smithies, *The Budgetary Process in the United States* (1955), 149.

15 *Organization of Congress* (Part 2), hearings before the Joint Committee on the Organization of Congress, 79-1 (1945), 207.

16 31 U.S.C. 665(e)(1) (1970).

17 *Effectiveness and Enforcement of the Antideficiency Act*, Interim Report of the House Committee on Appropriations, 84-1 (committee print, June 30, 1955). The study also mentioned two other reasons for deficiencies: "use of reimbursements prior to apportionment" and "claims adjudicated for an amount in excess of amounts obligated therein" (page 2). For problems with Post Office compliance, see 36 Comp. Gen. 699 (1957), 71 Stat. 440, sec. 1401 (1957), and 38 Comp. Gen. 501 (1959).

18 *Department of Defense Directive*, "Administrative Control

of Appropriations within the Department of Defense," No. 7200.1 (initially released March 20, 1952; revised Aug. 18, 1955 and March 3, 1958). Statistics on violations were obtained from the Office of Management and Budget. For unreported actions, see *Washington Evening Star-News*, Oct. 8, 1973, A2:1 and 119 Cong. Rec. E6322 (daily ed. Oct. 9, 1973); GAO concluded that the Army had overobligated by the amount of $104.5 million. Also, General Accounting Office, "Substantial Understatement of Obligations for Separation Allowances for Foreign National Employees," B-179343 (Oct. 21, 1974).

[19] Laird's letter and details on the violation: *Second Supplemental Appropriation Bill, 1973* (Part 3), hearings before the House Committee on Appropriations, 93-1 (1973), 417-582; H. Rep. 93-164, 93-1 (1973), 18-20; and H. Rep. 93-1255, 93-2 (1974), 17-19. For GAO study on the violation, see report of June 7, 1973, reprinted at 119 Cong. Rec. E4260-61 (daily ed. June 20, 1973).

[20] For example, see letter of Nov. 8, 1973, from Deputy Defense Secretary Clements to Speaker Carl Albert, referred to the House Appropriations Committee on Nov. 13, 1973, as Executive Communication 1542, with accompanying enclosures.

[21] Information obtained from the Office of Management and Budget.

[22] S. Rep. 1414, 89-1 (1966), 33; P.L. 91-510, 84 Stat. 1140.

[23] For examples, see 119 Cong. Rec. H21 (daily ed. Jan. 3, 1973), Executive Communications 6 and 10.

[24] 1 Stat. 54, sec. 3.

[25] Part of this section is based on a floor statement I prepared for Senator Abourezk, reprinted at 120 Cong. Rec. S9418-22 (daily ed. June 3, 1974).

[26] Detailed statistics are reprinted *ibid.*, at S9418-19. An official in the Pentagon told me that in some cases information might have been boxed and stored but that DOD could not trace it with their reference system.

[27] During hearings before the Senate Appropriations Committee in 1972, Senator Proxmire spoke of a movement within Congress to block any appropriation bill for defense, including any continuing resolution, unless it contained an amendment to withdraw all troops from Vietnam by Aug. 31, 1972. If such funding authority were denied, he asked Defense Secre-

tary Laird what spending power would be available to the President. Laird replied that "the only legislation which would permit us to operate would be the deficiency authorization legislation which was passed at the time of the Civil War . . . ." *Foreign Assistance and Related Programs Appropriations for Fiscal Year 1973*, hearings before the Senate Committee on Appropriations, 92-2 (1972), 837. See also 838-48. For treatment by the Senate Special Committee on the Termination of the National Emergency, see S. Rep. 549, 93-1 (1973), 320-21. A writer for the *Washington Post*, Sept. 30, 1973, A4:1, referred to the feed and forage law as a "Civil War stopgap financing measure." In an editorial, Oct. 7, 1973, the *Washington Post* asserted that the law "authorized deficiency spending to support Union troops in the field. . . ." Another article in the *Washington Post*, Jan. 6, 1974, B1:5, claims that the feed and forage law "dates back to the Civil War. . . ."

[28] 1 Stat. 754, sec. 24.

[29] Collection of bound bills, Library of Congress, 16th Cong., 1st Sess., H.R. 37, as committed to a Committee of the Whole House, Jan. 12, 1820. *Annals*, 16th Cong., 1st Sess., p. 934 (Jan. 22, 1820).

[30] Collection of bound bills, Library of Congress, 16th Cong., 1st Sess., H.R. 37, as committed to a Committee of the Whole House, March 6, 1820.

[31] General instructions for the Quartermaster's Department, Dec. 26, 1820, as reprinted in *American State Papers*, Class v, Military Affairs, ii, 248.

[32] 3 Stat. 568, sec. 6 (1820); see *Annals*, 16th Cong., 1st Sess., pp. 1616, 1620-21. 10 Stat. 107-08, sec. 2 (1852); see *Cong. Globe*, 32d Cong., 1st Sess., p. 2429 (Aug. 28, 1852).

[33] 74 U.S. (7 Wall.) 666, 684-85. See also 15 Op. Att'y Gen. 124, 209 (1876 and 1877).

[34] Thomas C. Cochran and William Miller, *The Age of Enterprise* (1961), 56.

[35] S. Stanley Katz, "The Federal Fiscal Year: Its Origins and Prospects," 12 *Nat'l Tax J.* 346 (1959). Pierce: Richardson, *Messages and Papers*, vi, 2927-29; 11 Stat. 147 (1856).

[36] Collection of bound bills, Library of Congress, 36th Cong., 1st Sess., H.R. 339, as reported out of the House Committee on Ways and Means, March 19, 1860, p. 35. Typical of legis-

lation of that era, there was no committee report to elaborate on the objectives and purposes of the section. For House debate and action, see *Cong. Globe*, 36th Cong., 1st Sess., p. 2282 (May 23, 1860). Regarding Senate action, see Collection of bound bills, Library of Congress, 36th Cong., 1st Sess., H.R. 339, as reported out of the Senate Committee on Finance, June 1, 1860, p. 38. See statement by Senator Hunter, *Cong. Globe*, 36th Cong., 1st Sess., p. 2914 (June 13, 1860), and *ibid.* at 2915, 2933. For compromise measure, see *Cong. Globe*, 36th Cong., 1st Sess., p. 3198 (June 20, 1860) and *ibid.* at 3206 (June 21, 1860); 12 Stat. 103-04, sec. 3 (1860).

[37] *Cong. Globe*, 36th Cong., 2d Sess., pp. 350-51 (Jan. 12, 1861), *ibid.* at 844 (Feb. 11, 1861); 12 Stat. 150, sec. 5 (1861).

[38] 12 Stat. 220, sec. 10 (1861). See *Cong. Globe*, 36th Cong., 2d Sess., pp. 1177-78 (Feb. 25, 1861), ibid. at 1341-42 (report of conference committee in the Senate, March 2, 1861), and at 1421 (report of conference committee in the House, March 2, 1861).

[39] 34 Stat. 255 (1906); 80 Stat. 993, sec. 612(e) (1966). The 1966 provision on reporting was recommended by the Senate Appropriations Committee; S. Rep. 1458, 89-2 (1966), 52-53. See also conference report at H. Rep. 1886, 89-2 (1966), 6. For floor debate on the reporting requirement, see 112 Cong. Rec. 20660, 20674, 24404, 26036, and 26066 (1966).

[40] For sample reports, see *Foreign Assistance and Related Programs Appropriations for Fiscal Year 1973*, hearings before the Senate Committee on Appropriations, 92-2 (1972), 844-47. DOD procedures are spelled out in *Department of Defense Directive*, "Policies and Procedure Governing the Use of the Authority of Section 3732, Revised Statutes," No. 7220.8 (Aug. 16, 1956).

[41] 73 Stat. 380, sec. 612(b) (1959); 75 Stat. 377, sec. 612(c) (1961). For contemporary example, see the defense appropriation bill for fiscal 1975, 88 Stat. 1227, sec. 813(b)(c) (1974).

[42] 120 Cong. Rec. S9803-08 (daily ed. June 5, 1974).

[43] *Second Supplemental Appropriations for Fiscal Year 1973* (Part 2), hearings before the Senate Committee on Appropriations, 93-1 (1973), 2025.

⁴⁴ The 1947 procurement act is codified at 10 U.S.C. 2304. A valuable description of the military contract system is by Richard F. Kaufman, *The War Profiteers* (1970), particularly chapters 4 and 8, and his article, "MIRVing the Boondoggle: Contracts, Subsidy, and Welfare in the Aerospace Industry," 62 *Am. Eco. Rev.* 288 (1972).

Early in 1975 Senator Thomas J. McIntyre claimed that the Defense Department was giving either tacit or explicit authority to contractors to use their own funds when Government funds had been exhausted toward the end of a fiscal year. The effect was to mortgage next year's budget. Funds necessary to repay the contractor for the amounts he laid out during that time would be repaid from the appropriations for the following year. See 121 Cong. Rec. S344-45 (daily ed. Jan. 16, 1975) and *ibid.* at S3886-92 (daily ed. March 13, 1975).

Agencies have some flexibility in switching from contracts to grants; legislation in 1974 (S. 3514) was reported by Senate Government Operations, S. Rep. 93-1239, and passed the Senate on Oct. 9. The House did not act.

⁴⁵ For the C-5A dispute, see Senator William Proxmire, *Report From Wasteland* (1970), 25-55, 239-40.

⁴⁶ P.L. 93-400, 88 Stat. 796. Goal of competitive procurement is in sec. 2(1). See also S. Rep. 93-692, 93-2 (1974), and H. Rep. 93-1268, 93-2 (1974). Major recommendations have been made by the Commission on Government Procurement, particularly Part C, "Acquisition of Major Systems," made a committee print in March 1975 by the Senate Government Operations Committee.

⁴⁷ 72 Stat. 972 (1958), codified at 50 U.S.C. 1431 (1970). Defense Department contention: H. Rep. 2232, 85-2 (1958), 2. Truman's proclamation: *Public Papers of the Presidents, 1950,* at 756. This issue was explored thoroughly during the 93d Congress by the Senate Select Committee on the Termination of the National Emergency.

⁴⁸ Annual reports on the use of the 1958 law were obtained from the Defense Department.

⁴⁹ *Ibid.,* particularly "Extraordinary Contractual Actions to Facilitate the National Defense (Public Law 85-804)," January-December 1971, Department of Defense, OASD (Comptroller), Directorate for Information Operations. For more on the Lock-

heed assistance, see *Cong. Q. Weekly Rep.*, Feb. 19, 1971, at 433-34, and *New York Times*, April 30, 1973, at 1:6.

⁵⁰ 87 Stat. 615, sec. 807.

⁵¹ See, for example, 42 Comp. Gen. 226 (1962). A GAO report states that decisions by the Comptroller General are "final and conclusive on the executive branch and are binding on the General Accounting Office in its audit." *Functions of the General Accounting Office*, S. Doc. 96, 87-2 (1962), 21. See also Elmer B. Staats, "The GAO: Present and Future," 28 *Pub. Adm. Rev.* 461 (1968), where he states that legal opinions by the Comptroller General regarding Government expenditures are "binding on the executive departments and agencies."

⁵² For contract modification law, see letter by Elmer B. Staats, Comptroller General of the United States, to the *New Republic*, Feb. 6, 1971 issue, page 35-36. Restrictions on GAO auditing are covered in General Accounting Office, *Legislation Relating to the Functions and Jurisdiction of the General Accounting Office* (January 1971), chapter C, and supplement dated Jan. 1973, chapter C.

⁵³ 41 Op. Att'y Gen. 507 (1960). Compare 74 Stat. 778, sec. 101(d) (1960) to 73 Stat. 253-54, sec. 401(h)(i) (1959). For other GAO conflicts with the Attorney General and the courts, concerning ultimate legal authority over expenditures, see Thomas D. Morgan, "The General Accounting Office: One Hope for Congress to Regain Parity of Power with the President," 51 *N.C. L. Rev.* 1279, 1285-1303 (1973).

⁵⁴ General Accounting Office, *Report to the Senate Committee on Foreign Relations on United States Economic and Military Foreign Assistance Programs* (committee print, 1971), 36-37. See also General Accounting Office, "Purchase Commitment Made to an International Organization Prior to Availability of Funds," Department of Defense, B-160154 (Oct. 2, 1970), unclassified digest.

⁵⁵ 49 Comp. Gen. 59 (1969).

⁵⁶ *Contractors Ass'n of Eastern Pa. v. Secretary of Labor*, 442 F.2d 159, 171 (3d Cir. 1971), *cert. denied*, 404 U.S. 854 (1971). The Philadelphia Plan had been upheld by a U.S. district court: *Contractors Ass'n of Eastern Pa. v. Secretary of Labor*, 311 F.Supp. 1002 (E. D. Pa. 1970). For Administration's

position, see 42 Op. Att'y Gen. 37 (1969), 115 Cong. Rec. S9953-54 (daily ed. Aug. 13, 1969), and *ibid.* at S11318 (daily ed. Sept. 25, 1969).

⁵⁷ GAO denied access: *Executive Privilege: The Withholding of Information by the Executive*, hearings before the Senate Committee on the Judiciary, 92-1 (1971), 303-15. Proposal for subpoena power: *Capability of GAO to Analyze and Audit Defense Expenditures*, hearings before the Senate Committee on Government Operations, 91-1 (1969), 105-06. During the fall of 1970 the Senate passed a bill (S. 4432, 91-2) designed to strengthen GAO access to departmental records, but the bill was not acted upon by the House.

⁵⁸ Louis Fisher, *President and Congress* (1972), 194-95.

⁵⁹ The Paris Agreement is reprinted at *Wkly Comp. Pres. Doc.*, ix, 45-50. The $7.5 billion program was described by President Nixon in *Wkly Comp. Pres. Doc.*, viii, 333 (President's report to Congress, Feb. 9, 1972). See newspaper reports: *Washington Post*, Jan. 28, 1972, A1:2; *Washington Evening Star*, Nov. 4, 1972, A1:3. Ford: *Wkly Comp. Pres. Doc.*, xi, 219 (News Conference of Feb. 26, 1975).

⁶⁰ Ford: *Wkly Comp. Pres. Doc.*, xi, 110 (Jan. 28, 1975). Rockefeller: *Washington Post*, Jan. 30, 1975, A2:4. I might have concluded that the Rockefeller statement was an error or distortion committed by the press, but I heard him give his statement during a radio news program.

⁶¹ Dean Acheson, *A Citizen Looks at Congress* (1956), 83.

⁶² 1 Stat. 239.

⁶³ Gallatin: *Annals*, 4th Cong., 1st Sess., pp. 426-28, 437, 466-74. Resolution: *ibid.* at 771-83. For official vote, see *House Journal*, ii, 499. The language of that resolution has been adopted on other occasions, such as on April 20, 1871; *Hinds' Precedents*, ii, §1523. See Ivan M. Stone, "The House of Representatives and the Treaty-Making Power," 17 *Ky. L. J.* 217 (1929).

⁶⁴ Chalfant Robinson, "The Treaty-Making Power of the House of Representatives," 12 *Yale Rev.* 191 (1903).

⁶⁵ Louis Henkin, *Foreign Affairs and the Constitution* (1972), 79. See also pp. 161-62, and Eli E. Nobleman, "Financial Aspects of Congressional Participation in Foreign Affairs," *The Annals*, Vol. 289 (Sept. 1953), 145, 146-49.

66 115 Cong. Rec. S7153 (daily ed. June 25, 1969). See Louis Fisher, *President and Congress* (1972), 225-27.

67 P.L. 92-403, 86 Stat. 619. 120 Cong. Rec. S19867-69 (daily ed. Nov. 21, 1974). A bill to permit congressional disapproval of executive agreements had been introduced by Senator Ervin on April 11, 1972 (S. 3475). See *Congressional Oversight of Executive Agreements*, hearings before the Senate Committee on the Judiciary, 92-2 (1972).

68 P.L. 93-148, 87 Stat. 555. See sections 2 and 3.

Conclusions

1 Hamilton, *Papers*, xix, 405. Madison: Federalist 48.

2 Richardson, *Messages and Papers*, xvii, 8846.

3 Paul Einzig, *The Control of the Purse* (1959), 71-72.

4 Clifford R. Hope, "Legislative-Executive Relationships in the Formulation of Public Policy as Viewed by the Legislator," in *Legislative-Executive Relationships* (1954), O. B. Conaway, ed., at 16.

5 This problem is of long-standing interest. See Marver H. Bernstein, *The Job of the Federal Executive* (1958), 56-62, 106-07.

6 James Madison, in a purist venture into the separation doctrine, opposed legislative participation in the designation of officers: "The Legislature creates the office, defines the powers, limits its duration, and annexes a compensation. This done, the legislative power ceases. They ought to have nothing to do with designating the man to fill the office. That I conceive to be of an executive nature." *Annals* i, 604 (June 22, 1789). The assumption here, which we can no longer make, is that administrators do indeed execute the laws passed by Congress. Madison generally advocated a less doctrinaire view of separation of powers. See Louis Fisher, *President and Congress* (1972), 20-26, 268-70.

7 *Youngstown Co.* v. *Sawyer*, 343 U.S. 579, 654 (1952).

8 Kenneth Culp Davis, *Discretionary Justice* (1969).

9 Woodrow Wilson, "The Study of Administration," originally published in 1887, reprinted at 56 *Pol. Sci. Q.* 481, 497-98 (1941).

Table of Cases

Index

Abourezk, James, 245
Accelerated spending, 138-39
Accountability, 202, 264-65
Accrued expenditures, 135-38
Acheson, Dean, 253
Adams, Arlin M., 294
Adams, Charles Francis, 274
Adams, Henry, 15
Adams, John Quincy: Monroe-Crawford clash, 15-16; financial policy as President, 16
Addabbo, Joseph, 115, 295, 296
Agency for International Development (AID): contingency fund, 67-70; deobligation-reobligation, 80; reappropriation, 131-33; access to carryover balances, 134-35, 142; spending under a continuing resolution, 145; confidential funds, 208; Laotian operation, 226
Agriculture impoundments, 131, 160, 166, 167, 177-84
Albert, Carl, 164, 176
Antideficiency Act, 28, 154-57, 233-38
Appointment power of the President, 43, 48-50, 53-54, 63, 259-60, 331
Apportionment of funds, 28, 38, 40, 112, 144-45

Appropriations, House Committee on: creation in 1865, 20; splintering of, 21-23; consolidation in 1920, 31-32, 36; supporting central clearance, 39; jurisdiction over recissions, 94, and tranfers, 106; policy on impoundment, 149
Appropriations, Senate Committee on: creation in 1867, 20; splintering of, 23-24; consolidation in 1922, 36-37
Arends, Leslie, 307
Armed Services Procurement Act of 1947, 247
Arthur, Chester, 25
Articles of Confederation, 10
Ash, Roy, 52-54, 57, 114, 154-55, 171, 183, 192
Atomic bomb, funding of, 214
Atomic Energy Commission (AEC), 207-08, 210, 318
Attorney General, 124-26, 127, 148, 250, 251

Ball, Joseph H., 155
Barry, William, 231-32
Bayard, James A., Sr., 101
Becker, Frank, 307
Bingham, Jonathan, 108
Blatnik, John, 49, 187

337

INDEX

INDEX

Feed and Forage Law, 238-47
Fenno, Richard F., Jr., 4, 176
Finance, Senate Committee on, 13-14, 20
Findley, Paul, 281
Fitzgerald, A. E., 248
Fitzgerald, John, 31
Fitzpatrick, Edward, 33
Fitzsimons, Thomas, 12
Floyd, John B., 231
Flynt, Joseph J., 295
Food for Peace, 226-27
Ford, Gerald R.: role of OMB, 57; committee clearance, 74; reprogramming, 83-84; impoundment of RS-70 funds, 164, and clean-water funds, 186; implementation of Impoundment Control Act of 1974, 199-201; commitment to South Vietnamese, 252-53
Forest Service, 77
Forrestal, James, 162
Fraser, Donald, 108
Free World Forces, 224-26
French, Burton Lee, 64-65
Fulbright, J. William, 107-08, 220, 224, 227

Gallatin, Albert: Secretary of the Treasury, 14-15, 60-61; critical of Washington's transfer of funds, 100-01; role of House in funding treaties, 254
Galloway, George B., 135
Garfield, James, 21-22, 232
Gasch, Oliver, 189-90
General Accounting Office (Comptroller General): Wilson vetoing bill because Comptroller General could be removed by concurrent resolution, 35; modified in bill signed by Harding, 35; interfering with executive responsibilities, 41-42; review of lump-sum funding, 65;

monitoring of reprogramming and deob-reob, 80, 97-98; study on reappropriation, 132; concept of obligation, 133; accounting on an accrual basis, 137; study on recoveries, 142; auditing of Federal drug treatment funds, 152; antideficiency language, 154-55; impoundment, 178, 199-200; auditing of confidential funds, 209-13; financing of Radio Free Europe and Radio Liberty, 217; financing of Free World Forces, 224-25; deficiency spending, 236; restrictions on review capability, 249-52
General Services Administration, 46
Gerry, Elbridge, 11
Giaimo, Robert N., 116, 295
Giles, William, 99-100
Gilmer Committee, 231
Gilpatrick, Roswell, 85
Goodhue, Benjamin, 11
Goodnow, Frank, 64
Grant, Ulysses S., 20-21, 165
Griffin, Robert, 53
Gross, H. R., 132, 210, 307

Halleck, Charles, 164
Hamilton, Alexander: Secretary of the Treasury, 12-13; line-itemization, 60; transfer authority, 99-100; unused balances, 123-24; power of the purse, 257
Harding, Warren G., 35, 38, 166
Harmon, Judson, 148
Harrington, Michael J., 227
Harrison, Benjamin, 27
Harrison, William Henry, 17
Harsha, William, 186-88
Hauk, A. Andrew, 190-91
Health, Education, and Welfare, Department of, 79, 142-43, 152, 160, 172

340

INDEX

342

Library of Congress Cataloging in Publication Data

Fisher, Louis.
  Presidential spending power.

  Includes bibliographical references and index.
  1. United States—Appropriations and expenditures. 2.
Budget—United States. 3. Finance, Public—United States.
I. Title.
HJ257.2.F57   353.007'222   75-4408
ISBN 0-691-07575-1
ISBN 0-691-02173-2 pbk.